World War One in Southeast Asia

D1594543

Although not a major player during the course of the First World War, Southeast Asia was in fact altered by the war in multiple and profound ways. Ranging across British Malaya, the Dutch East Indies, and French Indochina, Heather Streets-Salter reveals how the war shaped the region's political, economic, and social development both during 1914–1918 and in the war's aftermath. She shows how the region's strategic location between North America and India made it a convenient way-station for expatriate Indian revolutionaries who hoped to smuggle arms and people into India and thus to overthrow British rule, while German consuls and agents entered into partnerships with both Indian and Vietnamese revolutionaries to undermine Allied authority and coordinate anti-British and anti-French operations. *World War One in Southeast Asia* offers an entirely new perspective on anticolonialism and the Great War and radically extends our understanding of the conflict as a truly global phenomenon.

HEATHER STREETS-SALTER is Department Chair and Director of World History Programs at Northeastern University in Boston, Massachusetts. Publications include *Martial Races: The Military, Martial Races, and Masculinity in British Imperial Culture, 1857–1914*; *Traditions and Encounters: A Brief Global History* with Jerry Bentley and Herb Ziegler; and *Empires and Colonies in the Modern World* with Trevor Getz.

World War One in Southeast Asia

Colonialism and Anticolonialism in an Era of Global Conflict

Heather Streets-Salter

Northeastern University, Boston

CAMBRIDGE
UNIVERSITY PRESS

CAMBRIDGE
UNIVERSITY PRESS

University Printing House, Cambridge CB2 8BS, United Kingdom

One Liberty Plaza, 20th Floor, New York, NY 10006, USA

477 Williamstown Road, Port Melbourne, VIC 3207, Australia

4843/24, 2nd Floor, Ansari Road, Daryaganj, Delhi - 110002, India

79 Anson Road, #06–04/06, Singapore 079906

Cambridge University Press is part of the University of Cambridge.

It furthers the University's mission by disseminating knowledge in the pursuit of
education, learning, and research at the highest international levels of excellence.

www.cambridge.org
Information on this title: www.cambridge.org/9781107135192
DOI: 10.1017/9781316471487

© Heather Streets-Salter 2017

This publication is in copyright. Subject to statutory exception
and to the provisions of relevant collective licensing agreements,
no reproduction of any part may take place without the written
permission of Cambridge University Press.

First published 2017

Printed in the United States of America by Sheridan Books, Inc.

A catalogue record for this publication is available from the British Library.

Library of Congress Cataloging-in-Publication Data
Names: Streets-Salter, Heather, author.
Title: World War One in Southeast Asia : colonialism and anticolonialism in an era
of global conflict / Heather Streets-Salter, Northeastern University, Boston.
Description: Cambridge ; New York, NY : Cambridge University Press, 2017. |
Includes bibliographical references and index.
Identifiers: LCCN 2016043646 | ISBN 9781107135192 | ISBN 9781316501092
(paperback)
Subjects: LCSH: World War, 1914–1918 – Asia, Southeast.
Classification: LCC D577 .S77 2017 | DDC 940.3/59 – dc23
LC record available at https://lccn.loc.gov/2016043646

ISBN 978-1-107-13519-2 Hardback
ISBN 978-1-316-50109-2 Paperback

Cambridge University Press has no responsibility for the persistence or accuracy
of URLs for external or third-party Internet Web sites referred to in this publication
and does not guarantee that any content on such Web sites is, or will remain,
accurate or appropriate.

In loving memory of my father, Malcolm Gillis
(1940–2015)

Contents

Acknowledgments

This book has both personal and intellectual origins. In 1971, Suharto's relatively young government requested a team of economists from the United States to advise its ministers on everything from taxation to rice distribution and storage. My father was among them, and in that year he and my mother packed me and my two siblings up and moved us to Jakarta, Indonesia. The three years and many subsequent summers we spent there led all of us to develop not only a love for the region and for Javanese culture but also a strong curiosity about it. Once I became an historian of empire, one of my goals was to revisit Southeast Asia as a scholar in order to deepen my understanding about the legacies of its imperial past. The last eight years of research on this book has thus been a bridge between my own personal history and the profession I love.

The intellectual origins of this book began with a chance encounter in the French colonial archives in Aix-en-Provence. I had been conducting research about late nineteenth century connections between British Malaya, the Dutch East Indies, and French Indochina when I happened across a file called "Troubles de Singapour." The materials described a mutiny in 1915 Singapore that I had never heard of and demonstrated the ways in which French, Japanese, and Russian forces came to the rescue of the British as a result of wartime alliances. Suitably intrigued, I grew increasingly interested in following the many threads in the story to other colonies in Southeast Asia and also to India, China, Siam, Europe, and North America. As I continued my research, it became clear to me not only just how connected Southeast Asia was to the rest of the world in the early twentieth century, but also that World War I had a profound impact on the region.

I am grateful for the help and inspiration of many people who helped make this book a reality. Those who read drafts of chapters and commented on presentations include, among many others, Antoinette Burton, Trevor Getz, Marc Gilbert, Andrew Jarboe, Philippa Levine, Michele Louro, Patrick Manning, Lincoln Paine, Michael Vann, and the anonymous readers at the *Journal of World History*. The faculty and students at Northeastern University have provided intellectual stimulation at many stages during the research and writing of this book, as have the members of the World History Association, the American Historical Association, and the Asian Studies Association who have heard me present my work. I owe many thanks to the staff at the National Archives in Kew, the India Office Library in London, the Centre des Archives d'Outre-mer in Aix-en-Provence, the Archief Nationaal in Den Haag, the Singapore National Archives, and the Cornell University Library Division of Rare Books and Manuscripts for their help over several years. In addition, I am grateful for Michael Watson's patience and advice at the Cambridge University Press, and for his role in making this book a reality.

I owe my largest debt of gratitude to my family, who both encouraged and tolerated the many years of research and writing involved in completing this book. My mother and siblings, Elizabeth Gillis, Nora Bynum, and Stephen Gillis, have endured many conversations about World War I in Southeast Asia, and have provided unfailing love and friendship over a lifetime. My oldest children, Jessica and Travis, first came to know this project when they were still in school, while the impending birth of my youngest, Sarah, provided the final impetus for me to finish it. I am profoundly grateful to my husband, Steve Salter, for his limitless encouragement, his willingness to read draft after draft, and his enthusiasm for the travel necessary to complete such a book. I am also grateful to the project itself for providing the circumstances under which I would meet such a wonderful life partner. Above all, I wish to acknowledge the guidance and inspiration provided by my father: not only for giving me the initial opportunity to live in Southeast Asia, but for encouraging me in every academic pursuit, for reading all of my work, and for being a model of lifelong learning. It is bittersweet to be finishing this project with the realization that it is the last one for which he will be there to offer his cheerful support.

Maps

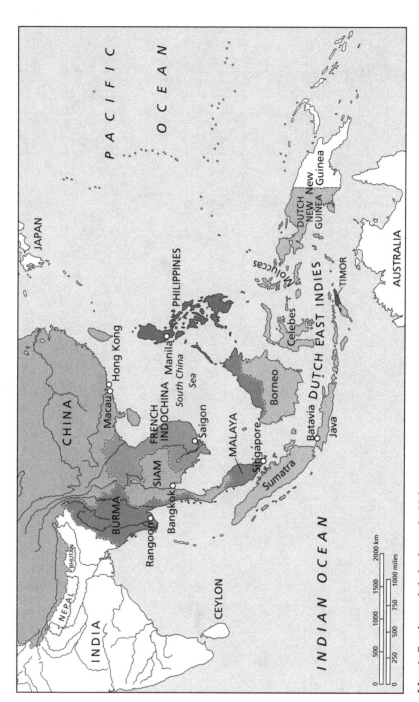

Map 1 Southeast Asia in the early 20th century.

Introduction

When we think about World War I, most of us picture the horrors of trench warfare in Western Europe. In our mind's eye, we might imagine the destroyed landscape of no-man's-land, rats and fetid water filling the trenches, and pointless, appalling casualties. When we think about empire and colonialism, most of us think of particular colonies – such as India, Algeria, or the Philippines – and their respective relationships to Britain, France, or the United States. For the most part, we operate under the assumption that colonies and their national metropoles functioned as more or less discreet units, and that the colonial/metropolitan relationship was more important than any other. Finally, when we think about world history, we tend to conceive of narratives that explore complex processes and large-scale connections over huge areas or long chronologies. For many of us, world history sacrifices minute, individual stories in order to tell big, abstract stories.

Yet in this book, the stories I tell about World War I occurred thousands of miles from the Western Front, in Southeast Asia. The stories I tell about empire and colonialism are about connections between colonies – and between colonies and independent states – rather than simply colonial connections with their various metropoles. And the stories I tell about world history begin with individuals in a small place and move outward, from the local to the regional and global. In the process, this book contributes to a growing historiography on World War I that seeks to understand it as a truly global conflict. More fundamentally, this book represents a contribution to a recent trend in which historians attempt to rethink the history of empire and colonialism as a global – rather than a national – phenomenon. Just as important, this book offers an approach to "doing" world history in a way that does not compromise archival research or individual stories.

World War I as Global War

Since the beginning of the twenty-first century, historians of World War I have focused increasing interest on the global nature of the conflict.[1] Many of their works explore the contributions of the millions of non-European soldiers and laborers who directly contributed to the war effort in Europe, often in the context of imperial relationships. As a result, we now have a better understanding of the experiences of the many hundreds of thousands of colonial subjects who served on the Western Front during the war, although more work remains to be done.[2] Other histories have demonstrated that World War I was global not only in terms of the people it drew to its main theaters of battle but also in terms of battlefronts outside of Europe altogether – particularly in Africa and the Middle East.[3] Still others have focused on the heretofore neglected subject of the effects of the war on non-European belligerents, including the Ottomans and the Chinese.[4] A growing number of studies have

[1] For general histories with a self-consciously global focus, see Hew Strachan, *The First World War* (New York: Penguin Books, 2005); Michael S. Neiberg, *Fighting the Great War a Global History* (Cambridge, MA: Harvard University Press, 2005); Lawrence Sondhaus, *World War I: The Global Revolution* (Cambridge; New York: Cambridge University Press, 2011); William Kelleher Storey, *The First World War: A Concise Global History*, 2nd edn., Exploring World History (Lanham: Rowman & Littlefield, 2014).

[2] See, for example, Andrew Tait Jarboe and Richard Standish Fogarty, *Empires in World War I: Shifting Frontiers and Imperial Dynamics in a Global Conflict* (London; New York: I.B. Tauris; Distributed in the U.S. and Canada exclusively by Palgrave Macmillan, 2014); Robert Gerwarth and Erez Manela, *Empires at War, 1911–1923* (Oxford University Press, 2014); Santanu Das, *Race, Empire and First World War Writing* (Cambridge; New York: Cambridge University Press, 2011). An early example concerning British India is DeWitt Ellinwood and S. D. Pradhan, *India and World War I* (Columbia, MO: South Asia Books, 1978). For France, see Jacques Frémeaux, *Les Colonies dans la Grande Guerre: Combats et Éprouves des Peuples d'Outre-Mer* (Paris: 14–18 Editions, 2006); Richard Standish Fogarty, *Race and War in France: Colonial Subjects in the French Army, 1914–1918* (Baltimore: Johns Hopkins University Press, 2013); Kimloan Hill, Nhung Tuyet Tran, and Anthony Reid, eds., "Strangers in a Foreign Land: Vietnamese Soldiers and Workers in France during World War I," in *Viet Nam: Borderless Histories* (Madison: University of Wisconsin Press, 2006), 256–89. For British India, see Andrew Jarboe, "Soldiers of Empire: Indian Sepoys in and Beyond the Imperial Metropole During the First World War, 1914–1919" (Ph.D. Dissertation, Northeastern University, 2013); David E. Omissi, ed., *Indian Voices of the Great War: Solders' Letters, 1914–18* (Houndmills, Basingstoke, Hampshire; New York: Macmillan Press; St. Martin's Press, 1999); DeWitt C. Ellinwood and S. D. Pradhan, eds., *India and World War 1* (Columbia, MO: South Asia Books, 1978).

[3] Strachan, *The First World War in Africa*; Anne Samson, *World War I in Africa: The Forgotten Conflict Among European Powers* (London: I.B. Tauris, 2012); David R. Woodward, *Hell in the Holy Land: World War I in the Middle East* (Lexington, KY: The University Press of Kentucky, 2006); Leila Tarazi Fawaz, *A Land of Aching Hearts: The Middle East in the Great War* (Cambridge, MA: Harvard University Press, 2014).

[4] Mustafa Aksakal, *The Ottoman Road to War in 1914: The Ottoman Empire and the First World War*, Cambridge Military Histories (Cambridge, UK; New York: Cambridge University Press, 2008); Guoqi Xu, *China and the Great War: China's Pursuit of a New*

explored the war as an opportunity for colonial dissidents to exploit the vulnerability of colonial powers by forming alliances with the Ottomans and the Germans, while others have focused on the global consequences of the peace.[5] Taken together, this recent scholarship has demonstrated in multiple ways and from many perspectives that World War I truly was a global war. This was so not only because it drew people and resources from around the world to the main theaters of battle, but also because the war's effects were felt by people and in places many thousands of miles from Europe.[6]

This book supports these recent developments in the field and extends their spatial limits to Southeast Asia. Very little has been written about Southeast Asia and the Great War, even in the historiography seeking to understand the war as a global phenomenon.[7] This is not difficult to understand: the region did not become a major theater of war, and of all the colonies in the area, only French Indochina sent soldiers and laborers to Europe.[8] In fact, much of the region – including the Dutch East Indies, Siam (until 1917), and the Philippines (until 1917) – remained officially neutral for all or most of the war.

Yet despite the fact that Southeast Asia did not significantly shape the course or the outcome of the war, the war did in fact shape Southeast Asia in multiple and profound ways. First, as in India and North Africa, representatives of the Central Powers – sometimes working in concert

---

National Identity and Internationalization, Studies in the Social and Cultural History of Modern Warfare (New York: Cambridge University Press, 2005).

[5] Maia Ramnath, *Haj to Utopia: How the Ghadar Movement Charted Global Radicalism and Attempted to Overtrhow the British Empire* (Berkeley: University of California Press, 2011); Sean McMeekin, *The Berlin-Baghdad Express: The Ottoman Empire and Germany's Bid for World Power* (Cambridge, MA: the Belknap Press of Harvard University Press, 2010); Peter Hopkirk, *Like Hidden Fire: The Plot to Bring Down the British Empire* (New York: Kodansha, 1997); Tilman Lüdke, *Jihad Made in Germany: Ottoman and German Propaganda and Intelligence Operations in the First World War* (Münster; London: LIT; Global [distributor], 2005). On the peace, see Erez Manela, *The Wilsonian Moment: Self-Determination and the International Origins of Anticolonial Nationalism* (Oxford: Oxford University Press, 2009).

[6] Robert Gerwarth and Erez Manela make a similar point in the introduction to *Empires at War: 1911–1923,* 3.

[7] Exceptions include Kees van Dijk, *The Netherlands Indies and the Great War 1914–1918,* Verhandelingen van Het Koninklijk Instituut Voor Taal-, Land- En Volkenkunde 254 (Leiden: KITLV Press, 2007); Kimloan Vu-Hill, *Coolies into Rebels: Impact of World War I on French Indochina* (Paris: Les Indes savantes, 2011). There is no monograph on the Great War in British Malaya, but John Murfett does include a chapter on Singapore in *Between Two Oceans: A Military History of Singapore from First Settlement to Final British Withdrawal* (Singapore: Marshall Cavendish Academic, 2004).

[8] Kimloan Hill, Nhung Tuyet Tran, and Anthony Reid, eds., "Strangers in a Foreign Land: Vietnamese Soldiers and Workers in France during World War I," in *Viet Nam: Borderless Histories* (Madison: University of Wisconsin Press, 2006), 256–289.

with Indian or Vietnamese revolutionaries – worked actively throughout the region to undermine Allied authority wherever it was manifested, particularly in British Malaya and French Indochina. In this respect, the neutral countries surrounding both colonies were crucial, as Germans and, to a much lesser extent, Ottomans used Siam, the Dutch East Indies, or China as bases from which to coordinate anti-British and anti-French operations. In Indochina, this meant that French authorities – whose defenses were already stretched thin because of the war – were forced to divert already limited police and military units to the Chinese frontier to quell frequent rebellions financed with German money. In Burma, a combination of German promises, the Ottoman call to jihad, and the work of Indian revolutionaries led to an aborted mutiny by the Indian garrison stationed in the colony. Far more seriously, the same combination led to a full-fledged mutiny of half the regiment of the Indian 5th Light Infantry in Singapore in February 1915 – a situation that required the help of the French, Japanese, and Russian navies to quell.

Various locations in Southeast Asia were also convenient way-stations for combined Indian and German schemes to transport arms and propaganda from the United States to India prior to 1917. Indeed, the ill-fated *Henry S* and the *Maverick* – supposedly meant to carry weapons bound for India – were halted in transit in Southeast Asia from San Francisco, while Singapore authorities made critical arrests among their crews. At the same time, German consuls worked in concert with Vietnamese and Indian revolutionaries in Siam, the Dutch East Indies, and China in order to encourage revolution in Allied colonies. For a short time in 1914, Allied ships plying Southeast Asian waters were even the site of German naval attacks, at least until the German cruiser *Emden* was sunk on November 9 of that year.

The intrigue fomented by the enemies of the Allies led not only to increased cross-border coordination between anticolonial activists, but also to the introduction of colonial intelligence agencies designed to monitor and control such activity in British Malaya, French Indochina, and the Dutch East Indies. Although these agencies were new and inexperienced during the war, in the 1920s and 1930s they grew increasingly efficient. Eventually, they became crucial in the fight to obliterate the communist threat from the region. World War I also provided the opportunity for Japan to play a more powerful role in Southeast Asia than ever before. As an Allied power, the Japanese navy took on the lion's share of the burden of patrolling the seas in East and Southeast Asia, while the British and the French diverted most of their naval resources to the theaters of war.[9] In the process, the Japanese not only took the opportunity to expand in China but also to become more visible in the economic affairs in Southeast Asia – particularly in the ownership of land and businesses. This increased activity struck fear into the hearts of Dutch administrators in the Indies in particular, as they feared the Japanese ultimately aimed to conquer the whole colony.[10]

Less dramatically but equally important, the Great War disrupted trade, travel, and communication across the region. Allied powers attempted to control shipping in order to prevent war materiel and food aid from reaching their enemies. Moreover, mail and telegraphic communications were subject to interception, monitoring, and confiscation. Finally, travel to Europe and to neutral countries in the vicinity was monitored in order to prevent German nationals from being transported to locations from which they could cause trouble for the Allies. These regulations were particularly harmful to the Dutch East Indies, which hosted a large population of German nationals and also carried on significant trade with Germany prior to the war. The resulting decline in revenues caused economic hardship in the archipelago, which in turn increased discontent among colonial populations.[11]

One of the contributions of this book, then, is that it demonstrates the global reach of World War I even beyond those who have sought to call attention to its effects outside Europe. In Southeast Asia, whose various states and colonies did not play much of a role in determining the outcome of the war, the Great War shaped the course of political, economic, and social developments not only for its duration, but for its aftermath as well. Indeed, it seems Hew Strachan's claim that "war for Europe meant war for the world" was true for even more of the world than we thought.[12]

Empire as a Global Phenomenon

Although this book is about World War I in Southeast Asia, it has two deeper methodological purposes. The first is to demonstrate the kinds of colonial histories that emerge when we complicate the metropole/colony relationships that have so dominated the historiography of empire. The

---

[9] Malcolm Murfett, *Between Two Oceans: A Military History of Singapore from the First Settlement to Final British Withdrawal* (Singapore: Marshall Cavendish, 2004), 156, 158.

[10] For a series of essays on this theme, see Elspeth Locher-Scholten, *Beelden van Japan in Het Vooroorlogse Nederlands Indië* (Leiden: Werkgroep Europese Expansie, 1987).

[11] This is a major theme in van Dijk, *The Netherlands Indies and the Great War 1914–1918*.

[12] Strachan, *The First World War*, 69.

focus on such relationships is an outgrowth of national history, in which the study of empire has overwhelmingly been conceived in national terms. Until very recently, one did not study "empire," but rather the British Empire, the French Empire, or the Spanish Empire, among others.[13] My own postgraduate training is a good example of this. My primary field was the British Empire, and my secondary fields were modern Britain and colonial India. Although I received excellent training in those fields, I was not encouraged to study the French, American, or Japanese Empires in tandem with the British, nor did I think to do so myself. This neglect was not out of hostility to the histories of other empires. Instead, we all seemed to operate under the assumption that colonies and their national metropoles functioned as more or less discreet units, and that colonial/metropolitan relationships were more important than any others.[14]

The problem with such an approach to the history of empire is that our enthusiasm for understanding the relationships between metropoles and colonies can obscure the many other structures, flows, and processes that were neither wholly defined by such bilateral relationships nor limited by national-colonial borders. In this book, I use the region of Southeast Asia in the early twentieth century to argue for a conceptualization of modern empires in a world that is messier, and more multilateral, than the colony/metropole model allows. On the one hand, I argue that both the colonies and the metropoles of all the modern empires were more connected to one another than is often imagined, particularly via

---

[13] Although I do not have hard figures, this pattern has clearly been changing in the twenty-first century. A variety of graduate programs now offer graduate fields in imperial or postcolonial history, broadly construed. Such configurations, no doubt, will continue to affect the histories of colonialism that scholars new to the field will tell.

[14] In fact, in the mid-1990s, it was cutting-edge to suggest that national histories and colonial histories were entwined and mutually constitutive. Prior to the mid-1980s, most national histories of the colonial metropoles were told as though the colonies did not exist. Historians of the British Empire led the way in reshaping mainstream perspectives about colonial/metropolitan relationships. The "New Imperial" history associated originally with John Mackenzie and his "Studies in Imperialism" series was devoted to demonstrating the impact of the colonies on the British metropole, beginning with his own *Propaganda and Empire: The Manipulation of British Public Opinion, 1880–1960* (Manchester: Manchester University Press, 1984). By the 1990s, both Antoinette Burton and Mrinalini Sinha, among others, argued not only that British colonial affairs had an impact on the metropole but also that metropolitan events and ideologies (beyond official colonial policy) also shaped colonial affairs, and in fact that the two could not be neatly divided. See Mrinalinia Sinha, *Colonial Masculinity: The 'Manly Englishman' and the 'Effeminate Bengali' in the Late Nineteenth Century* (Manchester: Manchester University Press, 1995); Antoinette Burton, *At the Heart of the Empire: Indians and the Colonial Encounter in Late-Victorian Britain* (Berkeley: University of California Press, 1998). Their work helped to dramatically reshape the history of modern imperialism, and was critical for encouraging historians to think beyond the "box" of the nation-state.

consular and diplomatic networks as well as anticolonial networks. On the other hand, I argue that colonial peoples and administrators alike were connected to, influenced by, and participants in larger global movements and events that sometimes had origins outside the colonial world altogether. In so doing, my goal is to contribute to a growing historiography that explores modern empires as porous, interconnected, and frequently disrupted by transnational or global forces.[15]

Early twentieth-century colonial Southeast Asia is a particularly fruitful region for this approach to the history of empire. By the turn of the twentieth century a wide variety of imperial powers laid claim to portions of the region, including the British in Malaya and Burma, the French in Indochina, the Dutch in the Indonesian archipelago, the Americans in the Philippines, and the Portuguese in Timor. Beginning in the late nineteenth century, successive Chinese governments and Chinese political parties also had strong interests in Southeast Asia because of the large Chinese populations distributed around the region. By the first decade of the century both the German and the Japanese governments entertained designs of achieving commercial or political influence in the region. In Siam, which remained independent, all of the major colonial powers and other contenders for imperial power jostled for influence and jealously guarded their prerogatives. Representatives of the Ottoman Empire and Arab teachers and travelers had long-standing interests in the Dutch East Indies and British Malaya, and Southeast Asian Hajis formed ever stronger contacts with areas in and around the Hejaz. Meanwhile, Vietnamese revolutionaries sought refuge from persecution in Siam and

---

[15] Some of these works have used an oceans framework to do this, including Sugata Bose's, *A Hundred Horizons the Indian Ocean in the Age of Global Empire* (Cambridge, MA: Cambridge, Mass: Harvard University Press, 2006); Enseng Ho's *The Graves of Tarim: Genealogy and Mobility Across the Indian Ocean* (Berkeley: University of California Press, 2006); and Thomas R. Metcalf's, *Imperial Connections India in the Indian Ocean Arena, 1860–1920* (Berkeley: University of California Press, 2007). Historians of colonial India have also made important contributions to this historiography, including Harald Fischer-Tiné, "Indian Nationalism and the 'world Forces': Transnational and Diasporic Dimensions of the Indian Freedom Movement on the Eve of the First World War," *Journal of Global History* 2, no. 03 (2007); Carolien Stolte and Harald Fischer-Tiné, "Imagining Asia in India: Nationalism and Internationalism (ca. 1905–1940)," *Comparative Studies in Society in History* 54, no. 1 (January 2012); and Michele Louro, "Where National Revolutionary Ends and Communism Begins: The League Against Imperialism and the Meerut Conspiracy Case," *Comparative Studies of South Asia, Africa, and the Middle East* (December 2013). Historians of Southeast Asia have also made critical contributions, including Eric Tagliacozzo, whose work includes *Secret Trades, Porous Borders: Smuggling and States Along a Southeast Asian Frontier, 1865–1915* (New Haven: Yale University Press, 2005), and Anne Foster, whose work includes *Projections of Power: The United States and Europe in Colonial Southeast Asia* (Durham: Duke University Press, 2010).

China, while Indian soldiers, merchants, and indentured laborers established communities in Burma, Malaya, Siam, China, and the East Indies.

As even this most cursory description indicates, Southeast Asia in the early twentieth century was a region composed not only of European and American colonies but was also criss-crossed by influences and movements connected to China, Japan, Germany, and the Ottoman Empire, to name only a few. Even decades before the First World War, colonized subjects and colonial administrators in the region had far more to think about than bilateral relations between colony and metropole. In fact, transnational and international flows and movements were defining features of colonial Southeast Asia in this period.[16] These flows and movements connected colonized subjects both with noncolonized travelers and with other colonized subjects in the region and beyond, and in many cases had the effect of strengthening international and national anticolonialisms. But they also began to connect colonial administrators, diplomats, and police with their counterparts in other locations, thus creating what would become an increasingly united front for combatting international anticolonialism.[17]

While the material for this book is largely drawn from the colonial archives of British Malaya, the Dutch East Indies, and French Indochina, the action takes place in many locations in and outside Southeast Asia. This includes not only the colonies associated with these archives but also Siam, India, China, and Japan. Actors in the story hail from an even wider set of geographical locations, including Germany, Britain, France, the Netherlands, the Ottoman Empire, and the United States. As I hope to make clear, it is simply impossible to tell the story of Southeast Asia during the First World War without attention to the many connections linking Southeast Asian colonies and peoples to each other and to the rest of the world.

World History

The second methodological purpose of this book is to add to the small body of work demonstrating that it is possible to write world history without sacrificing small-scale stories. World history is commonly associated

---

[16] For some recent works about these flows, see Eric Tagliacozzo and Wen-Chin Chang, *Chinese Circulations: Capital, Commodities, and Networks in Southeast Asia* (Durham, NC: Duke University Press, 2011); Eric Tagliacozzo, *The Longest Journey: Southeast Asians and the Pilgrimage to Mecca* (Oxford: Oxford University Press, 2013); Yen Ching-hwang, *The Chinese in Southeast Asia and Beyond: Socioeconomic and Political Dimensions* (Singapore: World Scientific Publishing Company, 2008); Gungwu Wang, "Greater China and the Chinese Overseas," *The China Quarterly*, no. 136 (1993), 926.

[17] Anne Foster, "Secret Police Cooperation and the Roots of Anti-Communism in Interwar Southeast Asia," *The Journal of American-East Asian Relations* 4, no. 4 (1995).

with works that focus, to borrow from Charles Tilly, on big structures, large processes, [and] huge comparisons.[18] Some of these works have had such an impact that they have reshaped the way historians across many fields understand the Columbian Exchange, the significance of global disease, the timing of western Europe's divergence from the rest of the world, or the global impact of human environmental damage in the twentieth century, to name only a few.[19] Because of the vast scale of their subjects, most world histories of this sort employ a panoramic view that allows readers to envision all (or most) of the moving parts at once. Like John McNeil's *Something New Under the Sun*, such world histories start big, at the level of the globe, and then move to more manageable sections, in this case to the hydrosphere, the lithosphere, and so on. But one of the drawbacks of such panoramic views is that the humans whose existence is implied in all of these works appear either as aggregates or abstractions. In other words, even while we know that people are presumed to be everywhere in these macro-level world histories, they often seem to be nowhere. Individual and local stories tend to disappear at the level of the bird's-eye view.

I believe macro-level world histories are important, but they do not represent the only way to write world history. In 1997, Donald Wright demonstrated that it is possible to write compelling world history by beginning at the micro-level and then tracing outward the threads that connect the local to the global.[20] My own fascination with world history comes from exploring the relationship between local events and individual agency on the one hand, and complex, global processes on the other. Like Wright, I believe it is worth remembering that the currents of world history have always involved individual people engaged in their own stories of survival, tragedy, or victory, even when their grasp of their connectedness to others was only partial. And for those of us who revel in a good story, exploring the interconnections of the global and the local allows us to explore world history via "the human dramas that make history come alive," as Tonio Andrade puts it.[21]

---

[18] This is the title of Tilly's 2006 book, published with Russell Sage Foundation Publications.

[19] I am thinking here of Alfred W. Crosby, *The Columbian Exchange: Biological and Cultural Consequences of 1492* (Westport, CT: Greenwood, 1973); William Hardy McNeill, *Plagues and Peoples* (New York: Anchor Books, 1989); Kenneth Pomeranz, *The Great Divergence: China, Europe, and the Making of the Modern World Economy* (Princeton, NJ: Princeton University Press, 2000); John Robert McNeill, *Something New under the Sun: An Environmental History of the Twentieth-Century World* (New York: W.W. Norton & Company, 2000).

[20] Donald Wright, *The World and a Very Small Place in Africa: A History of Globalization in Niumi, the Gambia*, 2nd edn. (M.E. Sharpe, 1997).

[21] Tonio Andrade, "A Chinese Farmer, Two African Boys, and a Warlord: Toward a Global Microhistory," *Journal of World History* 21, no. 4 (December 2010), 574.

In this book, I am interested in the ways global and trans-regional forces such as the alliance system, pan-Islam, revolutionary nationalism, and international diplomacy shaped the choices, actions, and fortunes of both anticolonial activists and colonial administrators in Southeast Asia. The drama of wartime – and the threat of subversion – encouraged colonial and foreign offices to keep copious records of activity in the region. In their efforts to track the many (real and perceived) threats to colonial rule both from within particular colonies and from without, they preserved an enormous amount of information about their participants. Because of this, the colonial archives in London, Aix-en-Provence, and the Hague are chock-full of reports generated by minor European officials and are peppered with testimony collected in the course of official inquiries, intercepted and translated correspondence, intercepted newspapers and propaganda in both European and non-European languages, photographs, and reports from paid informants. And although the circumstances under which such information was collected and preserved must be examined critically, taken together they allow us to get a glimpse of some of the individuals who chose to take part in anticolonial activities, the personal and political motivations behind such choices, and the networks within which they were imbricated.[22] In this sense, I read the sources created by the colonial governments "against the grain" in an effort to capture the lives and experiences of some of the people who sought to resist colonial rule in and around the region.[23]

These diverse sources shed light on the links that connected Southeast Asian colonies to one another, and also on the links that connected the region to forces and interests that literally spanned the globe. The individuals who feature most frequently in these pages came primarily from two anticolonial organizations: the Indian group that called itself Ghadar, and the Vietnamese group that called itself the Viet Nam Restoration Association. These groups were by their very nature international and intercolonial in outlook – a fact that was not lost on colonial

[22] Archives, of course, are not neutral repositories awaiting discovery, but instead have been imagined, ordered, and preserved as a result of a variety of political, social, and economic pressures. See Antoinette Burton, "Introduction: Archive Fever, Archive Stories," in *Archive Stories: Facts, Fictions, and the Writing of History* (Durham, NC: Duke University Press, 1995), 6.

[23] Although this project is different in many ways from Clare Anderson's *Subaltern Lives*, like her I agree that colonial archives can in fact tell us something about marginalized peoples. See her *Subaltern Lives: Biographies of Colonialism in the Indian Ocean World, 1790–1920* (Cambridge: Cambridge University Press, 2012). For an evaluation of recent approaches to writing imperial history, including those that seek to write against the grain, see Durba Ghosh, "Another Set of Imperial Turns?" *The American Historical Review* 117, no. 3 (June 1, 2012), 772–93, doi:10.1086/ahr.117.3.772.

administrators. And while there were many other anticolonial activists in French Indochina, the Dutch East Indies, and British Malaya, during World War I it was Ghadar and the Viet Nam Restoration Association that haunted both the British and the French out of proportion to other threats. As such, it should be clear that I am not trying to write a definitive history about the many and complex anticolonial movements in all of the Southeast Asian colonies. Rather, I seek to expose the ways in which certain anticolonial groups used multiple places within Southeast Asia and beyond to achieve their goals of violent revolution. I also seek to show how Southeast Asian colonial administrators responded to these groups by activating their own intercolonial and international networks in order to obtain information and to thwart their plans.

To make matters more complex, the story is not just about intercolonial or international links between anticolonial activists or administrators in different colonies. In fact, competing states sought to extend their influence in the region by aiding anticolonial activists or subverting the power of the colonial states. During the period covered by this book, Ottoman and German diplomats and activists sought to undermine colonial rule in Southeast Asian colonies by providing aid or support to pan-Islamists, the Ghadar party, or Indochinese nationalists, depending on the time and place. This story, then, is dotted with conspiracies to subvert colonial rule with help from allies near and far. It is also punctuated by opposing networks of colonial police, diplomats, and statesmen who sought to keep such conspiracies from reaching a successful conclusion. In short, it is a book about people whose strategies transcended colonial and national borders and who acted as members of organizations larger than the colony or the nation-state.

Structure

The structure of this book mirrors my own extended intellectual journey around this subject. I was originally attracted to looking more deeply into the effects of World War I on Southeast Asia when I accidentally came across archives associated with the 1915 mutiny of the 5th Light Infantry in Singapore. As an historian of the British Empire with deep interests in the Indian army, I was intrigued by an event I had never before heard of. As I dug into the research, I was struck by increasing evidence that suggested the mutiny could not be understood outside of its connection to global events and movements. But that was only the beginning. The more I pulled on the global strands connected to the mutiny, the more I realized that Singapore was just a microcosm of the ways the war affected the whole region of Southeast Asia. Indeed, I found that the issues of pan-Islam, Ghadar revolutionaries, and German collaboration were also important in the Dutch East Indies, Siam, and China, where Germans and Indian revolutionaries used neutral states to undermine British colonial possessions in the region. Further research revealed that this was not just a British problem, since Vietnamese revolutionaries also collaborated with Germans in Siam and China to undermine French rule in Indochina. What had started as a brief research side-trip into a local mutiny in Singapore, then, turned into a project that drew in most of Southeast Asia and parts of East and South Asia.

This book begins with a mutiny of the 5th Indian infantry regiment on the island of Singapore in February 1915, which is the subject of Chapters 1 and 2. Although the mutiny was a relatively minor affair in terms of world historical events, it perfectly encapsulated the ways in which larger forces associated with World War I came together to produce a violent, albeit short-lived, rebellion in a particular location in Southeast Asia. Two of its primary causes – anti-Allied propaganda and pro-German activists – played important roles in the region for the duration of the war. Chapter 1 focuses on the mutiny and its causes from the point of view of the rebels themselves and argues that pre-existing grievances in the 5th and the encouragement by pro-German, pan-Islamic print and people combined to produce the mutiny. Fortunately for us, the mutiny's rich documentary base allows us to glimpse the motivations of the sepoys as well as the influences acting on them – which can be traced as far afield as the Ottoman Empire, the United States, India, and Germany. When viewed in its wider global context, then, the mutiny allows us to see the influence of wartime global forces on individual actions, even when those individual actions did not affect the course of world history.

Just as the causes of the mutiny demonstrate the global webs that brought the war to Southeast Asia, so too did official and civil responses to it. Chapter 2 begins by setting the narrative framework for the coordinated response to the mutiny, which included actors from Britain, France, Russia, Japan, the Netherlands, China, India, and the Arab world. As a result of wartime alliances – which included military support from French, Japanese, and Russian troops – the mutiny ended in swift victory for the British and kept key civil populations quiet. The chapter then turns to look in more detail at the official and civil responses of three sets of actors: the British, French, Russian, and Japanese members of the Allies; the Dutch and Chinese neutrals; and the Japanese, Chinese, Indian, and Arab Muslim civil populations. In so doing, it aims to show the many different ways various actors perceived the mutiny itself, and also the variety of ways they understood wartime obligations. During the war in general and the mutiny in particular, wartime alliances determined how these actors interacted, which connections between them would grow stronger, and which would be closed off.

Chapters 3 through 6 zoom out from the very specific story of the mutiny in Singapore to consider a wider swathe of the region. In so doing, they demonstrate that the Singapore mutiny was not an anomaly but rather was just one of the more dramatic events in which the War made itself felt around the region. Moreover, these chapters argue that the war affected the neutral powers in the region as much as the belligerents, and especially that the neutral powers were crucial – wittingly or not – to furthering German, Indian, Ottoman, and Vietnamese conspiracies against the Allies. Chapters 3 and 4 focus on the Dutch East Indies, whose neutrality provided a convenient haven for pan-Islamic, Indian, and hostile German operatives to harass British Malaya, Burma, and India with incendiary propaganda and agents. Such schemes – both real and exaggerated – exercised British colonial and diplomatic officials from Batavia, Singapore, India, Siam, Burma, Hong Kong, Manila, San Francisco, New York, the Hague, and London. Their main concern was less the safety of British Malaya or Burma (though that was in fact a factor) than the safety of India, since British authorities were rightly convinced that their enemies were using the Dutch East Indies as a staging point for German-funded, Ottoman-inspired Indian revolutionaries from the United States to send arms and people to India. Dutch authorities were also concerned about these activities, mostly because they feared they would be dragged into the war on one side or another, and also because they worried about the effects of pan-Islamic propaganda on the Muslim population in the East Indies. Chapter 3 explores the massive impact of the war on the East Indies and outlines the various schemes of Germans and Indians to use the islands as both a base and way-station for carrying out anti-Allied schemes. Chapter 4 deepens the exploration of these schemes by focusing on the detention of two ships in Dutch waters during the war – the *Maverick* and the *Henry S* – and what they and their crews revealed about the global nature of these schemes.

Chapter 5 explores the role of neutral Siam in facilitating German attempts to foment unrest in Indochina, Burma, and India. In Siam, which remained neutral until 1917, German consuls collaborated with Indian and Vietnamese revolutionaries to facilitate and encourage armed insurrections in Burma and India on the one hand, and in French Indochina on the other. Since Siam was strategically located between British and French colonial interests, it – like the Dutch East Indies – became a convenient way station, safe haven, and training ground for anti-Allied activity in the region. Yet unlike the Dutch East Indies government, the Siamese government was under no illusions about which side it should support when push came to shove. The British influence on the Siamese government and economy, not to mention the proximity of the vast Indian army to the borders of Siam, led the Siamese king to cooperate fully with British requests for the arrest and extradition of suspected revolutionaries long before he formally joined his country with the Allies in 1917. As a result of the arrests made in Siam and the inter-rogations that followed, the British were able to learn a great deal about the larger regional and global plot to undermine the Allies through their colonies.

Chapter 6 explores the ways in which Vietnamese, Germans, and – to a lesser extent – Indians sought to export and finance revolution from the unstable but strategically located state of China. From China (until it entered the war on the side of the Allies in August 1917), German con-suls provided money and arms for bands of Chinese "pirates" willing to occupy frontier zones in Indochina, for Vietnamese anti-French activists such as Phan Bội Châu, and for Indian revolutionaries seeking funds for revolutionary activities in India. While these efforts did not successfully lead to widespread armed resistance in Indochina or India, in Indochina they did encourage sustained violence along the colony's frontier with China, which proved costly to the Indochinese government. At the same time, German schemes to foment unrest from China existed in tension with the Chinese government's desire to enter the war on the side of the Allies in order to have a voice at the bargaining table when the war was over. Yet the instability caused by the Chinese Revolution of 1911 and its aftermath meant that the Chinese government could do little to halt the activities of anti-Allied revolutionaries within its borders, even when it had the will to do so. The instability in China and elsewhere in the region also prompted the Allied powers to invest in the creation of fledgling intelligence networks designed to expose and root out the kinds of transnational, anticolonial subversive movements prompted by the war. The creation of these networks was in fact one of the more important long-term consequences of the war, for during the interwar period they would be employed with far greater efficiency in the fight against international communism throughout the region – although that is the story of another book.

A century has passed since World War I began. We are still learning about the ways the war was waged in the colonial world and also about the costs of the war to colonial subjects. I hope this book will add yet another layer of nuance to our understanding of the profound global consequences of the war, even in locations thousands of miles from the trenches on the Western Front. I also hope this book will provide a convincing argument that colonial administrators, colonial subjects, and anticolonial activists understood their actions not solely or even most importantly within binary colonial/metropolitan relationships but also within a variety of trans-regional networks that blurred the neat boundaries of national-colonial territories. My goal is to show that it is we who have tended to miss these larger connections, not they. Finally, I hope this book will demonstrate that it is possible to write meaningful world history by beginning with the micro-level and then tracing connections outward to multiple locations around the globe. Through the links between small-scale stories and large forces, we can see the many ways the global, the regional, and the local were mutually interdependent.

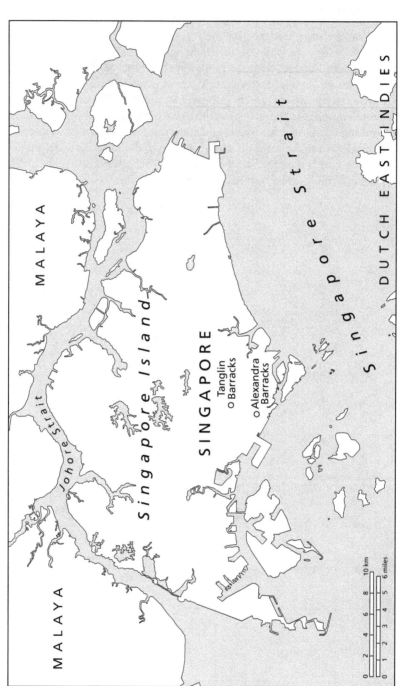

Map 2 The Singapore Mutiny.

1 The Singapore Mutiny of 1915

Global Origins in a Global War

On February 15, 1915, the right wing of the Indian Army's 5th Light Infantry mutinied on the island of Singapore. Although this mutiny did not affect most of the rest of the world, the rest of the world very definitely affected it. This book includes two chapters on the mutiny of the 5th because it encapsulates so clearly the ways World War I came to Southeast Asia. Indeed, two of its primary causes – German–Indian–Turkish anti-Allied propaganda and pro-German activists – played critical roles in the whole region for the duration of the war. Concern about pro-German, anticolonial schemes dominate the British, French, and Dutch official diplomatic and military archives from this period, and include an almost paranoid apprehension about the revolutionary potential for such schemes across Southeast and East Asia. For while activities intended to undermine colonial rule were never as successful, organized, or well-funded as colonial authorities imagined or feared, they nevertheless contributed to anticolonial unrest in many places during the war, including Malaya, the East Indies, and Indochina. Such anticolonial activity was doubly threatening because its networks of support went well beyond the orbit of colonial control, including places as close as Siam and China, and as distant as the Ottoman Empire, the United States, and Germany. And these networks did not respect colonial boundaries: Pan-Islamic, pro-German propaganda moved easily between the East Indies and Malaya, while pro-German activities originating in China were directed to Indochina, Malaya, Burma, and India. In this sense, the mutiny is also significant because it allows us to see the porousness of colonial and state territorial boundaries throughout the region, as well as the many avenues of connection between Southeast Asia and the rest of the world.

As a case study, the mutiny of the 5th in Singapore also illustrates the ways global, anticolonial forces generated during the war were mediated by colonized subjects. In order to win people over, anti-Allied propaganda and pro-German activists not only had to target issues that spoke to actual grievances of colonized subjects, but they also had to convince people that acting against colonial rule was worth the risk. The latter was far more difficult than the former, and is doubtless one of the reasons such efforts were not particularly successful over the course of the war. But in this case, the grievances of the 5th and the encouragement by pro-German, pan-Islamic print and people were sufficiently aligned that they produced a mutiny. Fortunately for us, its rich documentary base allows us to glimpse the motivations of the sepoys themselves in taking such a huge risk. In so doing, we can see the influence of wartime global forces on individual actions, even when those individual actions did not affect the course of world history.

It wasn't just the causes of the mutiny that capture the ways the World War I came to Southeast Asia – so too did the reasons for its defeat. Here too, wartime alliances and rivalries fundamentally shaped the outcome of the mutiny, even as they highlighted in microcosm shifting dynamics among the various powers in the region. This, however, is the subject of Chapter 2. In this chapter, we begin with the events of the mutiny in order to establish a baseline for "what happened" on February 15 and the days that followed. From there, we explore the causes of the mutiny, beginning with the initial disaffection of the Malay States Guides (who were also stationed on Singapore) and then moving to the German–Indian–Turkish plot and the role of German prisoners of war. We end by contrasting the available evidence on the causes of the mutiny with the public explanation in an attempt to understand why British authorities fought so hard to minimize the global context in which the mutiny had occurred. Throughout, the testimony and letters of sepoys themselves feature largely, both to demonstrate the impact of global forces on individual lives and also to remind us that they were more than mere pawns in a great game between European powers. In early 1915, the sepoys of the 5th were confronted with information about the war from sources that literally crisscrossed the world. They assessed the credibility of the information as best they could, explored their options, and then took action. While the mutiny occurred locally, the evidence indicates that sepoys in the 5th considered their place in the wider global context of anticolonial activity before making their choice to take local action.

Mutiny of the "Loyal 5th"[1]

Monday, February 15 was a holiday in Singapore in 1915. It was Chinese New Year, and since two-thirds of Singapore's population was

---

[1] The 5th Light Infantry were known as the "Loyal 5th" because of their role in helping to suppress the 1857 Indian Rebellion.

Chinese, the island city marked the occasion publicly as a day of cele-
bration and rest. By early afternoon, many men of the Indian Army's 5th
Light Infantry – which was completing a five-month garrison duty – were
involved in various light activities, including praying, napping, smoking,
taking care of regimental animals, and chatting. The regiment's British
officers were engaged in idle pursuits nearby: The commanding officer,
Colonel Martin, was sleeping at his house, several other officers were rest-
ing in their quarters, and one was returning from a picnic. Two weeks
earlier, the regiment had received orders to transfer to Hong Kong, and
most of the men's belongings were already packed. They were to embark
the next day, and only the final preparations for departure remained.

One of these preparations was to transfer small arms ammunition from
the regimental magazine to a truck destined for the Army Ordnance
Department. A small group of sepoys was ordered to complete this work,
and they began just after 2:00 p.m. At about 3:00 p.m., someone – it was
never clear exactly who – fired a shot in the direction of the truck, and
immediately afterward the outside sentry guarding the transfer charged
the men around the truck with fixed bayonet.[2] According to eyewitnesses,
all but one of the sepoys who had been loading the ammunition scattered,
and then both A and B companies of the regiment's right wing turned
out and looted the ammunition in the truck and the magazine.[3]

From all accounts, both Indian and British, confusion reigned for the
next few minutes. Many sepoys later testified they did not pay much
attention to the opening shots, thinking they were fireworks being lit in
honor of Chinese New Year. But as the companies that mutinied began
to move out and challenge bystanders to join or be shot, the gravity
of the situation became clear. Within fifteen minutes an Indian officer,
Subedar Khan Mohamed Khan, had reached Colonel Martin's house
to alert him. Since Martin was sleeping, it took some time for him to
telephone the city to let the newly arrived General Officer Commanding
the Troops in Singapore – Brigadier General Dudley Ridout – know what
was happening. In the confusion, Martin neglected to inform the officers

---

[2] Narrative of Events, Confidential Report from Governor Arthur Young to Lewis Harcourt, February 25, 1915, Report on Singapore Disturbances of 1915, WO 32/9559,
TNA. Imtiaz Ali was credited for firing the first shot later, but this is not entirely
clear.

[3] The half of the regiment that mutinied was the right wing, which the official report listed
as being composed mainly of "Rajput Muslims." T.R. Sareen, compiler. *Secret Documents
on Singapore Mutiny 1915, Vol. I* (New Delhi: Mounto Publishing House, 1995), 37. Both
volumes I and II are published versions of the Court of Inquiry held in the aftermath
of the mutiny, along with its supporting evidence, a few memoirs, and some newspaper
articles.

at Tanglin barracks, which was serving as a POW camp, or the municipal police in Singapore.[4]

In the meantime, the mutinous A and B companies of the right wing were joined by C and D companies, and they split into three groups. The first headed straight for the POW camp at Tanglin – where the officers and men of the German ship *Emden*, which had been sunk off the coast of Malaya, were being held along with other German nationals – and released the prisoners. In the process, they killed thirteen British and Indian officers and men and, apparently accidentally, one German prisoner.[5] A second, smaller group headed toward the center of Singapore, killing a Malay civilian and six British soldiers and civilians along the way. Once they reached the city center, they also wounded two police officers at the Central Police Station.[6] A third group proceeded to the barracks of the Malay States Guides artillery unit, where they attempted – with some success – to convince the soldiers there to join them.[7] At various points along the way, this third group killed nine British civilians – nine men and one woman – and one British officer.[8] This group also attempted to storm Colonel Martin's house but, after being beaten back, besieged it instead. It is worth noting that very few sepoys actively tried to defend against the mutinous right wing. A small group of Malay States Volunteer Rifles, who were in Singapore for a training course, stayed with Colonel Martin and helped defend his house, but the majority of the 818 men in the regiment either turned against the British or disappeared into the surrounding jungle.[9]

By late afternoon, news of the mutiny had spread to much of the island and well beyond. Brigadier General Ridout telephoned the Admiral Commanding-in-Chief, Martyn Jerram, to request authorization to land a party of eighty-five British seamen on the *HMS Cadmus*, which

[4] Ridout to Secretary of State for War, February 25, Report on Singapore Disturbances of 1915, WO 32/9559.

[5] Report on Singapore Disturbances of 1915, 22.   [6] Sareen, *Secret Documents*, 31.

[7] There is some confusion on this point. While Tarling and Harper argue that the 5th tried to force arms on the Malay States Guides, the papers included in the Memorandums and Telegrams Relating to Disturbances at Singapore, 1915, CO 273/420 indicate that about half of the ninety-six men of the unit joined with the 5th. See also Nicholas Tarling, "The Merest Pustule: The Singapore Mutiny of 1915," *The Malaysian Branch of the Royal Asiatic Society* 55 (1982); Tim Harper, "Singapore, 1915, and the Birth of the Asian Underground," *Modern Asian Studies* 47, no. 06 (2013).

[8] Sareen, *Secret Documents*, 30–31.

[9] Report 13548, March 23, 1915. Memorandums and Telegrams Relating to Disturbances at Singapore, CO 273/420, TNA. Sho Kuwajima makes this point about the behavior of the left, nonmutinous, wing of the regiment in "Indian Mutiny in Singapore, 1915: People Who Observed the Scene and People Who Heard the News," *New Zealand Journal of Asian Studies* 11:1 (June 2009), 376.

was in Singapore harbor.[10] He then called out the Singapore Volunteer Corps (SVC), which was a civilian force composed, in August 1914, of about 450 Malay and Chinese men. He also called out the Singapore Volunteer Rifles, a partially trained European infantry corps formed at the start of the war, and appointed about 200 special constables from among the European population.[11] Ridout proceeded to close all roads in and out of the city of Singapore in an effort to prevent mutinous sepoys from reaching the city center in force. Then, at dusk, he asked the Governor – Arthur Young – to declare martial law. Meanwhile, Ridout and Young sent small groups of volunteers and special constables to the European households in the surrounding area, and brought their members to the city center for protection. As many European women and children as possible were put out of harm's way on three ships in the harbor, while the men of the city – including 186 Japanese – were assembled to guard key buildings.[12]

The European population of Singapore had reason to be alarmed by the mutiny. The British regiment that had been stationed in Singapore before the war – the King's Own Yorkshire Light Infantry – had been recalled back to Europe at its start. As we have seen, the volunteer forces on the island were few in number and poorly trained. Singapore maintained a civil police force of about 1,200 Malays, Chinese, and Indians, but only 220 Sikhs among them were trained to use arms.[13] This meant that in February 1915, the 5th Light Infantry and the small detachment of the Malay States Guides were the only regular forces garrisoned for the defense of Singapore, and they were far better trained and armed than any of the auxiliary or civil forces. And now, in the middle of a world war, portions of both were in open rebellion and the rest were in hiding, leaving the colony almost completely undefended. To make matters more desperate, the rebel sepoys had made it clear that they were not afraid to

---

[10] The Admiral C-I-C China was in Singapore at the time. Ridout to Secretary of State for War, February 25, Report on Singapore Disturbances of 1915.

[11] Tim Harper, "Singapore, 1915, and the Birth of the Asian Underground," 1783.

[12] For more on the evacuation of women, see C. Doran, "Gender Matters in the Singapore Mutiny," *Sojourn: Journal of Social Issues in Southeast Asia* 17:1 (April 2002), 76–93. The elaborate protection of women and children from mutinous troops was reminiscent of the 1857 Indian Rebellion, when images of raped and murdered British women and children fueled British desires for revenge. See Heather Streets, *Martial Races: The Military, Race, and Masculinity in British Imperial Culture* (Manchester: Manchester University Press, 2004), chapters 1 and 2. Not surprisingly, the local government did not evacuate Chinese, Malay, or Indian women. For the Japanese volunteers, see Sho Kuwajima, *Mutiny in Singapore: War, Anti-War, and the War for India's Independence* (New Delhi: Rainbow Publishers, 2006), 96.

[13] W.R.E. Harper and Harry Miller, *Singapore Mutiny* (Singapore: Oxford University Press, 1984), 16.

kill the objects of their wrath, having taken thirty-one lives already in the first hours of the mutiny.

For these reasons, British authorities realized immediately that reinforcements from outside Singapore were necessary. Within hours after the start of the mutiny, Governor Young had telegrammed India to ask for a British regiment to be sent straight away. Realizing these reinforcements would take days to arrive, on the evening of the 15th Young also asked General Ridout to request that Admiral Jerram send a wireless message for help to a French cruiser, the *Montcalm*, which had just left Singapore harbor the previous day. Later in the evening, Young saw Admiral Jerram himself and asked him to try reaching one or two Japanese cruisers and any other friendly ships that might be of assistance. As a result of these efforts, help began to arrive from the waters around Singapore by the 16th. The French arrived first in the *Montcalm*, then the Japanese and Russian cruisers *Otowa* and *Orel* arrived on the 18th, and finally the Japanese cruiser *Tsushima* arrived on the 19th. By February 20, the 4th Shropshires, who had been sent from Burma by the Indian government, also arrived.[14]

In the interval, however, the mutiny had begun to fall apart. On the morning of the 16th, the eighty-five men of the British ship *Cadmus*, along with sixty Volunteers, raised the siege at Colonel Martin's house and retrieved the inhabitants.[15] Already on the 16th many men from the nonmutinous left wing left their hiding places in the jungle and surrendered to British authorities in small groups, and by the 17th, 300 of the approximately 400 of these men were in custody.[16] From that point on the British and their allies were on the offensive, capturing fugitives, retaking occupied areas, and receiving sepoys who decided to surrender. By February 24, all but 150 of the 818 men of the 5th Light Infantry and three of the ninety-six Malay States Guides were in custody.[17] The situation was so well in hand that the French *Montcalm* had departed the day before, and in the following few days so too did the Japanese and Russian ships.

The British authorities began meting out punishment for the mutiny almost immediately. On February 23, two sepoys were convicted by

---

[14] Report 8578, February 22, 1915. Memorandums and Telegrams Relating to Disturbances at Singapore.

[15] Report on Singapore Disturbances of 1915. They did not hold the house, but rather withdrew because their numbers were considered too small to hold it effectively.

[16] Report 13548, March 23, 1915. Memorandums and Telegrams Relating to Disturbances at Singapore.

[17] Report 14734, February 29, Memorandums and Telegrams Relating to Disturbances at Singapore.

summary court-martial and shot. But this was just the beginning. In all, 203 sepoys in the 5th Light Infantry were court-martialed, and 202 were convicted. Sentences included forty-one executions, sixty-three trans-portations for life, sixty-nine prison terms between ten and twenty years, and twenty-four prison terms between six weeks and seven years. A fur-ther fifty-two sepoys died in the fighting or in trying to escape Singa-pore, bringing the total death toll – soldier and civilian – to a grisly 124.[18] Nearly a quarter of the regiment had been killed or permanently removed.

The harsh response to the mutiny was meant to instill fear among both the armed forces and the civilian population, and executions were made public for this reason. The most dramatic episode occurred on March 22, 1915, when twenty-one of the principal instigators from the 5th were sentenced. A crowd of approximately 6,000 civilians turned up to watch. All twenty-one men had been court-martialed and found guilty: Six-teen were sentenced to transportation or imprisonment, while five were sentenced to summary execution by firing squad. The five condemned men – Subedar Dunde Khan, Jemadar Chisti Khan, Havildar Rahmat Ali, Sepoy Hakim Ali, and Havildar Abdul Ghani – were then marched, under heavy guard, to posts in front of the prison wall. Their feet and hands were tied together while the presiding Major loudly proclaimed that all of the men "have been found guilty of stirring up and joining a mutiny and are sentenced to death by being shot to death," and that "all these men of the Indian Army have broken their oath as soldiers of His Majesty the King."[19] For the benefit of the crowd assembled, the sen-tences were read in English, Malay, Chinese, and Urdu. Then, the firing squad of twenty-five men raised their rifles and fired multiple times while the crowd of civilians looked on. Executions continued to occur until April 18, although courts-martial continued to be held until September 1915 as the last remaining soldiers were brought in from their hiding places on the island.[20]

By all accounts, the mutiny was a failure. After liberating the German POW camp and causing panic on the island, the mutineers were unable to occupy the city, hold the military barracks, induce large numbers of other military or civilian groups to join them, or escape the island to freedom. Those who did make it across the narrow strait to Johore were

[18] Court Martial Proceedings on Mutineers of 5th Light Infantry, Singapore, 1915, L/Mil/7/7191; Report 8952, February 23, Memorandums and Telegrams Relating to Disturbances at Singpore. The death toll includes those killed by the mutineers as well.
[19] *The Straits Times*, March 23, 1915.
[20] Court Martial Proceedings on Mutineers of the 5th Light Infantry, 1915. India Office Records, (IOR) L/MIl/7/7191, Vol. II, 1.

sent back by its sultan, and several were believed to have drowned trying. In fact, almost every last sepoy who mutinied – and some who didn't – was either apprehended and punished, or died in the melee. Although the 5th had the element of surprise and military superiority, with outside help they were defeated in a matter of a few days.

For all its drama, the mutiny did not affect the course of the global war. Fighting continued in Europe, in the Dardanelles, and on the seas. Singapore remained in British hands, and no further violence erupted on the island for the war's duration. As we shall see, authorities in Singapore did their best to cast the event as a purely local phenomenon with little relevance to the rest of the world, and over the decades the event faded into relative obscurity. For these reasons, until recently the Singapore Mutiny has not attracted much scholarly attention. Only two monographs have been devoted to the event: One was written in 1984 for a popular audience, while the other was written in 1991 with an eye toward the Japanese role in the affair.[21] The mutiny has also been the subject of six scholarly articles. The first, written by Nicholas Tarling in 1982, discounts the role of external influences on the mutiny.[22] Three others explore particular aspects of the mutiny, including the role played by Russians in its suppression, the use of gender as a trope by Europeans, and the use of racial profiling by British authorities in its aftermath.[23] Three explore the mutiny in its global context. The first, written by Sho Kuwajima in 2009, explores this theme only superficially.[24] The final two appeared in print simultaneously in 2013 and explore the mutiny in terms of global radicalism and as a way of exploring the relations of the local and the global, respectively.[25] A few scholars have discussed the mutiny as part of the larger Indian nationalist movement or in terms of the development of British intelligence in Southeast Asia, but when it is

---

[21] These books are, respectively, R.W.E. Harper and Harry Miller's *Singapore Mutiny* (New York: Oxford University Press, 1984), and Sho Kuwajima's *Indian Mutiny in Singapore* (New Delhi: Rainbow Publishers, 2006).

[22] Nicholas Tarling, "'The Merest Pustule': The Singapore Mutiny of 1915," *Journal of the Malaysian Branch of the Royal Asiatic Society* 55:2 (1982).

[23] Karen Snow, "Russia and the 1915 Mutiny in Singapore," *South East Asia Research* 5 (1997); and Christine Doran, "Gender Matters in the Singapore Mutiny"; Farish Noor, "Racial Profiling Revisited: The 1915 Indian Mutiny in Singapore and the Impact of Profiling on Religious and Ethnic Minorities," *Politics, Religion, and Ideology* 12:1 (2011).

[24] Sho Kuwajima, "Indian Mutiny in Singapore, 1915".

[25] Tim Harper, "Singapore, 1915, and the Birth of the Asian Underground," *Modern Asian Studies* 47:6 (2013); Heather Streets-Salter, "The Singapore Mutiny of 1915: The Local Was Global," *Journal of World History* 24:3 (2013). The arguments in my own article preview, in much abbreviated form, some of the arguments I make in this chapter and Chapter 2.

mentioned at all it has most commonly been framed in the context of Singaporean national history.[26]

Despite the mutiny's apparent failure, it is an important case study for what it reveals about the ways larger global forces set in motion by the war affected Southeast Asia. The reason it provides such a rich case study is because it was documented extensively in multiple archives. The official British Court of Inquiry appointed to explore the causes of the mutiny compiled hundreds of pages of testimony from British, Indian, Chinese, and Malay witnesses. The sources also include courts-martial testimony, telegrams, reports, and eyewitness accounts.[27] The British sources are further bolstered by French sources compiled by the Admiral who commanded the *Montcalm* and the Governor of Indochina, by Dutch, Japanese and Russian sources, and by oral interviews of Singaporeans.[28]

[26] For example, Bhai Nahal Singh and Kirpal Singh mention the mutiny on pages 174–175 of their *Struggle for Free Hindustan: Ghadar Movement, Vol. I (1905–1916)* (New Delhi: Atlantic Publishers and Distributors, 1986), and Sho Kuwajima (*Mutiny in Singapore*) clearly sees the event as a part of an Indian nationalist history. Malcolm Murfett also devotes a chapter to the mutiny in his nationally based *Between Two Oceans: A Military History of Singapore From First Settlement to Final British Withdrawal* (Singapore: Marshall Cavendish Academic, 2004), while Ban Kah Choon discusses it in terms of the development of the British Special Branch in *Absent History: the Untold Story of Special Branch Operations in Singapore, 1915–1942* (Singapore: Horizon Books, 2001). The Singapore National Museum's permanent exhibit about the history of Singapore decidedly portrays the mutiny as a local event whose importance lies mostly in the development of the Singaporean nation.

[27] The British sources exist at both the National Archives (Report on Singapore Disturbances of 1915, WO 32/9559; Report on Singapore Disturbances Part Two, WO 32/9560; Memorandums and Telegrams Related to Disturbances at Singapore, CO 273/420) and at the India Office Library (Report in Connection with Mutiny of 5th Light Infantry at Singapore 1915, L/MIL/17/19/48, and Court Martial Proceedings on Mutineers of the 5th Light Infantry, 1915. India Office Records, L/MIl/7/7191, Vols. I and II). The Foreign Office papers of the Straits Settlements at The National Archives also contain voluminous reports and letters about the Mutiny, and about sedition in the Indian Army more generally. Many of these documents – especially those held by the India Office collection in the British Library, have also been helpfully reproduced in Sareen's *Secret Documents on the Singapore Mutiny.*

[28] French sources are located at the Archives Nationales d'Outre-Mer in Aix-en-Provence (Troubles de Singapore, FM indo/nf/1037). The Dutch sources are located at the Nationaal Archief at the Hague, mainly in the Ministerie van Kolonien: Geheim series but also in the Ministerie van Buitenlandse Zaken series. The Japanese sources have been used extensively by Sho Kuwajima in his *Mutiny in Singapore: War, Anti-War, and the War for India's Independence* (New Delhi: Rainbow Publishers, 2006), and the Russian sources by Karen Snow in her "Russia in the 1915 Mutiny in Singapore." The Singapore National Archives also maintains recordings (and transcriptions) of oral interviews, compiled mostly in the 1980s, of old Singapore residents who remembered the mutiny from their childhoods. However, these are mostly useful as a way of understanding how the mutiny has been remembered in Singapore rather than for their factual accuracy. Among the interviewees were Mabel Martin, William Martinus, Mohammad Javad Namazie, and Sng Choon Yee (SNA accession numbers 000388; 000446/09/07–08; 000189/11; and 000064/48/11–12, respectively).

Finally, the mutiny was well covered in newspaper articles from Japan, Hong Kong, Manila, and New York. While all of these sources must be used carefully when trying to reconstruct the voices of those who took part, they nevertheless allow unusual access, from a variety of international perspectives, to an event that brought the world – and the war – to Southeast Asia.

Causes

Why did the 5th mutiny? Certainly every soldier in the regiment understood that the price for mutiny, if unsuccessful, was death. In fact the regiment's history was steeped in defending the Raj against mutiny, as it had remained loyal during the Indian Rebellion of 1857 fifty-five years earlier.[29] When the 5th arrived in Singapore in October 1914 from India's Central Provinces, it came with a good record of service and was serving its first overseas duty in the regiment's history. And yet less than four months after arriving in Singapore, half the men had mutinied and the 5th would never be trusted again. In the circumstances, it seems logical to surmise that whatever had induced the men of the 5th to mutiny occurred during their time in Singapore.

Based on the available evidence, the disaffection that led to the mutiny seems to have come from three main influences: the earlier disaffection of the Malay States Guides, the impact of German–Indian–Turkish plans to undermine Allied rule, and encouragement by German prisoners of war. These three elements were in fact deeply intertwined, as the Malay States Guides were themselves influenced by the other two. Thus in spite of British protests to the contrary – about which we will hear more at the end of the chapter – the evidence collected by the court of inquiry and other sources indicate that local conditions alone could not account for the drastic decision to mutiny. Rather, the sepoys took action after a long period of assessing the news and information they received from events and people tied to places as far-flung as India, Canada, the United States, Britain, Germany, and the Ottoman Empire.

The Malay States Guides

Let us begin with the Malay States Guides, whose actions and overall demeanor played an important role in the outlook of the men of the

---

[29] Until 1902, the 5th had been numbered as the 42nd. It had gone through many changes in its composition since 1857, from high-caste Brahmins to completely Muslim troops from Eastern Punjab. Tarling, "The Merest Pustule," 27.

5th. The Guides had originally been formed for duties in peninsular Malaya, but were moved to Singapore in the fall of 1914 in anticipation of being deployed overseas for the war. The regiment was composed of Indians recruited both locally and in India, the bulk of whom were Sikhs, with the remainder comprising Pathans, Punjabi Muslims, and a few Hindus.[30] There was no history of trouble with the regiment, and in fact sources indicate British authorities thought of them highly. While being formally inspected in 1907, for example, the Field Marshal wrote that the commanding officer should be commended, because "the state of efficiency to which he has brought the Malay States Guides reflects the greatest credit on himself."[31]

Shortly after the war broke out, the commanding officer of the Guides had written to the War Office declaring that the regiment was willing and able to go on active service abroad in support of the war effort. He had done this on the advice of his highest-ranking Indian officer, who – it later turned out – might not have discussed the matter fully with his men.[32] But after they were moved to Singapore for redeployment abroad, it quickly became clear that all was not well in the Malay States Guides. The first indication occurred on November 24, 1914, when the Guides' Commanding Officer received an anonymous letter saying that some of the Indian officers were encouraging their men to refuse overseas service.[33] Shortly thereafter, when the regiment was ordered to proceed overseas to East Africa, the men made their unwillingness to go plain. In a letter signed "The Men of the Malay States Guides," they argued that their terms of service did not include the obligation to serve abroad.[34] As a result, in early December 1914 the Commanding Officer of the Guides was forced to withdraw the offer to serve overseas, much to his great embarrassment. Then in January 1915, all but one mountain battery of artillery was sent back to peninsular Malaya in disgrace.

What had happened to this efficient and dependable regiment during its brief stay in Singapore? An official British enquiry into the matter concluded, against substantial evidence, that the primary causes behind the Guides' unwillingness to serve had been because of disputes about

---

[30] When the regiment was inspected in 1907 at Penang, it consisted of 662 Jat Sikhs, 73 Punjabi Muslims, 69 Pathans, and 6 Hindus. Report 17871, May 20, 1907, Straits Settlements Original Correspondence: War Office, CO 273/334.

[31] Report 17871, May 20, 1907, Straits Settlements Original Correspondence.

[32] Tarling, "The Merest Pustule," 41.

[33] Malcolm Murfett, Between Two Oceans, 160.

[34] The progression of events relating to the Malay States Guides' refusal to serve overseas is documented in Malay States Guides: Withdrawal of Offer to Volunteer for Foreign Service and Subsequent Renewal of Offer, India Office Library, IOR/L/MIL/7/17261.

overseas pay and various nonpolitical "intrigues" by its Indian officers.[35] But statements made by individuals within the Guides clearly demonstrate that they conceived their discontent in terms of global events outside the immediate orbit of Singapore.

One of the most important of these events was the journey of the Japanese ship *Komagata Maru*.[36] The ship had been chartered in early 1914 by an Indian man, Gurdit Singh, to carry 376 Indian passengers (of whom 340 were Sikhs and twenty-four Muslim) from Hong Kong to Vancouver, with the purpose of deliberately challenging Canadian laws restricting Indian immigration.[37] However, once the ship arrived in the port of Vancouver it was not allowed to dock, nor were its passengers allowed to disembark. The passengers were forced to wait on board ship for two months in difficult conditions while their fate was decided, only to discover at the end that the entire ship had been ordered back to India. The *Komagata Maru* thus left Vancouver under escort by the Canadian military on July 23, 1914. When it finally reached Calcutta, India, on September 26, the outraged and weary passengers tousled with British authorities who were intent on treating them as prisoners. The altercation resulted in the passengers being fired upon by the authorities, during which nineteen of the Indians on board were killed.

The *Komagata Maru* incident galvanized anti-British sentiment among many Indians around the world, particularly among Sikhs and Punjabis. Soldiers in the Indian army were particularly outraged, since many of the potential settlers aboard the ship had served in the army themselves. News of the *Komagata Maru* easily reached the Malay States Guides, who informed their officers that the treatment of Sikhs and other Punjabis on the ship indicated that the colonial government did not hold the service of Indians in high regard, and that they therefore were not willing to sacrifice their lives abroad.[38] The letter they sent to their commanding officer refusing to serve in East Africa is worth quoting at length in this regard:

As our brethren who have been shot in the Komagatamaru [sic] case have troubled and grieved us, some of us have lost dear brothers and other blood-relations, we can never forget the kindness of the Indian Government (British) for shooting and slaughtering the dead who lost their livings in India in the hopes of earning

---

[35] Murfett, *Between Two Oceans*, 160.

[36] For a full account, see Hugh J.M. Johnston, *The Voyage of the Komagata Maru: The Sikh Challenge to Canada's Colour Bar* (Vancouver: University of British Columbia Press, 2014).

[37] Ramnath, *Haj to Utopia*, 47.

[38] For an extended treatment of the Komagata Maru and its impact on shaping the direction of the mutiny in Singapore, see Kuwajima, *Mutiny in Singapore*, 16–33.

money and better livings in America from which country they were expelled, and were not allowed to land and returned, but the Indian Government again taking the poor dead as seditious people, did not allow them to land at their own home even. When we have no right to walk freely on our own land then what do you want us for in other countries? As we are butchered in our own country we cannot expect better treatment from other countries, therefore we strongly tell you that we will not go to other countries to fight except those mentioned in our agreement sheets.[39]

In the court of inquiry prompted by the Guides' resistance to service abroad, the regiment's British officers testified they were aware that their men had heard damaging stories not only about the *Komagata Maru* but also about massive casualty rates in the War and the awesome power of the German military.[40] Thus, even though the court of inquiry finally concluded that external influences had not caused the disaffection in the Guides, its own summary contradicted its conclusions by noting that the unfortunate voyage of the *Komagata Maru*, not to mention sedition from outside the regiment, had in fact played a role.[41]

News of the refusal by Canadian authorities to let the ship land was widely reported in both mainstream and radical newspapers around the world. In Singapore, every stage of the voyage was covered in the English-language papers the *Straits Times* and the *Singapore Free Press and Mercantile Advertiser*, beginning in April 1914 when the ship arrived in Shanghai.[42] Between April and December 1914, no fewer than twenty-five stories appeared, many of them quite long and detailed, describing the struggles of the Indians to land in Vancouver and the violence used against them both there and in India. As we will see, radical revolutionary newspapers found in Singapore during the same period also reported the ship's journey and the suffering of its passengers. Thus during the fall of 1914, it would have been almost impossible for the Malay States Guides not to hear about the difficulties experienced by their co-religionists, either via discussion of English-language papers or through reports in Indian papers published in Urdu or Gurmukhi.

The Indian community in Singapore had another reason to be interested in the fate of the *Komagata Maru*, because Gurdit Singh, the Indian financial sponsor and organizer of the ship's voyage, had lived in British Malaya and Singapore for some years prior to the beginning of the ship's journey in April 1914. Because of this, reports in the papers were likely amplified by local individuals who knew Singh personally. And those

---

[39] Report 6471, February 9, 1915. Straits Settlements Original Correspondence: Foreign and India Offfices, 1915, CO 273/433.

[40] Murfett, *Between Two Oceans*, 160.   [41] Ibid., 160.

[42] *Straits Times* April 21, 1914, 8.

who identified with the struggles of those on board may have felt an even closer bond with the passengers when the ship anchored in Singapore for three days, from September 16 to 19, after being forced back to India from Canada. Even though the Singapore government did not allow the passengers in the *Komagata Maru* to come ashore for fear they would spread disaffection among the Indian community, news of its presence was widely known and discussed. Several months after the mutiny, the Governor admitted that "though the ship had no communication with the land, yet it left a bad effect" on the Indian troops stationed there.[43]

The outrage over the *Komagata Maru* expressed by the Malay States Guides in their anonymous letter of December 1914 appears to have been fed by a well-developed group of pro-German Indian revolutionaries active in Singapore at the time. One of the links to this revolutionary network was a merchant named Kasim Mansur. After the Guides' refusal to serve in December, a corporal in the unit persuaded Mansur to write a letter to the Turkish consul at Rangoon indicating that the Guides were ready to turn against the British, and asking the Turkish authorities to send a warship to Singapore to support them. The letter was intercepted by British authorities in Rangoon, and on January 23, 1915 Mansur was arrested in Singapore.[44] In light of the mutiny of the 5th less than a month later, Mansur's actions were deemed seditious enough that he was tried and hanged on May 31, 1915.

Mansur himself was a known supporter of the radical nationalist Indian Ghadar Party, about which we will hear more below.[45] What we need to know now is that the Ghadar Party was openly pro-German once war was declared, and that the Germans provided funds for Ghadar activists around the world to spread anti-British propaganda amongst Indian communities.[46] We also know that the Malay States Guides, in addition

---

[43] Letter from the Governor of the Straits Settlements to the Secretary of State for the Colonies Regarding Court of Inquiry and Causes of Mutiny, August 15, 1915. Sareen, *Secret Documents*, 711.

[44] Murfet, *Between Two Oceans*, 161. The letter was suspicious in any case because the Turkish consul left Rangoon once war was declared between the Ottomans and the British.

[45] Ramnath, *Haj to Utopia*, 191.

[46] There has been some very good work on this subject in the last decade, including Tilman Lüdke, *Jihad Made in Germany: Ottoman and German Propaganda and Intelligence Operations in the First World War* (Münster; London: LIT; Global [distributor], 2005); Kris Manjapra, "The Ilusions of Encounter: Muslim 'Minds' and Hindu Revolutionaries in First World War Germany and After," *Journal of Global History*, no. 1 (2006): 363–82; Andrew Jarboe, "World War I and the Imperial Moment" (Ph.D. Dissertation, Northeastern University, 2013); and chapter 10 in Suzanne L. Marchand, *German Orientalism in the Age of Empire: Religion, Race, and Scholarship*, Publications of the German Historical Institute (Cambridge: Cambridge University Press, 2010).

to likely hearing pro-German sentiments from people like Mansur, were detailed to guard German prisoners of war in Singapore, some of whom were hostile military prisoners. By December 1914, the British official in charge of the POW camp, Major General Reade, felt compelled to inform the Governor that "the German prisoners of war at Tanglin had attempted to tamper with the native sentries [of the Malay States Guides] guarding them."[47]

The point of all this is that once the Guides arrived in Singapore, the inflammatory nature of the *Komagata Maru* voyage – whose journey was being tracked at every step – reinforced deliberate schemes to spread disaffection among Indians worldwide. Moreover, the Guides were exposed to such ideas not only by revolutionary Indians like Mansur, but by Germans themselves who hoped to shift their loyalties. Clearly, these influences on the morale of the Guides indicate that the men imagined themselves as part of a global network of Indians abroad. British authorities certainly believed this to be the case when they suggested that the Guides had been in contact with revolutionaries in India weeks before writing the letter to their commanding officer, when they made their plans to refuse service known. As evidence of this communication, the British report noted that the *Simla Weekly Secret Diary* – a revolutionary paper in the Punjab – had predicted in November 1914 that "A local Regiment from Singapore will also refuse to go on Service."[48]

Notwithstanding later protests to the contrary, by late December 1914 it should have been reasonably clear to British authorities that not only was there already serious discontent within the Malay States Guides stationed in Singapore, but that clear avenues existed for sepoys to make contact with people outside the regiment – both Indian and German – who themselves had grievances with British authority. In fact, a letter from March 4, 1915 indicates that the decision to transfer the 5th out of Singapore in the first place stemmed from the belief that the Malay States Guides were part of a conspiracy against British rule, "and that the Indian Regiment here [the 5th] might be affected by it." Thus, the writer argued, "The authorities resolved therefore to send this regiment to Hong Kong."[49]

Let us step back now and visualize the situation of the 5th Light Infantry, garrisoned as it was on this small island with the Guides

---

[47] Letter from Governor Young to Secretary of State, August 19, 1915. Sareen, *Secret Documents*, 710.

[48] Malay States Guides: Withdrawal of Offer to Volunteer for Foreign Service and Subsequent Renewal of Offer, 1914, IOR/L/MIL/7/17261.

[49] Unsigned letter, March 4, 1915. Memorandums and Telegrams Relating to Disturbances at Singapore.

during the winter months of 1914–1915 until the latter's departure in late January. As we know, the 5th had arrived in Singapore in October 1914 from India's Central Provinces and was serving its first overseas duty. Its members were overwhelmingly from the Punjab – like many men of the Guides – and included four companies composed mostly of Rajputs, two of Jats, and two of Pathans. Unlike the Guides, the men of the 5th were almost all Muslim. While the two units were in Singapore together, the men had plenty of opportunity to interact, since individuals in the Guides and the 5th were at liberty to move about Singapore among the city's large Indian population.[50] Once the Guides had taken the step of refusing service overseas, it was common knowledge all over Singapore and would have easily reached the 5th. But there were also direct links between the men of the two regiments. A secret agent who had been employed by General Ridout to monitor the morale of the troops after the Ottoman Empire entered the war testified that Muslims in the Guides and Muslims in the 5th Light Infantry commonly attended the Kampung Java mosque together in the city. The imam of the mosque, Nur Alam Shah, was said to be hostile to the British, was believed to be a member of a revolutionary movement (Ghadar?), and was believed to have played a role in the Guides' refusal of service.[51] After the mutiny, he was arrested for sheltering some of the mutineers and giving them disguises so they could escape.[52] Another connection was Kasim Mansur, the Ghadar activist who had written the letter to the Turkish consul at Rangoon for the Guides. As he had done with the Guides, Mansur also made a point of becoming friendly with a number of officers and men of the 5th after their arrival.[53] The findings of the court of inquiry's report into the mutiny of the 5th indicated that Mansur had made a habit of visiting the lines of the 5th and had hosted men of both the Guides and the 5th in his home many times.

What this means is that immediately upon arriving in Singapore, the men of the 5th had ample opportunity to hear about the reasons for the dissatisfaction of the Guides, to share in their outrage over the fate of the *Komagata Maru* passengers, and to be exposed to the opinions of at least two anti-British activists. What seems plain is that even though British authorities decided to remove the Guides from Singapore in order to break their connections with such influences, they did not remove the influences themselves. The result was that the 5th ended up being

[50] The size of the Indian community in Singapore, as of the 1911 census, was 24,494. Kuwajima, *Mutiny in Singapore*, 5.
[51] Ramnath, *Haj to Utopia*, 288.   [52] Testimony of T. R. Sareen, *Secret Documents*, 616.
[53] Proceeding of Court of Inquiry. Sareen, *Secret Documents*, 39.

exposed to the same German–Indian–Turkish propaganda, and even the same German prisoners, as the Guides. The difference in the 5th was that the regiment actually mutinied.

The German–Indian–Turkish Plot

While the disaffection of the Guides surely influenced the overall morale of the 5th during the four months they were on Singapore together, sympathy with the grievances of another unit would have been unlikely to convince soldiers to mutiny. Rather, close interaction with an already deeply disaffected unit likely opened the eyes of some of the men in the 5th to anti-British perspectives. If receptiveness to such perspectives also translated into identification with the grievances of the Guides as fellow Punjabis serving an oppressive regime, it was not a far jump to grow increasingly receptive to the same influences that had sharpened the disaffection of the Guides. An escalating factor in the 5th was that, in contrast to the Guides, the regiment was almost entirely Muslim – and by late 1914 much of the Indian and German propaganda inciting revolution among colonial subjects was directed at Muslims. Thus when the 5th increasingly came into contact with both people and print that aimed to inspire sepoys to turn against the British, they were confronted with messages that appealed specifically to their identity as Muslims. In Singapore, one of the most important ways they came by these messages was through the activities of the Ghadar party, which during the war was directly funded by the German government.

Ghadar had developed independently of German aid in 1913 among Indian expatriates in California, many of whom were Sikhs from the Punjab. Sikhs in particular had settled along the west coast of North America in the early years of the twentieth century in order to escape conditions of poverty at home.[54] But once in the United States and Canada they experienced increasingly hostile discrimination, not only at the state level but also from white communities. In fact, "Asians" of any nationality faced harsh discrimination on the Pacific coast of North America at this time, and were subject to laws that sought to limit immigration and property accumulation as well as violence and race riots.[55] Explicit among the limitations white communities sought to impose was to restrict Indian

---

[54] Harish K. Puri, *Ghadar Movement: Ideology, Organization, and Strategy, 2nd edn.* (Amritsar: Guru Nanak Dev University, 1993), 15.

[55] Both the United States and Canada passed laws in the late nineteenth and early twentieth centuries designed to prevent "Asian" immigration, beginning with the Chinese Exclusion Act in 1882 in the United States, and followed by the 1903 Chinese Immigration Act in Canada. Exclusion of Chinese immigrants was followed by restricting

women from immigrating with their husbands and families. As a result, until 1912 the Indian immigrant population was composed entirely of men, which was a source of bitter complaint among them. The restriction on Indian women was intended to prevent Indians from establishing settled, self-propagating, racially distinct communities. By preventing female immigration, whites hoped the Indian population would be temporary sojourners for the purposes of work rather than permanent migrants.[56] Indians, for their part, argued that they possessed the same male rights to establish families and to head households as any white North American, and explicitly challenged these laws by attempting to gain entry for their wives.

Indians undergoing such hostile pressures sought help from the British authorities, only to discover that the authorities did not want to fight for Indian liberty in North America because of fears that it would create similar expectations in India.[57] Frustrated by British unresponsiveness, and taking it as yet another indication of British misrule over Indians everywhere, expatriate Indians in California determined that the solution to the problem was to overthrow British rule in India via armed rebellion. In 1914, one of the movement's leaders deplored the situation in which "our men, who valiantly shed their blood . . . can not have the privilege of bringing their wives and children in the lands of the British colonies." The response, he argued, must be "to remedy this situation, and acquire our inalienable rights."[58] The name Ghadar was descriptive of its intended methods, since the word means "mutiny." It was chosen deliberately to recall the Indian Rebellion of 1857, when a significant portion of the Bengal army and peasants in north-central India rose up against British power.

In November 1913, the party published the first issue of its newspaper – also called *Ghadar* – and distributed it in the United States, Canada,

---

the immigration of Japanese citizens in both countries. In 1908, the Canadian government passed legislation designed to restrict Asian immigration from any location by mandating that all immigrants possess at least $200 Canadian on arrival. Puri, *Ghadar Movement*, 31–32. For more context on the restriction of Asian immigration on the Pacific coast of North America, see Adam McKeown, *Melancholy Order: Asian Migration and the Globalization of Borders* (New York: Columbia University Press, 2008), and Andrew Gyory, *Closing the Gate: Race, Politics, and the Chinese Exclusion Act* (Chapel Hill: The University of North Carolina Press, 1998).

[56] Enakshi Dua discusses this is the context of Canada in "Racialising Imperial Canada: Indian Women and the Making of Ethnic Communities," in Antoinette Burton, ed., *Gender, Sexuality, and Colonial Modernities* (London and New York: Routledge, 1999), 123.

[57] Puri, *Ghadar Movement*, 37.

[58] Taraknath Das, *The Hindustanee*, April 1, 1914. Quoted in Enakshi Dua, "Racialising Imperial Canada," 127.

and India, and in other areas with significant Indian populations or garrisons, including South and East Africa, Hong Kong, Burma, Malaya, and Singapore. The first issue was unambiguous about the party's intentions:

A new epoch in the history of India opens today, the 1st November, 1913, because today there begins in foreign lands but in our country's language a war against the English Raj . . . what is our name? Mutiny. What is our work? Mutiny. Where will the mutiny break out? In India. When? In a few years. Why? Because the people can no longer bear the oppression and tyranny practiced under British rule and are ready to fight and die for freedom.[59]

Although Ghadar's leadership was made up mostly of literate Hindus (one of its founding members, Har Dayal, was a lecturer in Indian philosophy and Sanskrit), the party openly appealed to the grievances of other Indians as well. It was most successful, at least initially, with the poor Sikh peasants who had moved to the western U.S. and Canada and experienced first-hand anti-Asian discrimination. But the party's paper also made early efforts to include Indian Muslims, even though Har Dayal himself was known for being openly hostile to Muslims.[60] Just after the launch of the *Ghadar* paper, the December issue acknowledged that while "in the beginning few Mahommedans also belonged to this party . . . now all the young men are joining it."[61]

When the war began, *Ghadar* not only continued to insist that all groups of Indians must fight to overthrow the British but also began to focus special attention on sepoys in the vast Indian Army. These men, Ghadar leaders believed, would be particularly useful to win over because of their military training and access to weapons.[62] On August 4, 1914 the *Ghadar* paper exhorted:

Warriors. If you start to mutiny now you will put an end to the British government . . . Go to Indian [sic] and incite the native troops. Preach mutiny openly. Take arms from the troops of the native states and wherever you see British kill them.[63]

Not surprisingly, British authorities in India were alarmed at such calls to arms. They worked through the British consul in San Francisco to monitor the movements of Dayal and other Ghadar activists, and in February 1914 succeeded in convincing U.S. authorities to arrest and deport Dayal. Before he could be deported, however, Dayal escaped to

---

[59] T.R. Sareen, *Select Documents on the Ghadar Party* (New Delhi: Mounto Publishing House, 1994), 84.
[60] Manjapra, "The Ilusions of Encounter," 371.
[61] December 16, 1913. Sareen, *Select Documents on the Ghadar Party*, 88.
[62] Ramnath, *Haj to Utopia*, 55.   [63] Sareen, *Select Documents on the Ghadar Party*, 85.

Switzerland, and in early 1914 made his way to Germany.[64] In any case, removing Dayal from the United States did not stop the publication of *Ghadar*, which continued to be published in San Francisco under the leadership of Ram Chandra and distributed around the world. In March 1914, a British Foreign Office memorandum noted that copies had been found in Singapore, Hong Kong, and British concessions in China.[65] In such locations, Sikh Gurdwaras (temples) became centers of Ghadar activity, where worshippers read poems from the paper aloud and discussed politics after prayers.[66] In areas with large Indian Muslim populations, mosques served the same purpose, as the Kampung Java mosque in Singapore apparently did.

Once the war broke out, *Ghadar's* attention to Muslim disaffection grew sharper. This was due in large part to the formal connection Ghadar leaders forged with the German government immediately before the war. As we know, Har Dayal arrived in Berlin early in 1914, and by July other prominent Ghadar activists joined him. The Germans formalized the relationship by creating a Committee for Indian Independence, a department whose task it was to create anti-British propaganda for British colonial subjects and to coordinate the shipment of arms into India.[67] For Dayal and Ghadar more generally, the alliance with the Germans was an opportunity to attain financial, logistical, and technical support for furthering its own ends. For the Germans, it was a means of securing its explicit war aim of encouraging the collapse of the Raj via armed rebellion.[68] As the *Ghadar* put it on July 21, 1914, "All intelligent people know that Germany is an enemy of Great Britain. We also are the mortal enemy of the British Government and an enemy of my enemy is my friend."[69]

Once the war began, Ghadar activists began not only to send propaganda around the world but – with German money – they also sent people. Part of this effort was to send fighters directly to India. One source estimated that Ghadar had sent 8,000 people to India for this

---

[64] Richard Popplewell, "The Surveillance of Indian 'Seditionists' in North America, 1905–1915," in Richard Popplewell, Christopher Andrew, and Jeremy Noakes, eds., *Intelligence And International Relations, 1900–1945*, Exeter Studies in History (Liverpool: Liverpool University Press, 1987), 62, 65, 69.

[65] Sareen, *Select Documents on Ghadar Party*, 59; for the efforts made by British authorities to penetrate the Ghadar party, see Harold A. Gould, *Sikhs, Swamis, Students, and Spies: The India Lobby in the United States, 1900–1946* (New Delhi: Sage Publications, 2006), 210.

[66] Puri, *Ghadar Movement*, 85.

[67] Manjapra, "The Ilusions of Encounter," 372; Ramnath, *Haj to Utopia*, 73.

[68] This is the subject of Peter Hopkirk's *Like Hidden Fire: The Plot to Bring Down the British Empire* (New York: Kodansha USA, 1997).

[69] Sareen, *Select Documents on the Ghadr Party*, 85.

purpose.[70] But beginning in September and October 1914 – just months before the Singapore Mutiny – Ghadarites also left North America for the Far East. Specific target areas included Hong Kong, the Malay States, Rangoon, and Singapore – each of which had Indian Army garrisons that Ghadarites were eager to penetrate.

During this period, the *Ghadar* explicitly and regularly exhorted Indians to support Germany in any way possible during the war. On August 18, 1914, an article titled "O Hindus, Help the Germans" encouraged Indians to take the opportunity of Britain's weakness to mutiny. On September 8, 1914, the *Ghadar* prophesied "Germany is going to defeat England. German [sic] have taken the whole of France: and Russia too has been dismantled." And on December 8, 1915 an article cried: "Rise up: for the day will come when your flag will be respected throughout the world . . . Soon, with the aid of the Germans and Turkey, your enemies will be slain. This is the opportune time."[71]

Although the Indo-German partnership provided needed finances for the work of Ghadar, being in the pay of the German government meant an adjustment to German priorities – and one of those priorities was encouraging British Muslim subjects to rebel.[72] German interest in the potential of Muslims to weaken the British Empire was not new. Much to the irritation of the British, Kaiser Wilhelm II had been styling himself a special "friend" to the 300 million Muslims of the world since 1898. Wilhelm also gave much credence to the opinions of the eccentric Max von Oppenheim – a sometime consul in the Near East, legal counsel to the emperor and, during the war, chief of Intelligence Services in the East – who had been conceiving of ways to work with Muslim subjects against British rule since the early twentieth century.[73] As Kris Manjapra has argued, Oppenheim helped convince Wilhelm that Muslims could be radicalized and encouraged to revolt against British rule, particularly in India. But unfortunately for Oppenheim and the Germans who listened to him, his focus on Indian Muslims tended to blind him to the fact that the most visible Indian revolutionary groups – including those who made up the Committee for Indian Independence – were composed mostly of Hindus and Sikhs.[74]

---

[70] Ramnath, *Haj to Utopia*, 50.   [71] Sareen, *Select Documents on Ghadar Party*, 86.

[72] German efforts to stir up discontent among Muslims were not limited to Britain, and in fact included all the Allies. However, Manjapra argues that British Muslims were a special concern. Manjapra, "The Ilusions of Encounter," 366.

[73] Manjapra, "The Ilusions of Encounter," 365, 368–69.

[74] The Hindu/Muslim tension caused by the German connection, and German officials' belief that revolution would come from Muslims, created some odd situations. Germany sent Indians not only to the Far East but also to North Africa and the Middle East in order to incite Muslim rebellion. The fact that most of the Indians they sent were

After the Ottoman Empire entered the war on the side of the Central Powers on October 28, 1914, Oppenheim convinced the Kaiser – in the face of skepticism in German civilian and military quarters – of the viability of a jihadist strategy.[75] On the Ottoman side, although the ruling party was not initially convinced about the advisability of such a strategy, it was difficult, as Tilman Lüdke has argued, "to overlook the potential of Islam as a bond between the Muslim inhabitants of the Ottoman Empire and a tool for attracting sympathy and support throughout the Muslim world."[76] On entering the war, the Ottomans had already declared the liberation of occupied Muslim lands as a specific war aim. Then on November 14, 1914, the highest religious authority in the empire declared a jihad on behalf of the Sultan Caliph, Mehmed V, demanding that "the Moslem subjects of Russia, of France, of England and of all the countries that side with them in their land and sea attacks dealt against the Caliphate for the purpose of annihilating Islam" must "take part in the holy War against the respective governments from which they depend."[77]

From this point forward, both Germans and Ottomans sought to capitalize on the Sultan's claim to be caliph, the highest position of Islamic authority. The Committee for Indian Independence helped to spread propaganda, in *Ghadar* and other publications, indicating that Kaiser Wilhelm had converted to Islam, and that large segments of the German population had converted as well.[78] Muslim soldiers continued to be of particular interest to the Committee.[79] In order to reach as many Muslim soldiers as possible, the editors of *Ghadar* published special pamphlets in languages like Pushtu (spoken in Afghanistan and parts of Northwest India). One example, from August 1915, represented an attempt

---

Hindus induced the Germans to ask them to change their names in order to sound authentically Muslim. Manjapra, "The Illusions of Encounter," 372, 375.

[75] Lüdke argues that Oppenheim managed this almost single-handedly. Lüdke, *Jihad Made in Germany*, 48. Although this will be discussed in later chapters, it is important to note that it was the Ottomans who pushed the Germans for a formal alliance and not the other way around. At least initially, neither side entered the alliance with the goal of creating a platform for a jihadist strategy, and Lüdke makes it clear that the Ottomans were not at all enthusiastic about this idea at first (48). For an excellent monograph on Ottoman strategy during World War I, see Aksakal, *The Ottoman Road to War in 1914*.

[76] Lüdke, *Jihad Made in Germany*, 49.

[77] Cemil Aydin, *The Politics of Anti-Westernism in Asia: Visions of Pan-Islamic and Pan-Asian Thought* (New York: Columbia University Press, 2007), 94, 110; McMeekin, The Berlin-Baghdad Express, 124. Text of the fatwa taken from *Source Records of the Great War*, Vol. III, Charles F. Horne, ed., National Alumni 1923. www.firstworldwar.com/source/ottoman_fetva.htm.

[78] Peter Hopkirk, *Like Hidden Fire*, 3.   [79] Puri, *Ghadar Movement*, 107.

to reach soldiers fighting for the British on the Northwest Frontier. This
particular pamphlet claimed:

The wicked English and their allies are now attacking Islam, but the German
Emperor and the Sultan of Turkey have sworn to liberate Asia from the tyranny.
Now is the time to rise . . . Only your strength and religious zeal are required.[80]

Closer to Singapore, in January 1915, British censors in Burma intercepted 104 envelopes containing copies of the *Ghadar* paper, in three
languages. Among and within these papers were also copies of a Turkish paper called the *Jahan-i-Islam* (Islamic World). The paper contained
a speech by Enver Pasha, War Minister and Commander-in-Chief of
Ottoman forces, that declared:

This is the time that the Ghadar should be introduced in India . . . Hindus and
Muhammedans, you are both soldiers of the army and you are brothers, and
the low degraded English man is your enemy; you should become ghazis by
declaring jihad and combining with your brothers to murder the English and
liberate India.[81]

It is not certain whether similar material produced by Turkish sources
also reached Singapore, although given the vast amounts of illicit materials constantly circulating through the island colony, it seems perfectly
reasonable that some would have done so. We do know, however, that
Ghadar was found in Singapore and that individual pro-German Muslims
like Kasim Mansur and Nur Alam Shah – reportedly members of Ghadar
themselves – were believed to have encouraged sepoys and civilians alike
to align themselves with Britain's enemies.

The court of inquiry collected two types of evidence from the men
of the 5th. The first was testimony taken in the immediate aftermath of
the mutiny, and the second was letters that had been intercepted by the

Thus far, we have a lot of circumstantial evidence that the men of
the 5th had opportunities to interact with the Guides and with Ghadar
activists, and that pan-Islamic, pro-German printed material circulated
in Singapore. We also have undisputed evidence that the 5th did in fact
mutiny on February 15. In many instances like this, such a circumstantial case marks the limits of what we can know, leaving us to make the
connections between the fragments of evidence. In this case, however,
the massive amount of evidence collected and preserved by the Court of
Inquiry into the causes of the mutiny allows us to hear – albeit imper-
fectly – from some of the officers and men of the 5th themselves.

The court of inquiry collected two types of evidence from the men
of the 5th. The first was testimony taken in the immediate aftermath of
the mutiny, and the second was letters that had been intercepted by the

[80] Puri, *Ghadar Movement*, 110.   [81] Kuwajima, *Mutiny in Singapore*, 41.

censor. The first kind of evidence is of course deeply problematic, not least because the forty-three days in which the court sat – February 20 to April 4 – occurred simultaneously with the court-martials of those suspected of involvement in the mutiny. What this means is that the court was taking testimony from hundreds of sepoys in the 5th as their comrades were being sentenced and executed. A huge amount was at stake for each man, and many – if not all – must have feared either for their own lives or for the lives of their friends and relatives if they were to say too much, or to say the wrong thing.[82]

Only those sepoys who were known to have actively helped the British were considered above suspicion: Everyone else was asked to explain and justify their actions during the mutiny. Since large numbers of sepoys had deserted their posts and remained in hiding for several days, they had a lot to explain. Many were intent on describing themselves as ignorant of the coming mutiny, afraid for their lives as it began, and eager to turn themselves in – unarmed – as soon as possible. Given the level of discontent in the regiment, it seems likely that many sepoys lied, feigned ignorance, or refrained from telling the whole truth when questioned by the court. The testimony of Bahadur Khan, a servant to one of the British captains in the regiment, responded like many others when asked to elaborate on his statement that he had heard trouble was brewing in the regiment. Khan insisted, "I cannot say who said it; men were talking. I cannot say why there should be trouble. I don't know what kind of trouble. I heard it from lots of people. I cannot remember anyone who told me."[83] Even more common were those who maintained, like Colour Havildar Mohammed Hassan, "I am absolutely unable to say what the cause of the mutiny was. I know nothing about any cause of discontent or anything of that sort."[84]

The second type of evidence collected from the men of the 5th was letters intercepted by the censor in the days and weeks just prior to the mutiny. While such letters might be seen as more reliable than testimony taken in life and death circumstances, nevertheless they have their own difficulties. For starters, many men were not literate, and thus had an intermediary compose their letters. Not only that, only the translated English copies of the letters now exist, which means the translation cannot be checked against the originals. Finally, the sample size is quite small: There are only about ten surviving letters, and we do not know

---

[82] A number of men in the 5th had relatives serving in the unit, both by blood and by marriage.

[83] Sareen, *Secret Documents on Singapore Mutiny 1915, Vol. 2*, 72.

[84] Sareen, *Secret Documents on Singapore Mutiny*, 60.

how many other, "harmless" letters may have been sent at about the same time.

Notwithstanding these problems, the evidence collected from the 5th can give us at least a partial glimpse into the kinds of things the men were saying and observing just before and during the mutiny. Both letters and testimony indicate that the men had heard rumors about German sympathies for Islam. For example, just before the mutiny, Lance Naik Fateh Mohammed wrote to his father in the Punjab:

The Germans have become Mohammedans. Haji Mahmood William Kaiser and his daughter has married the heir to the Turkish throne, who is to succeed after the Sultan. Many of the German subjects and army have embraced Mohammedism. Please God that the religion of the Germans (Mohammedism) may be promoted or raised on high.[85]

When confronted by the court of inquiry about the letter, Mohammed admitted writing it but insisted, "I do not think this is true but it is what I heard in the lines. Abdul Hamid (bugler) told me. I wrote it through foolishness."[86] At that point, the court decided to question Abdul Hamid, who said he had seen reports about the Germans being Muslim in a newspaper. When asked to identify the paper, he said "I never saw the newspaper myself. I don't know what newspaper."[87]

It is very likely that both Mohammed and Hamid lied to protect themselves in their testimony before the court. In Mohammed's letter, there is no indication that he did not believe what he was saying. In Hamid's testimony, it would have been quite damaging if he admitted to having read proscribed material such as *Ghadar* or other propaganda produced by the Committee for Indian Independence. What is important here is not whether or not each man was telling the truth, but that the combination of the censored letter and the testimony allows us to see that at least some men had seen reports about Germans converting to Islam and had shared it with other sepoys, and that at least some men seemed to believe it. Whether Hamid had actually seen the paper himself or not, the testimony of his fellow soldiers indicates that many sepoys were hearing pro-German sentiments regularly from other soldiers.

Snippets gleaned from the testimony of a wide variety of men indicate that they were exposed to pro-German, pan-Islamic sentiments not only via newspapers but also via other people as well. For the most part, the people mentioned in this regard were not the "outside influences" mentioned in the court of inquiry, such as Kasim Mansur or the Imam

---

[85] Sareen, *Secret Documents on the Singapore Mutiny*, 731.
[86] Sareen, *Secret Documents on the Singapore Mutiny*, 122.
[87] Sareen, *Secret Documents on the Singapore Mutiny*, 122.

Nur Alam Shah. In fact, although many men of the 5th admitted to either having heard of Nur Alam Shah or to having occasionally attended the Kampong Java mosque, nearly all denied ever having heard the holy man raise seditious ideas. On the other hand, two secret agents in the employ of British authorities said exactly the opposite. In the words of one secret agent:

He [Nur Alam Shah] is always talking sedition and against the British government. He preaches fanatical doctrines daily. Batches of 5th Light Infantry used to listen to his preachings and used to give him offerings of money.[88]

Whether or not the evidence of the secret agents was reliable, the men of the 5th were adamant on the subject. If what the secret agents were saying was true, however, it is possible the sepoys were afraid to admit having attended ceremonies in which seditious things were being said, or even that they hoped to protect men like Nur Alam Shah from the British.

In contrast to their reticence to discuss the role played by outsiders, many men of the 5th implicated their fellow soldiers as the agents of "seditious ideas." Several in particular were mentioned over and over, particularly the Indian officers Jemadar Chiste Khan, Subedar Dunde Khan, Jemadar Abdul Ali, the NCO Colour Havildar Imtiaz Ali (reputed to have fired the first shot), and Taj Mohammed.[89] For example, when asked about the causes of the mutiny, Lance Naik Fazal Asim said:

All I can tell you is this: that Chiste Khan used to talk to my section in "D" Company and tell them all the news with regard to the war that was unfavorable to the Sirkar [British government]. We used to hear news of the successes of the British, at which we were very pleased. Chiste Khan would say the exact opposite; that the British had been defeated, etc.[90]

Similarly, Lance Naik Maksud testified that he heard Dunde Khan, Abdul Ali, and Chiste Khan saying that "Germany was making progress and that there would soon be a German Raj instead of a British Raj."[91] Sub-assistant surgeon R.S. Bell, who was part Indian, also testified that "I saw Jemadar Chiste Khan drawing maps with a stick on the ground showing the theatre of war. There were some fifteen or twenty men around. He said Belgium is taken, France is taken, Japan has left her friendship with England. The Germans will invade England. When I heard him

---

[88] Sareen, *Secret Documents*, 616. This testimony was corroborated by a second secret agent.
[89] Jemadars and Subedars were commissioned officers. Each company had one of each: subedars wore two stars and jemadars one. Tarling, "The Merest Pustule," 28. Each of the men listed here were executed for their role in the mutiny.
[90] Sareen, *Secret Documents*, 139–140.   [91] Sareen, *Secret Documents*, 79.

going on like this I used to walk away."[92] Again, Arshad, a sepoy in C company, said "I heard Chiste Khan, Jemadar, say about a fortnight ago, 'German has taken certain places, Austria has done likewise and Turkey has taken certain places. You people remain watchful."[93]

Problematic as the court of inquiry testimony might have been, it seems clear that certain men in the regiment – especially the officers Chiste Khan, Dunde Khan, and Abdul Ali – played key roles in spreading the kind of pro-German information found in Ghadar propaganda to other soldiers. In light of testimony that these officers had been talking this way for "two or three months" before the mutiny, it seems likely they were convinced in their views by contact with the Guides, Ghadar propaganda, and Ghadar supporters prior to the turn of the new year in 1915.[94]

But in January 1915, some of the men of the 5th had a chance to test their views on real Germans, who were being held as prisoners of war at the Tanglin Barracks just outside Singapore. Incredibly, even after British army authorities in Singapore had formally reported to the Governor in December 1914 that the Malay States Guides had been "tampered with" by the German prisoners from the *Emden* at Tanglin, and further that only "white" soldiers should therefore guard them, men of the 5th were nonetheless detailed to replace the Guides for guard duty at the POW camp.[95]

In January 1915, the camp housed 309 German men who were being interned for the duration of the war.[96] Most of the men were German nationals who had been residents in Singapore before the hostilities began. After the declaration of war between Britain and Germany, these men and their families were initially allowed to remain in their homes under a liberal interpretation of house arrest. Things changed in October 1914, however, when on the 28th the German cruiser *Emden* steamed into Penang harbor in British Malaya and promptly sank the Russian cruiser *Zhemtchug* and the French patrol boat *Le Mousquet*.[97] On 9 November, the *Emden* herself was sunk by an Australian cruiser, and several of its officers and men were brought to Singapore as prisoners of war. There, they joined the crew of the *Markomannia*, which had been

---

[92] Sareen, *Secret Documents*, 98.   [93] Sareen, *Secret Documents*, 129.
[94] Testimony of sepoy Nazim Ali, Subedar Dunde Khan's orderly. Sareen, *Secret Documents*, 109.
[95] Governor Arthur Young of Singapore wrote that after the mutiny he was "astonished to find . . . that the 5th Native Light Infantry had been mounting guard at the prisoners of war camp at Tanglin," despite recommendations to the contrary. Letter from the Governor of the Straits Settlements to the Secretary of State for the Colonies Regarding Court of Inquiry and Causes of Mutiny. Sareen, *Secret Documents*, 710–11.
[96] Murfett, *Between Two Oceans*, 163.   [97] Harper and Miller, *Singapore Mutiny*, 17.

sunk near Dutch waters on October 20.[98] During this time, German activities so close to Singapore increased suspicion about the loyalties of German residents on the island. In fact, one of the proprietors of the Singapore branch of a German-owned company called Behn, Meyer, and Company, August Diehn, was believed to have been arranging for the provisioning of the *Emden*.[99] Thereafter, on instructions from London, all German men were interned with the *Emden* and *Markomannia* crews at Tanglin Barracks.[100]

Many of the German prisoners did not do anything to indicate they were interested in stirring up trouble during their incarceration. For example, when a large group of sepoys liberated the camp on February 15, 292 of the 309 inmates ultimately decided not to leave. Instead, they remained in the immediate vicinity of the camp until a British and Japanese force returned to secure the area several days later.[101] But some of the men, like the crews of the *Emden* and *Markomannia*, were hostile military prisoners captured in battle, while others harbored grievances about being interned. It therefore seems reasonable to assume some prisoners had reason to relish the chance of wreaking whatever havoc they could, especially if such havoc might also lead to their escape. In fact, seventeen Germans did take the opportunity provided by the mutiny to escape. Among these, ten were from the ships' crews – including the Lieutenant Commander of the *Emden*, Julius Lauterbach – and three were employees of Behn, Meyer, and Company, including August Diehn himself.[102]

Did some of the German prisoners encourage the men of the 5th to mutiny? As we will see, the British court of inquiry's report made light of this possibility. Yet the evidence suggests that the German prisoners played a far more important role than the official report allowed. Especially when placed in the context of the larger German efforts to subvert Allied colonial rule during the war, the evidence linking some of the prisoners to the mutiny is difficult to ignore.

Let us begin at the liberation of the POW camp and work our way back. When the mutiny broke out, the largest of the three groups of sepoys marched straight away to Tanglin, overpowered and killed the guards, and

---

[98] "The *Markomannia*," *Straits Times*, October 20, 1914, 9.

[99] Karen Snow, "Russia and the 1915 Indian Mutiny in Singapore," *Southeast Asia Research* 5, no. 3 (1997), 309.

[100] Harper and Miller, *Singapore Mutiny*, 18.

[101] Sho Kuwajima, *Mutiny in Singapore*, 106. This did not necessarily mean the prisoners were well-disposed toward the British, and in fact the German prisoners Hageman and Hanke both testified that anti-British feelings were high among many of the prisoners. For example, Hanke testimony in Sareen, *Secret Documents*, 209.

[102] Of the seventeen, six were recaptured. Report 14734, February 29, 1915. Memorandums and Telegrams Relating to Disturbances at Singapore.

opened the gates. Two of the German prisoners, Mr. Hageman and Mr. Hanke, testified independently that, upon entering the camp, the sepoys went directly to the building in which the *Emden* crew was quartered and began shaking hands with them.[103] Clearly, the sepoys knew exactly where they were going and with whom they wanted to communicate in the camp. Hageman and Hanke also reported that, upon being liberated, the crews of the *Emden* and the *Markomannia* were ordered to form up, and that August Diehn of Behn, Meyer, and Company ordered the entire camp of Germans to be ready to march to Singapore at 7:00 a.m. the next morning.[104] According to both men, the rumor in camp was that German warships were waiting in the harbor to collect the prisoners and the mutineers and that the sepoys had taken all the forts.[105] As it turned out, of course, there were no German ships, and the sepoys were not in control of the island. Most of the German prisoners ended up staying where they were. Not a single German helped the sepoys. Instead, seventeen prisoners armed themselves and stole away, and eleven of them escaped to freedom while nearly all the sepoys were captured or surrendered and then punished severely.

It might be tempting to see the escaped Germans as mere opportunists, who took advantage of a moment of confusion to find their way off the island. But there was more to the situation than simple opportunism. First, it is worth remembering that German war aims to foment discontent among colonial peoples and troops around the world were widely known in German military and official circles. We know that August Diehn was interned because the British believed he had been instrumental in provisioning the *Emden*. Diehn's activism in anti-British schemes quickly appeared vindicated when he was later sought – along with two German brothers in the Dutch East Indies – as a key player in an operation smuggling weapons and propaganda to India.[106] And Lauterbach, the commander of the *Emden*, was only too happy to recount in his memoir how he had encouraged the sepoys to see Germans as allies during his internment at Tanglin.[107] Second, we know that some German prisoners had already tried, and succeeded, in influencing the Malay

---

[103] Testimony of Hageman and testimony of Hanke. Sareen, *Secret Documents*, 197, 205.
[104] Testimony of Hageman and testimony of Hanke. Sareen, *Secret Documents*, 198–99, 207.
[105] Testimony of Hageman and testimony of Hanke. Sareen, *Secret Documents*, 198, 209.
[106] van Dijk, *The Netherlands Indies and the Great War 1914–1918*, 329. We will hear more about these schemes later. In August 1915, Brigadier General Ridout said that it had "just come to light" that Diehn was in fact a leader in a scheme to bring revolution to India. Sareen, *Secret Documents*, 699.
[107] Julius Lauterbach, *£1000 Belooning Dood of Levend: Avontuurlijke Vlucht door de Hollandsche Koloniën van den Voormaligen Prijsofficier van de 'Emden'* (Amsterdam and Rotterdam: Van Langenhusen, 1918), 20.

States Guides in this same way. As a result, it seems reasonable to believe they would renew their efforts with a different group of sepoys. Third, and somewhat startlingly, Brigadier General Ridout himself acknowledged that German prisoners were attempting to influence the men of the 5th prior to the mutiny. As he reported to the court of inquiry, "there is no doubt that the 5th Light Infantry had come to think that the Germans were Mahommedans. It came to my notice about the middle of January 1915, that the German Prisoners were beginning to talk "at" the native sentries – were in the habit of saying prayers at sundown in Mahommedan fashion, and pretended to recite the Koran."[108] Fourth, we know that at least some of the German prisoners, Diehn and Lauterbach among them, wanted to escape the camp, and had been in the midst of digging a tunnel for that reason when the 5th liberated them.[109] By encouraging the men of the 5th to see them as allies with common grievances against the British, they were leaving the way open for another potential path to freedom.

Did some of the German prisoners promise help from German warships if the 5th were to rebel against the British? Sepoy Nizam Ali, one of the men posted at Tanglin, testified that while he himself had not spoken with the Germans, a fellow guard – sepoy Ali Ulla – said the "Germans told him that if he would release them, in a couple of hours they would get a German ship here to take them all away."[110] Whether they said this or not, it seems clear that at least a few of the men who were posted for this duty became friendly with some of the prisoners. A number of sepoys testified that certain men – Taj Mohammed in particular – had spent a lot of time in the German quarters, and then had long meetings with Chiste Khan and other sepoys later implicated in the mutiny.[111] Taj Mohammed's presence was confirmed by German witnesses themselves, one of whom – Hanke – testified that prior to the mutiny Mohammed had saluted a portrait of the Kaiser that he was painting. When questioned by Hanke, Mohammed was supposed to have said, "He is my king."[112]

Given the evidence, it seems probable that many men of the 5th had already been exposed to both people and propaganda that encouraged strong pan-Islamic, pro-German, and anti-British discontent in the regiment by the time they were posted to guard the German prisoners at Tanglin. When the 5th began their duties, some of the prisoners – already

---

[108] Report from Brigadier General Ridout on Proceedings of the Court of Inquiry. Sareen, *Secret Documents on Singapore Mutiny 1915*, 699.

[109] van Dijk, *The Netherlands Indies and the Great War 1914–1918*, 323.

[110] Sareen, *Secret Documents*, 109.

[111] For example, the testimony of Lance Naik Maksud and Sepoy Nizam Ali. Sareen, *Secret Documents*, 79, 109.

[112] Testimony of G.R. Hanke. Sareen, *Secret Documents*, 210.

experienced at encouraging dissatisfaction among the Guides – made a point of deepening that discontent, and of demonstrating their common grievances with the sepoys. Some of the guards may genuinely have believed that the Germans would call in warships if they were to mutiny, or at least that they would take up arms and help secure the island. Their hopes in this direction may explain why they liberated Tanglin first. Perhaps, too, the failure of the Germans to join them or help in any way may explain the subsequent lack of direction displayed by many of the sepoys just hours after the mutiny began.

Thus, instead of seeing the mutiny as a spontaneous affair with no clear leaders as some have done, I would argue instead that its causes can be clearly traced to the revolutionary influences to which the sepoys had been exposed since their arrival in Singapore.[113] These influences hailed from myriad channels, many with origins as far afield as North America, Germany, Britain, the Ottoman Empire, and India. The discontent produced by these influences was sharpened by contact with the German prisoners, who had clear reasons for egging them on, and who may have promised help in the event of mutiny. The situation was volatile.

Let us fast-forward now to the days just prior to the mutiny. On January 27, 1915, the commander of the regiment – Colonel Martin – was notified that the 5th were being transferred from Singapore to Hong Kong.[114] Hong Kong was not a combat post, and the 5th would be performing there the same kinds of garrison duty they already performed in Singapore. But the news was not welcomed by some of the Indian officers in the regiment. In response to the news, men like Chiste Khan, Dunde Khan, Abdul Ali, Taj Mohammed, Imtiaz Ali and others began to tell their fellow soldiers disquieting stories about the upcoming transfer. Some soldiers testified they had been told that because of certain German victory in the war, the British no longer needed sepoys, and that their ship would be intentionally sunk at sea. As Lance Naik Maksud, D company, testified, "They . . . said that as Germany was making so much progress the British would have no use for them and would send them away in a ship and sink them."[115] Other soldiers reported learning that even though the regiment was being transferred to Hong Kong initially, it would then be sent to the front.[116] Still others were led to believe that

---

[113] Karen Snow is among these. See Snow, "Russia and the 1915 Indian Mutiny in Singapore."

[114] Harper and Miller, *Singapore Mutiny*, 31.   [115] Sareen, *Secret Documents*, 79.

[116] A number of letters intercepted by the censor indicated this sentiment, including Shaikh Mohammed Ali, No. 2 Company, who wrote that the regiment "will go to Hong Kong. But don't know this, whether it is going to the war." Sareen, *Secret Documents*, 729.

the regiment was not going to Hong Kong at all, but that it was going straight to Europe or to Egypt.[117]

All of the intercepted letters registered concern and, often, confusion about the destination of the 5th. Lance Naik Najaf Khan and Munshi Khan wrote their brother that "the other news is that our Regiment is going to the war.... (We) will either go to Europe, France, or Africa. (We) don't know to which country we will go. Will embark the ship on the 18th.... And we know it by our sense that we will go to Europe."[118] Zaboor Ali Khan wrote, "And we cannot write any more letters now, as on the February 18th we will proceed to the war," and was echoed by Ghafoor and Nazir Khan who wrote, "We will go to Europe to war."[119] An unnamed sepoy wrote his father that he knew "we are being taken to Hong Kong from here," but followed by saying "God knows further where they are taking [us?] to."[120] Most dramatic was the letter written by Shaikh Mohammed Ali, who said "It is with sighing, crying, grief and sorrow to tell you that the transfer of the regiment on the February 20th is now a settled fact. It will go to Hong Kong. But don't know this, whether it is going to the war.... We are very much confused and shocked. All the regiment is in sorrow altogether."[121]

Widespread fears that the regiment was not going where the regimental commanders had promised were not, in fact, far-fetched. The men of the 5th knew that the King's Own Yorkshire regiment – which had been sent to the front at the start of the war – was originally told that it was being sent to India. As Arthur Young himself wrote, "the battalion believed it was going to Egypt, not to Hong Kong, in the same way as the King's Own Yorkshire Light Infantry when embarked went to Europe not, as anticipated/believed, India."[122] Given everything else the men had heard about German power, the untrustworthiness of the British, and the possibility of being forced to fight other Muslims over the last few months, such stories must have been particularly alarming. In the version where the regiment would be sunk at sea, the scenario was one of extreme British duplicity that would result in the death of everyone on board. In the version where the regiment would be sent to the front, death would take more time but was equally sure. In order to discourage relatives at home from enlisting, Ghafoor and Nazir Khan wrote, "In

---

[117] For Europe, letter from Lance Naik Najaf Khan and Munshi Khan. For Egypt, testimony of Lance Naik Maksud. Sareen, *Secret Documents*, 718, 83.

[118] Sareen, *Secret Documents*, 718–19.   [119] Sareen, *Secret Documents*, 726, 722.

[120] Sareen, *Secret Documents*, 724. Rahim Dad Khan also voiced the same suspicions, 720.

[121] Sareen, *Secret Documents*, 729.

[122] Report 9891, March 1. Memorandums and Telegrams Relating to Disturbances at Singapore.

one day alone sometimes two thousands, sometimes twenty thousands and sometimes one hundred thousand, no day passes without events, so many people perish.... No trusting in the employment."[123] Finally, in the version where sepoys would be sent to Egypt, the men faced the specter of having to fight against other Muslims when they arrived.

These rumors soon came to the attention of Major William Cotton, second in command of the 5th. In his testimony to the court of inquiry, Cotton admitted that a Muslim *moulvi* (a Muslim doctor of the law) who was returning to India had come to say goodbye just a few days before the mutiny. The moulvi told Cotton that a sepoy in the 5th had said that another moulvi was telling the men "not to go and fight against the Turks," and also that Chiste Khan "was lecturing every morning to the men to the same effect."[124] Cotton was not convinced of the reliability of this report. He did, however, discuss it with Colonel Martin, who declared that he would inquire into the matter once the men had reached Hong Kong. In the meantime, Cotton was made aware by some of the Indian officers that rumors were circulating that the regiment was not going to Hong Kong. To dispel these, Cotton gathered the Indian officers under his command and showed them a telegram from Hong Kong advising the regiment of its housing situation.[125]

These efforts, however, did not deter the main instigators. It is impossible to know whether or not men like Chiste Khan truly believed they were being sent to the front (or drowned, or to Egypt), or if they used a plausible story to inspire other men to join them in their already well-developed desire to rebel. Whatever the case, upon learning of their transfer to Hong Kong, at least some men of the 5th decided they were not going. Lance Naik Maksud, "B" company, testified that on February 14 Dunde Khan and Abdul Ali had said, "we intend to raise a disturbance and we have no intention of going on service."[126] Whether or not the men did in fact say something to that effect, we do know that they did play critical roles in the mutiny that occurred the very next day. On the 14th, it is possible that the instigators still believed they had a few days to plan, because the original transfer day had been scheduled for February 18. However, the ship arrived early, and the departure date was set for the 16th. Time was short.

On the morning of the 15th, the regiment assembled for a final inspection by Brigadier General Ridout. His speech had been given to Colonel

---

[123] Sareen, *Secret Documents*, 722. Also Najaf Khan, who said, "No one has escaped who has gone to the war. All have perished," 720.
[124] Testimony of Major W.L. Cotton, 5th Light Infantry. Sareen, *Secret Documents*, 383.
[125] Major Cotton. Sareen, *Secret Documents*, 384.
[126] Sareen, *Secret Documents*, 82.

Martin the day before, so that it could be translated for the men. After Ridout complimented the regiment on their good service in Singapore, the men heard the following translation:

In saying goodbye to the regiment [the general] would remind them that though it is not their good fortune to go to EUROPE, they are going where there is need of their services. It is the duty of all of us to go where we are ordered, no matter what our own feelings are. The Empire is vast and the duty of guarding it great. At the same time he hopes that it may soon be their luck to go to EUROPE and fight side by side with the Indian troops against our powerful enemy.[127]

Although the general had clearly stated that the regiment was not going to Europe, at the same time he did not specifically say that they were going to Hong Kong. Given the tense state of the regiment, such vagueness did not reassure the men whose loyalties had been tested from so many quarters for the past several months. Thus when the first shot was fired later that afternoon, it was a local expression of a truly global set of pressures.

The Official Version

That is not how the British authorities decided to explain the mutiny, a least publicly. An official version of events – produced by the court of inquiry – in fact did devote attention to all of the causes explored above, although its conclusions were somewhat different. The report itself was completed and submitted on May 20, 1915, exactly two months from the day the court first began its investigations. In its conclusions regarding the causes of the mutiny, the report maintained that it owed its origins to a set of "primary" and a set of "contributory" factors. First among the primary causes, it insisted, was serious tension between the regiment's British commanding officers – particularly between Colonel Martin and two of the British captains – the net result of which undermined discipline. Second, the report cited disagreements and dissension between the Indian officers and men in the regiment's mutinous right wing, particularly between Subedar Dunde Khan and Jemadars Chiste Khan and Abdul Ali on the one hand, and two other Subedars on the other. In fact, the evidence indicates that both problems did indeed exist within the regiment. Colonel Martin's British officers believed him to be an ineffective leader who had the tendency to say things in front of sepoys that undermined their own authority, while the disagreements between the

---

[127] Copy of Regimental Order no. 100 d. Report on Singapore Disturbances, Part II, WO 32/9560, 103.

Indian officers had apparently been going on for years.[128] In the view of the court of inquiry, this poor state of discipline is what allowed various "seditious" influences to find such a "ready and fertile field" in the regiment in the first place, and thus must be considered the most important causes of the mutiny.[129]

But the official report did take other causes seriously, even though it demoted them to mere "contributory" causes. Of these, the report cited "outside influences" from seditious elements filtering through Singapore, the poisonous influence of the Indian merchant, Kasim Mansur, who preached "fanatical unrest" among the troops, the influence of German POWs, the seditious work of a few Indian officers and men (including those whose execution was recorded at the start of this essay), and jealousies over promotions among the men.[130] Of particular note, among these "contributory" causes, was the court's acknowledgment of Ghadar activism in the region:

The town and settlement of Singapore, together with the neighboring states, enjoy a widespread and unenviable notoriety as being a focus for Indian seditionists passing to and from the Far East and America. It is also well known to harbour many rank seditionists of Indian nationality amongst its residents.[131]

Included among these "rank seditionists" were both Kasim Mansur and Nur Alam Shah, the latter of whom had specifically "incited sepoys to rise against the British, telling them that a German warship was about to arrive at Singapore." To make matters worse, the report continued, "we have evidence, fragmentary it is true, but circumstantial, of collusion with the German prisoners of war" at Tanglin.[132]

Perhaps not surprisingly, the conclusions of the court of inquiry were hardly unbiased. Its three members were all British men whose careers were vested either in Singapore or in the Indian Army, and thus none were likely to have sympathy with the sepoys' cause.[133] In addition, while the court was in session more than two hundred sepoys were executed, exiled,

---

[128] Proceedings of Court of Inquiry. Sareen, *Secret Documents*, 36–37.
[129] Proceedings of Court of Inquiry. Sareen, *Secret Documents*, 38.
[130] Proceedings of Court of Inquiry. Sareen, *Secret Documents*, 39.
[131] Report in Connection with Mutiny, IOR, L/MIL/17/19/48, 8.
[132] Proceedings of Court of Inquiry. Sareen, *Secret Documents*, 40.
[133] The three members were Brigadier-General F.A. Hoghton, president, sent from India; Lieutenant-Colonel Ferguson, Royal Artillery Medical Corps; and Mr. Chancellor, Inspector-General of the Police, Straits Settlements. Two other prominent Singapore Britons, a lawyer and a banker, had served on the committee prior to Hoghton's arrival from India.

or imprisoned – a factor that almost certainly hindered the collection of honest testimony by the sepoys it interviewed.[134]

As imperfect as the final report may have been, it was nevertheless far more balanced than the public explanations offered by the British metropolitan government and the government of Singapore in the immediate aftermath of the mutiny. In fact, the final report from the court of inquiry was never publicly released, which gave British authorities the opportunity to "spin" the event for their own purposes. The public explanation of the mutiny, therefore, was significantly different from the version reconstructed by the court of inquiry. Most importantly, the public version denied the importance of external causes and instead held that the Singapore mutiny had been a strictly local affair caused by lack of discipline in the regiment. This was the intentional result of furious collaboration between authorities in Singapore and London in the days immediately following the mutiny, in which each word of the official communiqué was scrutinized for its impact.[135] The official press release given to Reuters thirteen days afterwards read:

Owing to jealousy about recent promotions, a portion of the 5th Light Infantry (late 5th Bengals) at Singapore refused to obey orders, causing a serious riot. This was quelled by the local forces assisted by British and Allied ships. The casualties were – Killed: six officers, fourteen British soldiers and fourteen civilians. Wounded: nine British soldiers. Some of the rioters were killed, and a large number surrendered and were captured. There has been no destruction of property. All is now quiet.[136]

One thing that stands out in this public press release is that the event was reduced from a mutiny to a "serious riot." More importantly, its global origins were completely erased, and instead were ascribed to "jealousy about recent promotions." In spite of the complex, international networks that influenced the men of the 5th to take the dramatic decision to mutiny, their actions – for which many paid with their lives – were reduced to petty infighting. In the hopes that this version of events would eventually prevail, the government of Singapore maintained tight censorship over newspapers and letters to and from the island.[137] And because the report of the court of inquiry was never made public and was only declassified

---

[134] Court Martial Proceedings on Mutineers of the 5th Light Infantry, 1915. India Office Records, (IOR) L/MIl/7/7191, Vol. II. Letter from Dudley Ridout, General Commanding the Troops in Singapore, August 26, 1915.

[135] See Reports 8188, 19 February; 8189, 19 February; 8577, 22 February; 8578, 22 February, in Memorandums and Telegrams Relating to Disturbances at Singapore.

[136] Press Bureau Account of the Emeute, February 28, 1915. Sareen, *Secret Documents*, 828.

[137] An internal memo from the Governor of the Straits Settlements, Sir Arthur Young, indicated that "... instructions were issued to the Censor on the 16th instant that

in 1965, the official version of the mutiny as a purely local affair has cast a long shadow over later interpretations.

Conclusion

British insistence, at least in public, that the mutiny was caused solely by local conditions flatly contradicted not only the evidence but also what many authorities – including Arthur Young himself – said in private and official reports. Part of the motivation for making light of the situation was surely to avoid censure for fostering an environment of international sedition and lax discipline. Young had in fact responded to the court of inquiry's castigation of Singapore as a site with a notorious reputation for sedition by countering, "I will only say that this reputation was unknown to the Government of the Straits Settlements and to the Government of the Malay States, and that no communication on the subject was ever received from the Government of India . . . or from any Government or from any person."[138] Given the strong evidence that Young and the General Commanding the Troops were aware of these problems at least since the first publication of *Ghadar* in 1913, this statement seems disingenuous and self-serving at best.

But public explanations of the mutiny as a local affair were allowed to go unopposed by other authorities who knew better, including the Government of India and the court of inquiry itself. This was because British authorities were desperate to maintain a façade of confidence in the face of what they believed to be a coordinated conspiracy by the Central Powers and their sympathizers to undermine colonial rule. They feared emphasizing the external causes of the mutiny would only fuel discontent among other Indian regiments and Indian civilians both in India and abroad, as well as among colonized populations elsewhere.[139] For all of these reasons, British authorities were keen to avoid adding fuel to the fire of discontent, and especially to avoid publicizing an event that could inspire emulation elsewhere.

no papers were to be permitted to leave for abroad, and that letters except for the United Kingdom were to be censored." Arthur Young to Government House, February 25, 1915. Report on Singapore Disturbances Part Two, WO 32/9560, The National Archives, London.

[138] Sareen, *Secret Documents*, 710.

[139] Of special concern to British authorities were the Indian regiments stationed in places such as Hong Kong and Burma. They were also highly conscious of how Chinese populations in China and Southeast Asia might regard the mutiny. For concerns about Chinese populations, see Ching-hwang, *The Chinese in Southeast Asia and Beyond*, 191–204; Leo Suryadinata, "Overseas Chinese" and Southeast Asia in Chinese Foreign Policy: An Interpretive Essay (Research Notes and Discussion Paper No. 11: Institute of Southeast Asian Studies, 1978), 9.

When viewed in the larger context of German–Indian–Turkish intrigue in World War I Southeast Asia, the mutiny was only a dramatic episode in a much larger story that endured for the rest of the war. Such intrigue was a constant feature in the communications of not only the British in Malaya but also the French in Indochina. British and French authorities believed those responsible for anti-Allied plots had found safe havens in nearby neutral territories – especially the Dutch East Indies, Siam, China, and the Philippines – and that they were using these havens to wreak havoc on Malaya, Indochina, Hong Kong, the Chinese Concessions, and India. After the mutiny of the 5th, British authorities were well aware that the suppression of the mutiny did not eliminate the problem of anti-Allied sedition in the region. By insisting on the purely local origins of the mutiny, they hoped to be able to stem its progress. In the meantime, they did not waste time martialing the help of their wartime allies in what they hoped would be a massive demonstration of power – and it is to that we now turn.

2   The Defeat of the Singapore Mutiny
Regional Expression of Global Alliances

If the causes of the mutiny demonstrate the global webs that brought the war to Southeast Asia, so too did official and civil responses to it. The conditions created by World War I played a critical role in shaping the actions taken by representatives of various governments and civil populations during the mutiny. This was because decisions made at the centers of government about whether (and on whose side) to enter the war reverberated around the world as a result of empire. In Southeast Asia, colonial governments in Malaya and Indochina whose home countries joined the Allies now found themselves in even closer relationships of obligation with Japan and Russia. Meanwhile, colonies and states whose governments remained neutral – in this case the Dutch East Indies and China – nevertheless found it necessary to respond to the events of the mutiny. In the case of China, the desire to stay in Britain's good graces led the government to instruct the huge Chinese population in Singapore to remain calm. In the case of the Dutch East Indies, British calls for help led the Dutch to respond by playing both ends against the middle in order to prevent being dragged into the war on either side. Finally, civil populations of Japanese, Chinese, Indians, and Arab Muslims were either guided by their consuls to make their orientation to the war clear, or else found it expedient to do so for their own reasons.

These official and civil responses to the mutiny allow us to see the concrete impact of wartime alliances as they played out on the ground on one small island in Southeast Asia in early 1915. While Chapters 3–6 will explore the effects of these alliances over a larger area and a longer chronology, here we are able to see the complex ways they were expressed in response to a single event. This chapter begins by setting the narrative framework for the coordinated response to the mutiny, which included actors from Britain, France, Russia, Japan, the Netherlands, and China. It then turns to look in more detail at the responses of three sets of actors: the French, Russian, and Japanese members of the Allies, the Dutch and Chinese neutrals, and the Japanese, Chinese, Indian, and Arab Muslim populations living in Singapore. In so doing, it aims to demonstrate not only that wartime alliances and rivalries fundamentally shaped the outcome of the mutiny, but also that the mutiny itself helped, in its own small way, to reshape wartime alliances. It also shows how the conditions of war made it difficult even for neutral powers and civilian populations to remain aloof from the events of the mutiny.

A persistent theme in this chapter is the communication networks that linked colonies not only to their metropoles but also to neighboring colonies, to other imperial metropoles, and to independent states around the world. If Chapter 1 demonstrated that colonized subjects had access to ideologies, print materials, and people from all over the globe, this chapter shows how governments and colonial administrations acquired information about both the colonized and noncolonized world. In many cases, such information was collected and transmitted by low-level administrators such as consuls, who were literally stationed around the world for this purpose. This chapter demonstrates, then, that colonial rule was not simply about information passing between colony and metropole and vice versa: rather, in large part because of the consular system each colony was connected to foreign metropoles and to other states. As we will see in the case of the mutiny, information moved quickly in these multinodal networks, with results that often affected the outcome of local events.

A second theme in this chapter is the ways in which civil populations in Singapore responded to the mutiny based on their awareness of both local and global political conditions.[1] In the Japanese and Chinese cases, civil populations were guided by their own experiences in the island city, and also by information provided by the Japanese and Chinese governments via consuls. In the case of Indians and Arab Muslims, this multinational community took it upon themselves to convey their loyalty to the British crown in the punitive, anti-Muslim atmosphere that prevailed in Singapore after the mutiny.[2] Like official responses to the mutiny, civil responses were shaped by larger global conditions, alliances, and rivalries, even as they highlighted networks of information between colonies and independent nations all over Southeast and East Asia.

---

[1] Unfortunately, there is very little information about the Malay population, of whom there were more than 40,000 in Singapore around the time of the war. Most archival and secondary sources, whether British, French, Russian, or Japanese, explore the other civil populations on the island.

[2] Farish Noor likens the anti-Muslim atmosphere in postmutiny Singapore to the anti-Muslim racial profiling in the west in the aftermath of 9/11. Noor, " 'Racial Profiling Revisited': the 1915 Indian Mutiny in Singapore and the Impact of Profiling on Religious and Ethnic Minorities.".

Response to the Mutiny

As we know, when news of the mutiny at Alexandra Barracks reached the civil and military authorities in Singapore on the afternoon of the 15th, a flurry of activity ensued. Within hours, Arthur Young had requested troops from India, and had asked his military commanders to hail the French cruiser *Montcalm* – which left port the day before – to request its immediate return.[3] This was critical because in addition to having no regular land forces in Singapore, the only British naval ship at port was the *H.M.S. Cadmus*, a survey sloop with a contingent of just eighty-five sailors.[4] Later in the evening on the 15th, Young authorized a second call for help from any allied vessel in nearby waters.[5] The call for help yielded four allied ships: the French cruiser *Montcalm*, the Japanese cruisers *Tsushima* and *Otowa*, and the Russian *Orel*.

The first allied ship to make it to Singapore was the *Montcalm*. When its commander, Rear-Admiral Huguet, received a cryptic message from Admiral Thomas Martyn Jerram calling it back to port as soon as possible, the ship was off the tip of northern Sumatra in the midst of heavy storms.[6] Although Huguet had other duties to attend, he wrote that because of his familiarity with Jerram's character and the general helpfulness of the British to the French in the Pacific, he decided it was necessary to go "as quickly as possible to assist our allies."[7] Ten minutes after receiving the wireless message, at 11:30 p.m., Huguet turned the *Montcalm* around. The ship made it back to Singapore harbor at 5:10 p.m. the next day, where an impatient and anxious Jerram boarded the ship and briefed Huguet on the situation. At 10:15 p.m. Huguet's 190 men debarked, and by 2:00 a.m. they were being transported by car to the north and northwest of the island to round up mutineers.[8] This force marched around the area in the pouring rain until February 22, but aside from shooting and killing one sepoy, its searches for additional fugitives was unsuccessful.

Next to arrive in Singapore, on the night of February 18, was the Japanese cruiser *Otowa*, followed by the *Tsushima* on the 19th. Although Jerram had sent a telegram to the Japanese squadron headquarters on the evening of the 15th, it was only forwarded to the commander of the third

---

[3] R.W.E. Harper and Harry Miller, *Singapore Mutiny* (Singapore: Oxford University Press, 1984), 97.

[4] Arthur Young to Lewis Harcourt, February 17, 1915. Report on Singapore Disturbances of 1915, WO 32/9559, 28.

[5] Harper and Miller, *Singapore Mutiny*, 102.

[6] Admiral Huguet à Gouverneur General de L'Indochine, Mutinerie de Singapour. Troubles de Singapour, Aix-en-Provence, FM indo/nf/1037, February 22, 1915, 8.

[7] Admiral Huguet, Ibid.   [8] Admiral Huguet, Ibid.

squadron – Rear Admiral Tsuchiyu Mitsukane – the next day, much to Jerram's irritation. Moreover, Tsuchiyu expressed initial hesitation about getting involved in internal colonial affairs and declined to land his troops immediately after arrival.[9] Eventually, Tsuchiya did land his 150 sailors and placed them under British command. These men assisted British forces in re-taking the Alexandra Barracks, where the mutiny had begun, and in securing the Tanglin Barracks.[10] During their time ashore, Japanese forces came under fire on one occasion and captured twenty-two fugitive sepoys, who they promptly turned over to British authorities.[11]

Close behind the *Otowa* was the Russian ship *Orel*, which had been in Penang, off the coast of peninsular Malaya.[12] The *Orel* arrived on the evening of the 18th with a force of forty-two men and was promptly combined with a French unit and sent to apprehend fugitives in the north of the island.[13] The Russians were ordered to position themselves at the entrance to the Straits in order to prevent sepoys from trying to cross over to Johore on the Malay peninsula, and by February 21 they had assisted with the capture and disarming of 180 men.[14] Following this, the Russian sailors were attached to automobile patrols, and on February 25 two sailors were wounded – one quite seriously – during an armed engagement with a group of sepoys on a pineapple plantation.[15]

During the military actions against the sepoys, the multinational civil population in Singapore also responded to the mutiny. We know from Chapter 1 that several hundred British men volunteered to serve as special constables to help guard the city, and that British and European women and children were put on ships in the harbor to ensure their safety. Additionally, all of the foreign consuls in the city notified their home governments as well as relevant neighboring colonies that were part of

---

[9] Sho Kuwajima, *Mutiny in Singapore: War, Anti-War, and the War for India's Independence* (New Delhi: Rainbow Publishers, 2006), 103–104.

[10] Young to Harcourt, March 3, 1915. Report on Singapore Disturbances, Part II, WO 32/9560, 91.

[11] Kuwajima, *Mutiny in Singapore*, 106. Kuwajima notes that only the crew of the *Otowa* were involved in the capture of fugitives.

[12] Karen Snow, "Russia and the 1915 Indian Mutiny in Singapore," *Southeast Asia Research* 5, no. 3 (1997), 303.

[13] Young to Harcourt, March 3, 1915. Report on Singapore Disturbances, Part II, WO 32/9560, 91. Karen Snow puts the Russian force at 40 men. Snow, "Russia and the 1915 Indian Mutiny in Singapore," 304.

[14] Snow, "Russia and the 1915 Indian Mutiny in Singapore," 304. The Sultan of Johore also assisted the British by capturing and returning fugitive sepoys who had successfully crossed the Straits into his territory. For example, on February 17 the Sultan's forces captured sixty-one men. Report 14734, February 29, 1915, Memorandums and Telegrams Relating to Disturbances at Singapore, TNA, CO 273/420.

[15] Telegram February 26, 1915. Report on Singapore Disturbances of 1915, WO 32/9559; Snow, "Russia and the 1915 Indian Mutiny in Singapore," 305.

their regular network of communications. As a result, most of the diplomatic world with any stake in Singapore or Southeast Asia knew what was happening within about twenty-four hours. This, in turn, allowed the various governments to react to the situation, to send instructions to their nationals and, if it was so decided, to take action. The French, Russian, and Japanese consuls each received telegrams authorizing their national communities to aid the British in putting down the mutiny. Of great concern to the British was the very large Chinese community in Singapore, which had for decades been the source of most anxieties about unrest in the city. However, for reasons we will discuss more fully below, the Chinese government sent a message through its consul in Singapore urging the Chinese to remain calm during the mutiny.[16] For this and other reasons, the mutiny did not spark a general conflagration among the Chinese population. Nor did it elicit widespread participation among the Muslim civilians in the city, in spite of the support pro-Ottoman, pan-Islamic propaganda seemed to have enjoyed in the months preceding the mutiny. Even the civilian Indian population, Muslim and Hindu, remained quiet.

In order to apprehend the German prisoners of war who had escaped Singapore after being liberated by the sepoys, British authorities called on Malaya's neutral southern neighbor – the Dutch East Indies – for help. Only six of the prisoners were caught before leaving the island, meaning that eleven successfully made their way off the island and were presumed to be heading toward Dutch waters. In accordance with the British request, the Dutch Governor General – A.W.F. Idenberg – ordered Dutch ships to patrol the waters between Singapore and Sumatra, though without result.[17]

What this means is that within a few days of the first shots of the mutiny, ships from all of the Allied powers had arrived to help put it down, the most worrisome civilian populations had chosen not to join the mutineers' cause, and even the neutral Dutch East Indies appeared to give pro forma assistance in searching for escaped prisoners. Within a week, the British were confident they had the situation well in hand, and the Allied forces began to leave in more or less the order they had arrived: the French on February 23, the Japanese on the 25th, and the Russians on March 3.[18] Executions of mutineers began on February 23 and continued through April 18, and were attended by orderly crowds of

---

[16] Kuwajima, *Mutiny in Singapore*, 94.

[17] van Dijk, *The Netherlands Indies and the Great War 1914–1918*, 323.

[18] Young to Harcourt, March 3, 1915. Report on Singapore Disturbances, Part II, WO 32/9560, 91. The Japanese ships did not actually leave Singapore harbor at that time, but they withdrew their men to their ships. As an extra measure of security for the

Singapore's multinational civilians. What seems abundantly clear from all this is that while the war had provided the opportunity and the context for the mutiny to occur in the first place, the military alliances created by the war also provided the context in which it was put down.

Assembling the Allies in a "Time of Need"

There was little that was natural or comfortable about the Allied effort to help the British in Singapore. Although the alliances between Britain and Russia, France, and Japan were already eight, eleven, and thirteen years old (respectively) by 1915, at the turn of the twentieth century this particular combination of foreign help would likely have seemed inconceivable to a contemporary. In fact, it is safe to say that rivalries between all of the European powers with colonies in Southeast Asia had long been more characteristic of the region than friendly feelings and alliances. As late as 1903, for example, British army authorities in India had commissioned a secret report to discover exactly what it would take to conquer Indochina from the French.[19] Anglo-Dutch relations in Southeast Asia had been tense since the early nineteenth century and remained so in the twentieth, including during the war.[20] As for Anglo–Russian relations, rivalries between the two powers could hardly have been more tense right up until the entente brokered between them in 1907.[21] In fact, until 1902 the defense of Singapore was directly tied to the expansion of Russian power in Central and East Asia – especially after the Russians established a strong naval fleet at Port Arthur in Manchuria in 1897, which allowed it to threaten both China and Japan. As a result of this threat, British authorities felt it necessary to send a squadron of ships to the area in order to defend its interests from Russian advances.[22] The desire to position itself more strongly against a potential Russian menace in East Asia also explains, at least in part, the British willingness to conclude an alliance with Japan in 1902. But even this historic alliance had its own

British, Admiral Huguet left three French cruisers to the discretionary use of Jerram after the *Montcalm* departed.

[19] Frank Rennick, Strategical Memorandum on French Indochina, TNA, WO 33/287, 1903.

[20] A variety of issues during the war produced recurring tension between British and Dutch authorities, which we will return to in Chapters 3 and 4.

[21] By the late nineteenth century, these rivalries included Southeast Asia specifically, as Russia sought to intervene in both Burma and Siam to counter the influence of both the British in Burma and the British and French in Siam. See Karen Snow, "Russia as the 'Western Other' in Southeast Asia: Encounters of Russian Travelers in the Second Half of the Nineteenth Century," *The Russian Review* 71 (April 2012).

[22] Murfett, *Between Two Oceans*, 154.

tensions, particularly after India was brought into the Anglo-Japanese alliance at its first renewal in 1905. This was because the Government of India was deeply suspicious of Japan with regard to its territorial ambitions in China, and thus Anglo-Japanese relations in the Far East were often tinged with mutual apprehension.[23]

That representatives of all four powers could come together in common cause was one of the more remarkable aspects of the mutiny, notwithstanding the formal alliances between them. From the Allied perspective, this was a happy outcome, and in fact the collaboration modeled in Singapore had diplomatic repercussions in all of the concerned metropoles. British sentiments of goodwill were understandably effusive after the mutiny, given the perception that Allied help had averted a grave danger to the colony. Arthur Young, Dudley Ridout, and Thomas Martyn Jerram each made particular mention of the outstanding and important assistance of all Allied parties in their homeward correspondence and memoranda. This atmosphere of warmth overflowed from the grateful authorities of Singapore and their naval rescuers. Thanks to the reports received in London by Young and his military commanders, the Foreign Office activated the British consular network in Paris, Petrograd, and Tokyo and directed their representatives there to convey a "further expression of thanks for the effective and admirable services rendered by the landing parties from their warships."[24] Closer to home, the Singapore authorities also reached out to individual naval commanders with formal letters of thanks, and publicly acknowledged the service of each force with a parade and inspection before they disembarked from the island. Was this abundant thanks just a momentary expression of relief after a near miss, or were these warm feelings shared by Britain's allies to produce more lasting changes in their respective relationships? Let us look closer at both the public and private reactions of the French, Russians, and Japanese to find out.

On the morning of February 23, the Singapore authorities staged the first of three public spectacles to mark their appreciation for the help offered by Allied naval forces in quelling the mutiny. The *Straits Times*, which carried a full report of the event, professed that "all of Singapore" had turned out on the grounds of the Singapore Cricket Club to express their gratitude to the French forces, whose help "will for all time, in these parts, cement the bond which has grown up between the two

---

[23] Antony Best, "India, Pan-Asianism and the Anglo-Japanese Alliance," in Phillips Payson O'Brien, ed., *The Anglo-Japanese Alliance, 1902–1922* (London: RoutledgeCurzon, 2004), 237.

[24] Foreign Office to Consulates in Paris, Petrograd, and Tokyo, February 27, 1915. Report on Singapore Disturbances, Part II, WO 32/9560, 13.

nations."[25] The symbolism was thick. The French sailors of the *Mont-calm* were assembled in the center of the cricket field at attention, the French flag flying. British troops were assembled on the outside of the field, accompanied by the highest British military authorities, Admiral Huguet, and the French consul. When Governor General Young arrived at about 8:00 a.m., he walked onto the field with Huguet, Ridout, and Jerram to inspect the troops, while the French band played the British national anthem. When Young completed the inspection, he addressed the French forces in English, and then the French consul, Monsieur Bondy, translated for the French troops. Young thanked them "for the ready help we required," which "saved us many days of anxiety." He went on to say that "cheerfulness and zeal are two of the attributes of the great French nation," and called attention to their mutual bond of alliance in the war by offering the hope that "you may have your wish and come into close reach of our chief enemy, the Germans," who had "set aside the laws of humanity and stained its honour." He concluded by quoting the French premier and by promising that "the French and her Allies" would not lay down arms until "Prussian Militarism is wholly and finally destroyed."[26]

Privately, Huguet admitted that he was surprised by Young's enthusiastic and emotional speech, since, as he noted, such a reception was "not usual for French sailors in an English colony."[27] Although the mission had gone well, Huguet had not had a chance to see Young's speech beforehand, and so only prepared "a few vague words" that were in a "less warm tone."[28] But his own speech, read in French and then translated into English by the French consul, nevertheless called attention to the warm bonds of alliance between the French and the British. He began by saying that the whole crew of the *Montcalm* keenly felt the call on their friendship with the British, and that they were very happy to render their assistance to the best of their abilities. He went on to say that "what happened here, in a theater so far from the places where our destinies are being decided, is testimony to our solidarity and to the solidity of our friendship."[29]

Huguet directed his reports to the Governor General of Indochina – the French civil authority in closest range. After reviewing the events of

---

[25] "Governor Reviews the French Contingent: A Stirring Scene," *Straits Times*, February 23, 1915.

[26] "Governor Reviews the French Contingent: A Stirring Scene," *Straits Times*, February 23, 1915.

[27] Huguet to the Governor General in Indochina, February 25, 1915, Troubles de Singapour, CAOM FM indo/nf/1037.

[28] Huguet to the Governor General in Indochina, ibid.

[29] Huguet to the Governor General in Indochina, ibid.

the mutiny from Huguet's reports, the Governor General of Indochina made a point of writing to the French Minister of Colonies in Paris. Even though the mutiny had no visible repercussions in Indochina, he felt it was important because the alacrity with which the French responded had a "happy effect" on Franco-British relations. In fact, he thought French assistance "from colony to colony" demonstrated the true scope of the entente cordiale, and that this was well noted on the British side, both by the civil and military authorities and by the European population in Singapore.[30] The Governor General even took the unusual step of offering, via the French consul, a contingent of Indochinese soldiers to help put down the mutiny.[31]

In fact, intercolonial support for putting down internal colonial unrest was quite a new development. In the past, rival colonial powers were normally content with taking a wait-and-see attitude to rebellions occurring in neighboring colonies. But the mutiny demonstrated that wartime alliances could trump intercolonial rivalries. In so doing, it offered the possibility of a new kind of colonial security – one that could benefit from pooled resources rather than those of a single nation. This, Huguet thought, could have the benefit of making colonial subjects think twice before rebelling, even when colonial forces were stretched thin. As he told the Governor General of Indochina, he noticed with pleasure that one of the purposes of the pomp and circumstance displayed during the inspection was, no doubt, to "strike the native imagination, Chinese or Malay, and to demonstrate that British forces were not alone, and that they must count on the solid support of allied forces" in times of crisis. In this, he argued, "Indochina has the same interest."[32] By February 1915, when it was becoming ever more clear that the global war then in progress would not be over quickly or won easily, such small examples about the true potential of the wartime alliance may have gone a small way toward improving the good will between the British and the French.

In the Russian case, Karen Snow believes that the mutiny played an important role in improving the tense Anglo-Russian relations that characterized the early months of the war.[33] For much of the nineteenth

---

[30] Governor-General Hanoi, March 18, 1915. Troubles de Singapour, CAOM FM indo/nf/1037.

[31] February 19, 1915, Troubles de Singapour, CAOM FM indo/nf/1037. Young declined the offer, because the *Montcalm* had already arrived by that point.

[32] Rear-Admiral Huguet to the Governor General in Indochina, February 25, 1915, Troubles de Singapour, CAOM FM indo/nf/1037.

[33] This is one of the main points in Snow, "Russia and the 1915 Indian Mutiny in Singapore."

century, Anglo-Russian rivalry on India's northwest frontier was so well known that it was literally the stuff of storybooks.[34] The rivalry also raged in China at the turn of the twentieth century, as the British sought to block Russian expansion in the country's north, while the Russians sought to protect their economic and strategic interests there. Mutual concern about Russian expansion, in turn, helped push the British and the Japanese together in 1902. While it is true that Anglo-Russian tensions lessened after the end of the Russo-Japanese war, and that these decreased tensions paved the way for the 1907 Anglo-Russian entente, old feelings nevertheless died hard.[35]

Those old feelings were rekindled in Southeast Asia in October 1914, at Penang Harbor in British Malaya. In the early morning of October 28, the German ship *Emden* – the same ship whose crew ended up being interned in Singapore – steamed into the harbor flying a Russian flag.[36] There, it drew up next to the Russian cruiser *Zhemchug* and fired a torpedo, followed by a round of shells and gunfire. Before the Russian crew had time to respond, the *Emden* fired a second torpedo into the front of *Zhemchug*, causing it to sink abruptly with many of its crew aboard.[37] After sinking the *Zhemchug*, the *Emden* was confronted by the French cruiser *Mousquet*, which was returning from patrol. The *Emden* then fired on the *Mousquet* and sank it as well before steaming out of the harbor. Casualties were high for such a short battle: a number of the French crew died on the *Mousquet*, though the German ship did take the time to rescue thirty-six men who survived the initial attack. The *Zhemchug* sustained the highest casualties: out of a crew of 355 men, 89 were killed in the initial battle, 123 were wounded, and 143 escaped unharmed. One hundred fourteen of the wounded were brought to the British General Hospital in Penang, where a further five men died from their wounds.[38]

The sinking of the *Zhemchug* did not improve Anglo-Russian relations. Already in the first months of the war the Russian consul in Singapore, N.A. Rospopov, had expressed concern that the Singapore newspapers were not sympathetic to the difficulties Russia faced in its early battles

[34] Rudyard Kipling's *Kim*, for example, originally published in series in 1900–1901.

[35] Snow, "Russia and the 1915 Indian Mutiny in Singapore," 296, 297.

[36] There is some disagreement about which flag the *Emden* was flying: Karen Snow says it was Japanese, while the *Straits Times* claimed it was Russian. The point is that the German ship had disguised itself to gain access to the harbor.

[37] "Emden at Penang: Terrible Morning Scene in Harbour," *The Straits Times*, November 2, 1914, 7.

[38] Report 6948, Treatment of Wounded Russians from Russian Warship Zhemtchug, CO 273/420, February 12, 1915. Many of the unharmed had been ashore at the time of the attack.

against the Central Powers.[39] Rospopov's frustrations with the British in Singapore were not out of line with those of his predecessors: since the first establishment of a Russian consul in Singapore in 1890, the general tone of correspondence between the consuls and the Russian Asiatic Department had been consistently anti-British. When the *Zhemchug* was sunk, therefore, Anglo-Russian tensions flared as each side seemed ready to malign the other for its occurrence. On the Russian side, Rospopov's report suggested that the British authorities had not done enough to prevent such an occurrence – especially since they were already aware of the *Emden's* exploits in the region. On the British side, rumors suggested that Russians on the *Zhemchug* had tried to escape rather than fight, and that all but one Russian officer was involved in various hedonistic pleasures on shore when the attack occurred.[40]

Arthur Young's report on the treatment of the *Zhemchug's* wounded made an effort to paper over these tensions by demonstrating the good will of the British toward the fallen Russians, arguing that all 114 "were in bed with first dressings applied within three hours." As further proof of the excellent care to which the Russians had been treated, Young pointed out that no further deaths had occurred aside from the five "hopeless cases" who had sustained very great wounds in the attack, and that by the end of 1914 ninety-four had been released from the hospital.[41] Notwithstanding such cheerful-sounding reports, the attack on the *Zhemchug* had sharpened old Anglo-Russian tensions to a new intensity.

The mutiny of the 5th occurred only three and a half months after the sinking of the *Zhemchug*. In fact, the Russian ship that came to the aid of the British – the *Orel* – was in Penang to aid in the salvage of the *Zhemchug's* guns when it was ordered to Singapore.[42] Because of this, the men on the *Orel* would undoubtedly have been familiar with the ill will the attack by the *Emden* generated between Russians and Britons. Nevertheless, when the *Orel* arrived in Singapore on February 18, Rospopov followed the example of the French and Japanese and placed the forty men on board under British command. Karen Snow argues that this was quite an unusual step, especially given recent feelings between Britons and Russians in Malaya. In fact, Rospopov was so unsure

---

[39] Snow, "Russia and the 1915 Indian Mutiny in Singapore," 300.

[40] Ibid., 297, 299. Snow argues that although Rospopov initially thought the British had started these rumors, he eventually decided they had originated with a Russian woman in Singapore who was hostile to the consul and to the command of the *Zhemchug*.

[41] Arthur Young to Lewis Harcourt, Colonial Office, January 14, 1914. Treatment of Wounded Russians from Russian Warship Zhemtchug, TNA, CO 273/420.

[42] Snow, "Russia and the 1915 Indian Mutiny in Singapore," 303.

about the decision that he discussed its propriety with the French Admiral Huguet. Huguet reassured Rospopov by suggesting that such an act of friendliness would have a positive effect on inter-Allied relations.[43] As we know, the small Russian contingent went on to play a role in capturing a number of sepoys, and two of the men were wounded in a firefight.

The salutary effects of Russian aid in the mutiny began to be felt in official circles within days of the *Orel's* arrival. On February 21 Admiral Jerram went to Rospopov personally to thank the troops for their good service. That same evening, Rospopov and Captain Vinokurov of the *Orel* visited the troops to convey Jerram's appreciation. Rospopov also communicated British gratitude back to his superiors in Russia.[44] By the time the men of the *Orel* were ready to leave Singapore, the tone of the discourse between British and Russian officials had shifted from mistrust to warmth. The parade and inspection of the troops by Governor General Young, held on March 2, provided a public venue in which to pronounce this shift. Although it was the last of these events, the *Straits Times* noted that attendance seemed even greater than the previous parades for the French and Japanese troops.[45] Together with British and Russian officers and the Russian consul, Young inspected the troops as they were lined up at attention on the pavilion. When the inspection was complete, he expressed his sincere gratitude for the "valuable support" provided by the Russian contingent. Much more dramatically, he went on to say "Your powerful nation has, in the Eastern area of the war, been fighting practically the whole strength of Austria and a large portion of the German forces and the brilliant strategy of . . . the Grand Duke Nicholas . . . greatly relieved the stress in the western area." Tying the larger alliance to their present location, Young added, "our unity has been further demonstrated during the last few days in the way in which Russians, French, Japanese, and British have fought side by side for the preservation of peace and order in this distant colony."[46] He ended by saying that, in the future, he hoped to see more Russian flags flying from ships in the port of Singapore.

Not to be outdone, Captain Vinokurov graciously accepted the Governor General's thanks, and dramatically replied:

the Russian blood spilt in defence of a right cause, on this British soil, may unite us – the Allies – better than any treaty and may give to that union a great and holy sanction. Long before the treaty of peace destined to crown the present war for Freedom and National dignity in Europe, we now may be allowed to say that we

[43] Ibid., 303.   [44] Ibid., 304–305.
[45] "Our Allies: Governor Inspects Russian Detachment," *Straits Times* March 3, 1915, 8.
[46] "Our Allies: Governor Inspects Russian Detachment," *Straits Times* March 3, 1915, 8.

have already passed here a treaty of fraternity which, I hope, will not only prove indissoluble, but ever destined to grow and gather in strength.[47]

Times had definitely changed. Just a few months earlier the Russian consul had been certain that British officers were inventing stories to discredit the crew of the *Zhemchug* – a conviction that was in line with decades of Anglo-Russian antagonism in Singapore. And yet after the mutiny both sides were talking about "unity," fighting "side by side," and an "indissoluble" "treaty of fraternity."

Of course, some of these pronouncements might have simply been mere words on an occasion when the authorities were expected to expound on the bonds of friendship. But British and Russian private correspondence back to their respective metropoles suggest there was more to it than this. For Young, Jerram, and Ridout, the men of the *Orel* transformed their vision of Russians from representatives of a malevolent and antagonistic power into real allies, fighting together for the same purpose. These sentiments were conveyed to the Colonial Office and the War Office in London, which were then conveyed to the Russian ambassador and the Russian government. Then, as a practical gesture of appreciation, the British government decided not to charge the Russian government for the hefty expense incurred during the hospital care of the wounded crew of the *Zhemchug*.[48] The same was true for the Russian side: although Rospopov remained unconvinced of the official British explanation of the causes behind the mutiny, he did believe that the mutiny had brought Russians and Britons together as partners. Like the British officials in Singapore, Rospopov also conveyed these ideas to his superiors in the Ministry of Foreign Affairs.[49]

Even though the Singapore mutiny was not a major event in the war, the fact that it had drawn the French, British, and Russians together seemed to go at least a small way toward improving inter-Allied relations between them. Given their history of tension – particularly between Britain and the other two powers – perhaps it is not surprising that both colonial and metropolitan authorities wanted to make as much as possible out of the example of mutual aid demonstrated in the mutiny. In addition, since the outcome of the mutiny was a clear and quick victory for the Allies, it may well have provided a welcome distraction from the horrifying news on both the western and the eastern fronts, and a ray of hope for better outcomes in the future.

While the result of mutual aid during the mutiny seemed to have a positive effect on relations between the European Allies, the Japanese case

---

[47] "Our Allies: Governor Inspects Russian Detachment," *Straits Times* March 3, 1915, 8.
[48] Snow, "Russia and the 1915 Indian Mutiny in Singapore," 307.   [49] Ibid., 315.

was more complicated. First, in contrast to the French and Russian cases, there was a small but active community of Japanese citizens in Singapore, and within hours of the outbreak of the mutiny the Japanese consul had organized its men into a volunteer defense force. Second, although the Japanese sent two cruisers to Singapore and provided important support to British forces, the aid was given with noticeable hesitation. Third, although both sides declared their mutual friendship publicly during the parade and inspection, private correspondence and print material indicated significant Anglo-Japanese antagonism even after the mutiny was over.

At the beginning of the war, there were 1,830 Japanese nationals in Singapore. Although two-thirds were involved in "respectable" business interests such as rubber plantations and retail, the remaining third were involved in the business of specialized Japanese brothels – and it was for this that the Japanese in Singapore were best known.[50] As a result, other Singaporeans – especially the British – tended to look down on the Japanese. Many of the "respectable" Japanese chafed under this condescension, and by 1913 had already begun to try to improve their reputation by attempting to close down the brothels.[51] In their view, the poor reputation of Japanese in Singapore was in conflict with their growing national pride, and with the fact that the British were now dependent on the Japanese navy for protection in East and Southeast Asia.[52] Thus when the mutiny broke out, both the Japanese consul and the leading men of the community saw it as an opportunity to demonstrate to the British not only their worthiness, but also their equality as men and allies.

The Japanese consul, Mr. Fujii, received word of the mutiny in the late evening of the 15th. That night he conveyed the situation to his government by telegram.[53] British and Japanese sources diverge slightly about what happened next. According to Japanese sources, an agitated Arthur Young called Mr. Fujii at about 11:00 p.m. to ask him to recruit a force of special constables from among the Japanese men living in the city. Fujii recorded that after meeting with some twenty prominent Japanese expatriates, the Japanese agreed to form such a corps, but only under specific conditions that guaranteed they would be treated as equals and not like colonial subjects. For example, they stipulated that the corps must be

---

[50] Kuwajima, *Mutiny in Singapore: War, Anti-War, and the War for India's Independence*, 7.

[51] Between 1913 and 1920, the "respectable" Japanese succeeded in closing down the Japanese brothels. Kuwajima, 10–11.

[52] For the Anglo-Japanese alliance, see Philips Payson O'Brien, *The Anglo-Japanese Alliance* (London: Routledge Curzon, 2004).

[53] Kuwajima, 95.

under Japanese command, and must be used only to defend the city of Singapore from attack. They also insisted that the force be disbanded as soon as Japanese naval ships arrived, and that anyone killed or wounded as a result of defending the city would be given the same treatment as any European.[54] Only when these terms were agreed, according to Japanese sources, did Fujii tell Young that the Japanese agreed to form the unit. In this version, the undertone of mistrust by the Japanese toward the British is quite strong.

Arthur Young told the story slightly differently in his homeward report. Young's report leaves the impression that it was not Young who approached Mr. Fujii, but the other way around. In Young's version, the Japanese consul "interviewed the General Officer Commanding and myself and arranged to obtain the services of a number of nationalists to assist the military."[55] Young also did not mention any of the conditions outlined in the Japanese sources, saying only that the 182 men assembled did good service but were not needed after February 22.[56]

The differences between Young's and Fujii's accounts of the conditions under which the volunteers were formed are minor but are indicative of deeper Anglo-Japanese tensions in 1915. At a local level, it is certainly clear that many of the leading Japanese men felt that the British were inclined to treat them with haughty arrogance, and thus they were not willing to jump to the defense of the British unless it also served Japanese interests. On the British side, Young's homeward reports about the mutiny included a number of obfuscations typical of authorities who find themselves in crisis situations. It is likely he simply did not want to admit the necessity of pleading with the Japanese for help, in the same way that he confidently asserted, contrary to all the evidence, that the mutiny had produced "no panic" in Singapore.[57]

But at the time of the mutiny, there were more than just local Anglo-Japanese tensions at stake. When the Great War began, the existence of the Anglo-Japanese alliance allowed the British to withdraw their five battleships from the Far East for use in Europe, with the understanding that the Japanese navy would help protect British interests in the waters of East and Southeast Asia. This meant that the Japanese navy became

[54] Kuwajima, 95.

[55] Arthur Young to Lewis Harcourt, M.P., February 25, 1915. Report on Singapore Disturbances, Part II, WO 32/9560, 90, 91.

[56] Kuwajima gives the number of Japanese volunteers as 186. Kuwajima, *Mutiny in Singapore*, 96.

[57] Young to Colonial Office, February 17, 1915, Report on Singapore Disturbances of 1915 (Kew: TNA, 1915), WO 32/9559.

the dominant naval power in the region, which the British considered an acceptable risk in 1914.[58]

This dominance was extended when the British Foreign Secretary requested the help of the Japanese navy in capturing armed German merchant ships that were using German concessions in Tsingtao (Qingdao), China, as a base. In Japanese naval circles this request was viewed as an unprecedented opportunity for extending Japanese power in China while the Europeans were otherwise occupied. Not quite three weeks after Britain entered the war, the Japanese also declared war on Germany and set their sights on conquering the German territory of Tsingtao.[59] With the blessing of the British and the assistance of two British battalions, the Japanese assembled a force of 60,000 men and attacked Tsingtao by sea. Although the action violated Chinese neutrality, both British and Japanese strategists justified it for their own reasons: the British because it removed the threat of an active German naval base in the region, and the Japanese because it strengthened their position in China.[60] By November 7 the German contingent on the base surrendered, leaving Japan in control of Tsingtao.

What the Japanese did after taking Tsingtao, however, brought the Anglo-Japanese alliance under serious strain.[61] Not content with the former German base, on January 18, 1915 the Japanese government secretly presented Yuan Shikai's Chinese government with what became known as the Twenty-One Demands. These demands included a dramatic extension of Japanese control on the Shantung peninsula as well as southern Manchuria and Inner Mongolia, and would have given Japanese interests the same privileges as those previously enjoyed by the European powers in China.[62] If all the demands had been accepted by the Chinese government, China would have become a virtual protectorate of Japan.[63] Thus, in the hope that the demands would spark outrage amongst the British – which had heretofore been the most influential foreign power in China – the Chinese government let their contents be known to the wider world. The effects were explosive. In China and among the

---

[58] Murfett, *Between Two Oceans*, 156, 158. The Dutch were much more worried about this risk, as we will see in Chapter 4.

[59] Strachan, *The First World War*, 72. The Japanese declared war on Germany on August 23.

[60] Hew Strachan, *The First World War*, 73.

[61] Phillips Payson O'Brien, *The Anglo-Japanese Alliance, 1902–1922* (London; New York: RoutledgeCurzon, 2004), 5.

[62] Hew Strachan, *The First World War*, 74.

[63] Odd Arne Westad, *Restless Empire: China and the World since 1750* (New York: Basic Books, 2012), 115–116.

Overseas Chinese, communities responded with outrage.[64] More importantly for our purposes here, it was also a turning point for the Anglo-Japanese alliance, because at that point the British began to have grave concerns about Japanese expansion in China and, more particularly, how such expansion would affect established British interests there.

When the mutiny occurred in mid-February, then, all was not rosy between the British and the Japanese, either in Singapore itself or on a wider, regional scale. As we have already seen, the British request for help from the Japanese Third Squadron resulted in the dispatch of two ships, the *Otowa* and the *Tsushima*. As a precaution, the Japanese also dispatched a third ship to Hong Kong, in case the Indian regiment stationed there also mutinied.[65] But according to Kuwajima, the commander of the Third Squadron, Rear Admiral Tsuchiya Mitsukane, had misgivings about intervening in an internal colonial affair, and thus he delayed landing his men. Apparently, Tsuchiya did not believe that the Anglo-Japanese alliance obligated him to help the British in the case of internal colonial unrest.[66]

In spite of Tsuchiya's initial hesitation, his Third Squadron did respond, and the men from the *Otowa* and the *Tsushima* did good service during their limited time on Singapore. British homeward reports about the Japanese were not effusive but were diplomatic and complimentary. At the end of their service on land, Young conducted an inspection of the Japanese troops just as he had done for the French and would later do for the Russians. The *Straits Times* reported the event as fully as the other inspections, arguing that "the public of Singapore proved just as eager to pay their tribute to our Eastern friends as they were to wish good luck to the Frenchmen, and their repeated cheers, whole-hearted and spontaneous, must have assured every single member of the force, officers and men alike, that what they have done for the Colony will not be forgotten."[67]

Following the inspection, Arthur Young and Rear Admiral Tsuchiya made speeches translated by the Japanese consul, Mr. Fujii. Young began by offering his thanks to the Japanese force and then pointed to the wider struggle in which both the British and Japanese were involved. "Your nation has accounted for Tsingtau," he argued, "that powerful stronghold in the East of our common enemy the Germans: the

---

[64] Xu, *China and the Great War: China's Pursuit of a New National Identity and Internationalization*, 97.

[65] Kuwajima, *Mutiny in Singapore: War, Anti-War, and the War for India's Independence*, 104.

[66] Ibid., 101.

[67] "The Japanese Parade: Colony's Thanks to our Allies," *The Straits Times*, February 26, 1915.

overthrow of that fortress was conducted in the methodical and thorough manner with which your nation characterises her deeds." But, he also reminded them that "during that siege a body of the forces of our King fought with you," and thus that the Japanese still had to contend with the British presence in China. Young continued by commending the "cordial manner" of Japanese cooperation with the British in this and other wartime operations, and by singling out Mr. Fujii for bringing together the force of Japanese special constables prior to the arrival of Japanese troops.[68] Overall, his remarks were friendly but hardly as warm and emotional as those he had directed to the French or the Russians.

Admiral Tsuchiya's reply matched, and even exceeded, Young's reserve. He began by saying, "It really is an honour to me that I have been able to help you, though it was very little that I could do." He continued by saying that the British arrangements for accommodating the Japanese troops were "appropriate," and that the ceremony marking their contribution was "courteous." He then pointed out that his ships were going to remain in and near Singapore for "some time," and suggested "if you should need again any assistance from their crews we shall at any time be ready and delighted to give it," thereby reminding the colony of Japanese naval predominance in the region.[69]

In contrast to the words exchanged between Young and either the French or Russian commanders, the remarks between the British and the Japanese were markedly more distant. The Twenty-One Demands had recently become public knowledge, and mutual mistrust was high in spite of the formal wartime alliance. While it is impossible to know how prevalent these feelings of mistrust were, it is worth considering the Japanese perspective outlined in a book by M. Tsukuda, who worked as a journalist for the *Nanyo Nichi-Nichi Shimbun* newspaper in Singapore at the time of the mutiny. *From Nanyo* was published in Tokyo in 1916, and was distributed in Singapore in the same year. Tsukuda had little charitable to say about British conduct during the Great War in general and the mutiny in particular. He complained about British attitudes toward the Japanese, arguing that the Japanese in Singapore were initially treated as a suspect population in spite of the Anglo-Japanese alliance. Once the mutiny broke out, however, Tsukuda was gratified to observe that "the British, until recently so arrogant, now had their tails down and their wings tucked in, and had come greatly to value us." He ended his account by proudly claiming that the mutiny represented the first time

[68] "The Japanese Parade: Colony's Thanks to our Allies," *The Straits Times*, February 26, 1915.
[69] "The Japanese Parade: Colony's Thanks to our Allies."

"we were in military possession of a portion of British territory," even if only for a short time.[70] For Tsukuda, the story of the mutiny was about the arrogant British being brought low, and about the rise of the Japanese to their rightful position in the region.

Several clues also indicate that British military officials were not as pleased with Japanese aid as Young professed in his inspection. One of these comes from the French Admiral Huguet, who reported that Admiral Jerram had told him he was doubly grateful for French aid because he could get only limited action that was "full of hesitation" from the Japanese.[71] The second was recorded well after the mutiny in 1917, when British authorities in Singapore read the first English translation of Tsukuda's book. At that point they argued that Japanese civilians hadn't done much in the mutiny because they refused to engage in real battle, and that the naval landing party mostly sat around in Alexandra Barracks while ashore.[72] Whether these opinions reflected widespread feelings at the time of the mutiny is unclear, but they do suggest a higher level of mutual tension than existed between the British and either the French or the Russians once the mutiny was over.

In spite of lingering Anglo-Japanese tensions, Japanese aid during the mutiny did at least provoke the British Colonial Office to direct its Tokyo ambassador to convey Britain's thanks to the government and included a special acknowledgment of the actions of the Japanese consul in Tokyo for raising a volunteer force.[73] And while relations between the British authorities in Singapore with either Fujii or Tsuchiya may not have been warm, both Japanese men had fulfilled their obligations as representatives of an Allied power in wartime. Notwithstanding a certain amount of resentment on the part of some individuals on both sides, the mutiny had nevertheless demonstrated the material consequences of the wartime alliance.

When the responses of each of the Allies are viewed together, one of the things that becomes clear is the surprising strength of wartime global alliances even far from the centers of battle in Europe, and even among nations with histories of tension and rivalry. In the case of the mutiny, a key factor in lubricating the diplomatic machinery that helped maintain these alliances so far from their metropolitan centers were the consuls. Each of the consuls in Singapore obtained local information and conveyed it to their home governments multiple times during the

---

[70] Straits Settlements Original Correspondence: Foreign, 1918, CO 273/475.
[71] Huguet to Governor General Indochina, February 25, 1915, Troubles de Singapour.
[72] Kuwajima, 109.
[73] Foreign Office to Consulates in Paris, Petrograd, and Tokyo, February 27, 1915. Report on Singapore Disturbances, Part II, WO 32/9560, 13.

mutiny. They served as translators, intermediaries, and leaders. They awaited instructions from their metropoles on how to proceed, but they also helped shape their governments' perceptions of the host authorities. On a practical level, the existence of these relationships helped ensure that the crisis of the mutiny was communicated to the metropolitan centers of all of Britain's allies within hours of its occurrence, and that each had the opportunity to assemble and coordinate a thoughtful response.

The military nature of these responses virtually ensured that the mutiny of the 5th would fail, and that British control of Singapore would not be under threat for long. But the experience of all the Allies having "boots on the ground" together at the same time, and the successful outcome that arose from it, seemed to also have effects that reverberated far beyond Singapore. This was particularly true for British relations with the French and the Russians, the latter of which had been rocky immediately prior to the mutiny. Yet even the discourse between the British and Japanese, whose relations had come under considerable strain by February 1915, appeared publicly united by the events of the mutiny – and in fact Japanese aid during the mutiny may have played a role in muting British anger over Japan's recent attempts to extend its control over China.

Role of the Neutrals: China

We have just seen how the alliance system in the Great War shaped the ways Britain's allies responded to the mutiny. But Britain's allies were not the only ones who found it necessary to respond to the mutiny. The Chinese and the Dutch – both neutral in 1915 – also had a stake in the game, albeit for very different reasons. In the Chinese case, the fledgling republican government under Yuan Shikai sought to build on several decades of government involvement in claiming responsibility for overseas Chinese by issuing instructions for the large population of Chinese in Singapore to remain calm during the conflict. At the same time, the Chinese experience of the war at the hands of the Japanese – especially in light of the recent Twenty-One Demands – meant that the government needed Britain's help to defend itself from being forced to become a Japanese protectorate. Although the evidence is only circumstantial, this may also have influenced the Chinese government's desire to avoid having its overseas populations cause trouble for the British.

For decades prior to the mutiny, Chinese Singaporeans had been the community of greatest concern to the colonial government. Chinese communities had been the source of serious riots in both Singapore and the Malay Peninsula during the late nineteenth century, and for more than thirty years the British colonial government had been deeply concerned over the destabilizing effects of interference among Singapore Chinese by the Chinese state as well as Chinese reformers and revolutionaries.[74]

There were good reasons for the British to be concerned about Chinese matters in Singapore, because the Chinese composed by far the largest community on the island. Out of a population of 303,261 in 1911, 219,577 were classified as Chinese – which included five different language groups from China as well as Straits-born Chinese. When contrasted with the 5,711 Europeans, 4,611 Eurasians, 41,806 Malays, and 27,755 Indians on the island, the numerical superiority of Chinese Singaporeans is stark.[75]

Until the late nineteenth century, the Qing government largely ignored the Chinese who emigrated overseas and washed its hands of responsibility for them. But as part of the state's desire to modernize in the wake of increasing threats to its sovereignty after the Opium Wars, the Qing government found it prudent to revise this attitude. By the 1870s, the Qing began to recognize the importance of participating in the international diplomatic system, and also of taking responsibility for Chinese who had emigrated overseas. Thus in 1877, the Qing established diplomatic embassies in London, Berlin, and Tokyo, and created its first consulate in the location where the largest and wealthiest community of overseas Chinese lived: Singapore.[76]

The establishment of the Singapore consulate was just the beginning of the Qing state's increasing involvement in the lives of the overseas Chinese. In 1893, the Qing formally rescinded its long-standing ban on Chinese emigration. Thereafter, the government referred to such emigrants as *Huaqiao*, or Chinese sojourners, emphasizing their status as *temporary* emigrants abroad and affirming the responsibility of the Chinese state for their well-being. In 1909, the government increased its claim to jurisdiction over Overseas Chinese by legislating that all children of Chinese fathers – regardless of where they were born – would

---

[74] Eric Tagliacozzo, *Secret Trades, Porous Borders: Smuggling and States Along a Southeast Asian Frontier, 1865–1915* (New Haven: Yale University Press, 2005), 133.

[75] "Military Report on The Straits Settlements," printed booklet, (1915), L/Mil/17/19/47, 6. The census also recorded 3,801 "miscellaneous" people.

[76] So Fion, Wai Ling, Ulbert, Jörg, and Prijak, Lukian, "The Rise of the Chinese Consular Service Abroad," in *Consuls et Services Consulaires Au XIXe Siecle = Die Welt Der Konsulate Im 19. Jahrhundert = Consulship in the 19th Century* (Hamburg: DOBU, Dokumentation & Buch, 2010). The establishment of this consulate was negotiated by the first Chinese ambassador to London, Kuo Sung-Tao.

be recognized as Chinese nationals, and that any Overseas Chinese who wished to return to China would be granted a Chinese passport.[77]

This shift in attitude toward the Overseas Chinese was aimed at redirecting the allegiance – and the money – of the *Huaqiao* toward China at a time when the Qing government was desperate to fund its modernization plans and regain full sovereignty over China.[78] This was a highly practical strategy, because Overseas Chinese communities – especially those in Southeast Asia, known as *nanyang* – had become extremely wealthy and had the means to contribute to state-building programs in China. Since the British government in Singapore already claimed jurisdiction over the Chinese there, however, by the 1890s this strategy caused increasing friction between the Qing and the British.[79]

Adding to the tensions on both sides was the fact that, in the two decades before the Great War, both Chinese reformers and revolutionaries increasingly sought to enlist the support of *nanyang* Chinese for their plans to either reshape or eliminate the existing Qing state.[80] This meant that Singapore not only had an active Chinese consulate that was frequently trying to raise money and support for Chinese projects, but those individual Chinese activists – including revolutionaries like Sun Yat-Sen – often travelled to Singapore to raise money for their own programs.[81] The net result of all this activity in Singapore is that it encouraged the Chinese community there to see themselves ever more clearly as a unified group of Chinese nationals, separate from other colonized subjects, and to look to China as a homeland.[82]

In 1911, a revolution inspired by Sun Yat-Sen (and funded principally by Overseas Chinese) brought the Qing dynasty to an end.[83] The formal reins of government quickly fell to a former Qing general named Yuan Shikai. Yuan was no revolutionary, but he did take seriously the many efforts of the late Qing state, the reformers, and the revolutionaries to incorporate Overseas Chinese into the new Chinese state. Each of

---

[77] Philip A. Kuhn, *Chinese among Others: Emigration in Modern Times* (Lanham: Rowman & Littlefield Publishers, 2009), 241.

[78] Kuhn, 179.

[79] For an example of these tensions, see British Chinese Subjects, Report 2174, Straits Settlements Original Correspondence: Foreign, January 31, 1898, CO 273/243.

[80] Kuhn, *Chinese among Others*.

[81] Ching-hwang, *The Chinese in Southeast Asia and Beyond*. Sun raised $50,000 from Chinese in British Malaya and the Dutch East Indies, and $30,000 from Chinese in Indochina for his revolutionary plans.

[82] Ching-hwang, *The Chinese in Southeast Asia and Beyond*, 191–204; Leo Suryadinata, *"Overseas Chinese" in Southeast Asia and China's Foreign Policy: An Interpretive Essay* (1978), 9. This was not only true for Singapore, but for Chinese communities across Southeast Asia.

[83] Westad, *Restless Empire*, 141.

these groups had thought of Overseas Chinese as integral to financing China's bid "to join the world community as an equal member" – a goal that continued to exercise Yuan's regime.[84] As a result, Yuan's government remained committed to using the international diplomatic system – including its consuls in Southeast Asia and its ambassadors in Europe – to project Chinese aspirations to great power status around the world.[85]

From the perspective of British colonial authorities in Singapore, the political orientation of the majority Chinese population toward the war was not certain in 1915. The authorities were wary because of the historic turbulence within Chinese communities, and because of the recent political instabilities in China that increasingly brought Singapore Chinese into their orbit. In fact, as World War I was breaking out, colonial authorities across Southeast Asia were deeply concerned about the wider effects of a growing sense of Chinese national identity among *nanyang* communities. A fresh example – and one that caught the attention of neighboring colonies – was the context in which the Muslim, nationalist *Sarekat Islam* movement was founded in the Dutch East Indies. The movement was triggered in reaction to the "haughty and rude" behavior of some Chinese in the wake of the 1911 Chinese revolution, which caused native Javanese to form an organization to protect their own economic interests.[86] Quickly, however, it became a mass movement directed not only against the Chinese but also against Dutch colonial rule. By 1913, tensions between Javanese, Chinese, and Dutch were so high that the Dutch feared widespread massacres of Chinese by the Javanese.[87] Tensions like these were followed closely in neighboring colonies like Singapore, which were also home to large Chinese communities. Authorities were well aware of the lines of contact between Chinese communities across colonial borders and frequently worried that unrest among one portion of the colonial population had the potential to stir up unrest in other communities.[88]

When the mutiny broke out, then, colonial authorities did not fear that the Chinese would join forces with the mutineers, but that they would use the opportunity to express their own grievances through rioting and looting. These concerns, in fact, went well beyond Singapore: just days after the mutiny the French Rear-Admiral Huguet reported

---

[84] Xu, *China and the Great War*, 1.   [85] Ibid.

[86] Quoted in van Dijk, *The Netherlands Indies and the Great War*, 40; Michael Francis Laffan, *Islamic Nationhood and Colonial Indonesia: The Umma below the Winds* (London; New York: RoutledgeCurzon, 2003); Takashi Shiraishi, *An Age in Motion: Popular Radicalism in Java, 1912–1926* (Ithaca: Cornell University Press, 1990), 40.

[87] van Dijk, *The Netherlands Indies and the Great War*, 41.

[88] See, for example, the series of memos by the British ambassador at the Hague and the consul in Batavia on the early Sarekat Islam movement, in Islamic Movement in Netherlands East Indies, 1913, IOR/L/PS/11/58, 2771.

to the Governor General in Indochina that the British were bracing for possible unrest in Chinese communities on the Malayan peninsula in the wake of the mutiny. If that were to occur, he added, such unrest could even reach Indochina. For several days, administrators from Singapore to Indochina held their collective breath to see how Chinese communities would respond.[89]

As it turned out, fears that the Chinese in Singapore would add to the chaos were completely unfounded. Instead, Arthur Young wrote the Colonial Secretary that the Chinese population in the city was quiet "almost to the point of unconcern."[90] This was not entirely accurate, according to the Chinese newspaper *Kok Min Jit Poh*. Eight days after the mutiny the paper reported that some Chinese were so careless of the danger that they continued celebrating the New Year and lighting off fireworks, but that others "fell into a complete panic."[91] Nevertheless, the much-feared rioting never happened. In fact, some groups of Chinese Singaporeans – especially Christians and Straits-born Chinese – went out of their way to help round up, turn in, and arrest mutineers in and around the city. The court-martial proceedings of the accused mutineers indicate that Chinese farmers and shopkeepers were responsible for turning in a number of sepoys who had hidden themselves in the surrounding jungle after the Mutiny.[92] Other Chinese who did not wish to take an active role in suppressing the mutiny simply carried on with their business, apparently assuming this was not their fight. According to one Chinese man interviewed years later, he and his fellow Chinese Singaporeans watched the executions of the sepoys with "no reaction at all . . . [they] caused a lot of troubles here, you see."[93]

While it seems clear that most Chinese living in Singapore did not see common cause with the Indian sepoys who mutinied, it is equally clear that the Chinese government sought to play a role in instructing the

[89] Troubles de Singapour, CAOM FM indo/nf/1037. A month after the mutiny, the Governor General noted with relief that the event had not had a single effect in Indochina owing to the loyal attitude of the Chinese in Singapore.

[90] Young to Harcourt, February 25, 1915. Report on Singapore Disturbances, Part II, WO 32/9560, 82.

[91] Quoted in Kuwajima, 103.

[92] Examples include the cases of Sepoy Karrim Baksh, Lance Havildar Niaz Mohammed, and Sepoy Taj Mohammed. Court Martial Proceedings on Mutineers of the 5th Light Infantry, 1915. IOR/L/MIl/7/7191. On the other hand, a few of the sepoys were helped by Chinese men who gave them food, including Lance Naik Immamudin Khan.

[93] Sng Choon Yee, *Interview of Sng Choon Yee by Mr. Lim How Seng*, 1981. This oral testimony was part of the National Archives of Singapore project called "Pioneers of Singapore." Most recordings were done in the 1980s, which means that Sng Choon Yee, born in 1897, was eighty-four at the time of the interview. We should keep in mind the potential problems of such oral histories, even though this particular story reinforces contemporary sources.

Chinese in Singapore how to behave once the mutiny occurred. Having learned of the mutiny from the Chinese consul within hours after its start, the Chinese Foreign Office directed the consul to encourage the Chinese population in Singapore to remain calm, and to conduct business as usual.[94] On February 17, the daily Chinese paper *Kok Min Jit Poh* contained an appeal by the consul to the entire Chinese population, asking them "to conduct their business as usual and not to be misled by hearsay and create disorder."[95] The consul added that the situation was well in hand by the authorities.

These instructions were entirely consistent with the decades-long Chinese governmental strategy of taking responsibility for the Chinese in Singapore through the consul. Like all the other consuls in Singapore, the Chinese consul sought to use the authority of his office to encourage Chinese Singaporeans to act in accordance with official wishes. As such, the actions of the consul reflect continuing efforts by the Chinese government to follow modern standards of international diplomacy.

At the same time, it is possible that conditions caused by the Great War were also behind instructions to avoid disorder. The mutiny occurred just a little over a month after the Japanese presented Yuan Shikai's government with the Twenty-One Demands – which, as we know, represented a major threat to Chinese sovereignty. Yuan's government prevaricated after receiving the demands and leaked the document in hopes of provoking outrage among other powers with interests in China, including Britain. The Twenty-One Demands also convinced the regime that the best way to regain China's possessions from the Japanese – not to mention China's rightful status as a fully sovereign world power – was to enter the war on the side of the Allies.[96] This, they believed, would give them an equal seat at the bargaining table at the end of the war, and thus a chance to regain their territories. Although the Chinese government did not make it clear to the British that they were ready to join the Allies until November 6, 1915, the idea may already have been floated at the time of the mutiny. Given the need to keep the British in their good graces under those circumstances, it would have been doubly important to urge Chinese Singaporeans not to make trouble during the mutiny.[97] Faced with the Japanese aggression that had been made possible by wartime

---

[94] Kuwajima, *Mutiny in Singapore*, 94.   [95] Kuwajima, *Mutiny in Singapore*, 94.
[96] This is the main theme of Xu, *China and the Great War*.
[97] Westad, *Restless Empire*. As it happened, the Japanese were the main obstacles to the Chinese entering the war, and their objections kept the British from insisting on China's participation until August, 1917. By that time, the rest of the Allies had begun to see Japanese ambition in China not as a convenient replacement for German authority, but as a threat in itself.

conditions, Yuan Shikai's government needed all the help it could get – even from the power that had first encroached on Chinese sovereignty. In the end, then, even though the Chinese population of Singapore was probably not inclined to rise against the British during the mutiny in any case, the neutral Chinese state nevertheless had its own reasons to take an active role in directing its "nationals" about how to respond.

Role of the Neutrals: The Dutch East Indies

The events of the mutiny also forced the neutral Dutch East Indies to respond. When the eleven remaining German prisoners of war escaped Singapore, Arthur Young made an appeal (through the British consul in Batavia) to Governor General Idenburg, asking the Dutch navy to patrol their territorial waters in search of the men. A few weeks later, when it turned out that the escapees did in fact reach Dutch territory without being intercepted at sea, Young requested that the Dutch detain and intern any and all of the Germans for the duration of the war.[98]

These requests put the Dutch in an awkward position, for the government's main objective was to maintain Dutch neutrality during the war.[99] The situation was already tense, because British authorities in Singapore believed pan-Islamic activists had used the Dutch East Indies as a distribution point for anti-Allied Ghadar material prior to the mutiny. This was, in fact, correct. As we will see in Chapters 3 and 4, German, Indian, and Ottoman activists took advantage of the neutrality of the Dutch East Indies for most of the war, since it was an ideal location from which to launch conspiracies against Malaya, Burma, and India. This was a constant source of irritation and apprehension for the British in Malaya, whose difficult and sometimes bitter history with their colonial neighbors led them to believe the Dutch harbored pro-German sentiments.[100] Their belief, moreover, was only reinforced once the German escapees from Tanglin reached the Dutch East Indies without being apprehended by Dutch authorities.

Since the beginning of the war, the Dutch had been exercised by the fear that the British would find deliberate fault with Dutch efforts to abide by the laws of neutrality in the East Indies, thus providing an excuse to invade. This fear reached a peak in early 1915, and caused so much anxiety that on February 19 – during the crisis caused by the mutiny – the British ambassador at the Hague asked the Foreign Secretary to

---

[98] Report 19605, April 29, 1915, Straits Settlements Original Correspondence: Foreign, CO 273/430.
[99] van Dijk, *The Netherlands Indies and the Great War 1914–1918*, 202–204.
[100] van Dijk, *The Netherlands Indies and the Great War 1914–1918*, 202–204.

make a public statement denying British interest in "touching the Dutch colonies."[101] Even though the Secretary obliged with a statement affirming the rights of small countries, Governor-General Idenburg continued to believe that the Dutch East Indies would somehow be dragged into the war, if not by Britain then by its ally Japan, or else by German actions in Europe.[102]

When Arthur Young asked Idenburg for help in tracking down the escaped Germans, therefore, Idenburg could neither refuse nor fully comply if he wanted to maintain Dutch neutrality. Idenburg had already sent the Dutch fleet to the Riau Archipelago, just south of Singapore, in case it was needed to protect Dutch citizens endangered by the mutiny. Because of this, it was already in a good position to patrol for the eleven missing Germans. But Idenburg was anxious about what to do in the event any of the Germans were found, since turning them over to the British would have angered the Germans. In the end, Idenburg agreed with the suggestion of his naval commander, Vice Admiral F. Pinke, that if any Germans were found they would be picked up, questioned, and released after finding "no legal reasons" for detaining them further.[103] This way, the Dutch would fulfill the British request for help without risking angering the Germans.

As it turned out, neither Dutch nor British ships found the escaped Germans, all of whom made it to the island of Sumatra, in Dutch territory. A few of the men, including the commander of the *Emden*, went to the city of Padang, where the German consul provided a warm welcome. Several others went to the city of Medan, where they also remained at liberty. Within a matter of days the British consul in Batavia, J.W.D. Beckett, learned of the Germans' safe arrival in the East Indies and conveyed the news to Singapore. Young then directed Beckett to petition the Dutch to intern all of the former prisoners. Beckett had made it easy for the Dutch to comply by providing Idenburg with the names and whereabouts of each German escapee. But while interning the Germans would have made the British happy, it would have made the German government (and its representatives in the East Indies) quite angry, thus potentially risking Dutch neutrality. After a flurry of letters and telegrams, the Dutch successfully argued that Arthur Young did not have the legal right to insist on the internment of the escapees. As the Dutch pointed out, article thirteen of the Fifth Hague Convention of 1907 on the rights and duties of neutral powers stipulated "a neutral Power which

---

[101] Van Dijk, *The Netherlands Indies and the Great War 1914–1918*, 203.
[102] Van Dijk, *The Netherlands Indies and the Great War 1914–1918*, 205.
[103] Van Dijk, *The Netherlands Indies and the Great War 1914–1918*, 323.

receives escaped prisoners of war shall leave them at liberty." It seems clear that the argument went well beyond Southeast Asia, because at the end of April 1915 the British Foreign Office, which was communicating with the Dutch ambassador in London, directed Beckett not to press for the internment of the German escapees.[104] In the end, none of the Germans were recaptured by the British, and Lauterbach – the much sought-after commander of the *Emden* – made his way back to Germany and even wrote a book about his escapades.[105]

This was not the first time the Dutch found it necessary to respond to a situation created by the wartime alliances, and it was far from the last. In this case they managed to maintain their neutrality by doing the minimum necessary to appease British demands. It should be emphasized that the Dutch hesitation to help the British in no way indicated sympathy for the Indian sepoys, however. In fact, given long-term Dutch anxieties about the destructive effects of pan-Islamic ideas in the East Indies, and by the fact that their own Indies army was composed largely of Muslims, they were horrified by the idea of a rebellion that brought military rebellion together with Islamic ideas. Nevertheless, they had a neutrality to maintain, and in that respect they navigated the crisis of the mutiny successfully.

Muslims and Indians Within and Outside Singapore

Nearly a month after the mutiny, on March 6, 1915, the "leading Muslims" of Singapore took it upon themselves to respond to the mutiny by making their loyalties to the British, and thus the Allies, absolutely clear. The group was diverse, as it was composed of coreligionists from Egypt, the Hadramaut, India, and Malaya. No consul, of course, spoke for the Muslims, since they did not represent a national authority. In any case, India, Egypt, and Malaya were British colonial possessions, while the Ottoman consul had been expelled from Singapore after the Ottomans declared war. Lacking a formal spokesperson, they chose a leader among themselves. The situation was urgent, for the pan-Islamic aspect of the mutiny had brought deep suspicion on the Muslim community in Singapore. In addition, government efforts to identify fugitive mutineers resulted in what amounted to racial profiling, in which all Indians were suspect regardless of religion, and in which non-Malay Muslims could be mistaken for Indians. In light of these dangers, and to quell British

---

[104] Report 19605, April 29, 1915, Straits Settlements Original Correspondence: Foreign, CO 273/430.

[105] The book was published in Berlin in 1917, and was called *1000 £ Kopfpreis tot Oder Lebending*, or *1000 £ Reward, Dead or Alive*.

fears that unrest would spread from the Muslim and Indian communities in Singapore to other areas of the Empire, the "Muslims of Singapore" sought to ensure their own safety by taking a political stand meant to reverberate around the world.

In the days and weeks following the mutiny, British authorities took drastic steps in an effort to control the spread of the unrest among Indians in particular and Muslims in general. Arthur Young took the first step by declaring martial law on the evening of February 15. With this power he was able to supersede the process of civil law and to rule by proclamation.[106] The next day, on February 16, Young ordered that no newspapers from Singapore would be allowed to leave the island, and that all letters bound for anywhere but Britain were to be censored of all information regarding the event.[107] As we saw in Chapter 1, only a bland message about "riots" over internal regimental "jealousies" was distributed to Reuters. In this way, Young and other Singapore authorities hoped to limit the damage from news of the mutiny spreading to other colonial locations. In an effort to isolate the mutineers from civilians who might wish to help them, on February 19 Young also issued a proclamation stating that it was a criminal offense to "receive, harbor, relieve, comfort, or assist anyone who has committed the offence of mutiny," and that doing so would result in being apprehended and dealt with "the utmost rigour of the law."[108] Two days later, on February 21, Young issued another proclamation warning against the "offence of spreading reports calculated to create unnecessary alarm or despondency."[109] In this way, Young hoped to discourage people from spreading rumors about the mutiny, or even to talk about it with others.

Five days after the mutiny, with more than 150 mutineers still at large on the island, Young also initiated a registration program for all Indian men. Because Singapore authorities believed that many of the fugitives were pretending to be "milkmen or cow-keepers," on February 20 they proclaimed "all Indians of whatever race will report to the Police Station of their district for the purpose of obtaining passes to protect them from arrest."[110] Henceforward, all Indian men would be required to have passes that would "satisfy the authorities that they were not soldiers."[111]

---

[106] Proclamation of Martial Law, February 15, 1915, Report on Singapore Disturbances, Part II, WO 32/9560.

[107] Young to Harcourt, February 25, 1915. Report on Singapore Disturbances, Part II, WO 32/9560, 92.

[108] Proclamation, February 19, 1915, Report on Singapore Disturbances, Part II.

[109] Proclamation, February 21, 1915, Memorandums and Telegrams Relating to Disturbances at Singapore.

[110] Proclamation, February 20, 1915, Report on Singapore Disturbances, Part II.

[111] February 20, 1915, Memorandums and Telegrams Relating to Disturbances at Singapore.

If stopped without papers, an Indian man – or even a man who looked like an Indian – could be presumed guilty of participating in the mutiny. Finally, on February 23 the authorities began the succession of public executions by shooting two sepoys who had been convicted of mutiny. These public executions continued until April 18, when the last of forty-one sepoys – all Indian Muslims – were shot in the presence of silent crowds.

Beyond the obvious goal of trying to capture fugitive sepoys, these drastic measures by the Singapore government indicated an authority that was extremely worried about the potential for further unrest, particularly among Indians and other Muslims, in Singapore and beyond. Their methods utilized a combination of terror (via public execution), isolation (via punishment by association and censorship), and intimidation (via penalties for spreading discontent)– all designed to eliminate local unrest and to prevent it from spreading. The scope of these fears was evident in the government's reaction to the 25th and 26th Punjabi regiments – most of whom were Muslims or Sikhs – who passed through Singapore harbor on March 1. The regiments were on their way back to India from garrison duty in Hong Kong and had given no indication of disloyalty. When their officers offered to land the regiments to help restore order in Singapore, however, Young not only declined but only allowed the ship to stay in port for half an hour before being moved on.[112]

Singapore authorities also employed secret agents, in Singapore and on the Malayan Peninsula, to get a feel for the discontent among Indian and Muslim communities. On March 3, General Ridout reported to the War Office in London that he had placed "reliable" secret agents, "who know the F.M.S. [Federated Malay States] and Indian character well," in Kuala Lumpur to gauge the level of discontent among Indians in Malaya, particularly among the Sikh police. He was happy to report that the agents could not detect any unrest, and that the Sikh police "are quite all right." News from Ipoh, also on the Malay peninsula, was not as good, for Ridout had just received a report saying that "agitators have been at work for some time there." While the report did not anticipate further trouble since the Singapore mutiny had been put down, its author was certain that Muslims from Northern India in the area "are not to be trusted."[113]

Arthur Young also employed one of Ridout's Indian agents in Singapore to go to a meeting of the city's Muslims and to "mix among the

---

[112] GO Commanding the Troops to Secretary of War, March 3, 1915. Report on Singapore Disturbances, Part II, WO 32/9560, 100.

[113] GO Commanding the Troops to Secretary of War, March 3, 1915. Report on Singapore Disturbances, Part II, WO 32/9560, 99.

crowd . . . and ascertain their feeling." On March 11, he informed the Colonial Office that, based on the agent's observations, "there is little doubt that there is a certain amount of disaffection among the Indians and lower class of immigrant Arabs; sedition has been preached and five men are at present in custody for that reason." At the same time, even though the agent heard disloyal sentiments among the crowd, "he does not question the sincere loyalty of the leading Mohammedans in Singapore."[114]

In spite of such murmurs of discontent among some Indian and Muslim civilians, there was no general rising in these communities in the wake of the mutiny, and the unrest did not manifest itself in rebellions elsewhere. But the atmosphere of mistrust was oppressive, and Indians and Muslims likely perceived that their every move was now open to scrutiny, even if they had had nothing to do with the mutiny. It was well known that several prominent Singapore Muslims had been implicated in distributing pan-Islamic and Ghadar propaganda prior to the mutiny, and it was clear that Singapore authorities were looking for evidence of others.

It was in this context that the "leading Muslims" of Singapore, after securing permission by the government, organized a meeting at Victoria Memorial Hall on March 6 to "give expression to their loyalty to H.M. the King and Emperor."[115] The conveners were Egyptian Muslims from the prominent Alsagoff family, but the crowd of 3,000 attendees was mixed with Muslims of diverse origin. It was a well-choreographed event, designed to reassure the British that the disaffection that had caused the mutiny was not a general Muslim problem. The leaders chose bold (and, given the recent events of the mutiny, false) language for their telegram to the King-Emperor, proclaiming "the absolute loyalty of all Mahomedans in the Colony, a loyalty that has never changed, and never will change."[116] The telegram was sent on March 10 and was respectfully acknowledged by the King on March 11.[117]

Whatever the involvement of civilian Muslims in the lead-up to the mutiny of the 5th Light Infantry, the resulting climate of mistrust in the aftermath of its utter failure compelled prominent Muslims to take

---

[114] Young to Harcourt, March 11, 1915. Report on Singapore Disturbances, Part II, WO 32/9560, 18.

[115] "Loyal Moslems: Community Gives Proof of Allegiance," *Straits Times*, March 8, 1915, 8.

[116] "Loyal Moslems: Community Gives Proof of Allegiance," *Straits Times*, 8 March 1915, 8.

[117] Telegram exchange from Arthur Young to Secretary of State for the Colonies, 10 and 11 March 1915. Report on Singapore Disturbances, WO 32/9559, 54–56.

a stand on behalf of all their coreligionists. The exigencies of wartime, in which the Ottoman call for jihad seemed to have contributed to the mutiny in the first place, now made it necessary for these men to safeguard their position in Singapore society by publicly proclaiming their loyalty to the Central Powers' greatest foe.

Conclusion

For such a minor event in terms of the larger world war, the mutiny of the 5th Light Infantry nevertheless commanded a robust response from multiple actors from around the world. In spite of a history of strained relations, Britain's allies brought ships and men to defend Singapore and to search for fugitive sepoys. In spite of being neutral, both the Chinese and the Dutch East Indies government nevertheless found it difficult to remain aloof from the events – the Chinese state because of a desire to demonstrate its involvement, and the Dutch because the British demanded their involvement. Even communities with no formal spokespersons, like the "Muslims of Singapore," found it necessary to make a formal declaration about their orientation to the war in the wake of the mutiny. What all this demonstrates is that Singapore in 1915 was hardly an isolated outpost – the location itself and the people living and serving there were connected via multiple networks to the rest of Southeast Asia, the imperial systems of the Great Powers, and the global war then raging in Europe. Once the mutiny had begun, these networks first brought Singapore to the world via military, diplomatic, and consular communications. Unfortunately for the sepoys of the 5th, but fortunately for the British, these same networks then facilitated bringing the world to Singapore. And the world that came to the shores of Singapore in early 1915 was not just any world, but a world at war – a fact that, as we have seen, had devastating consequences for the short-lived rebellion.

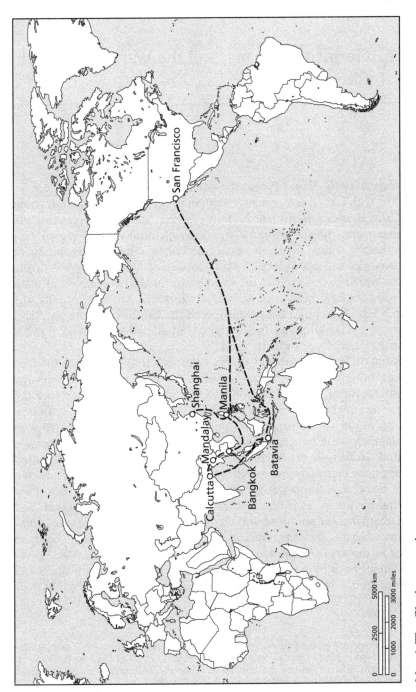

Map 3 The Ghadar networks.

3   Germans, Indians, and the War in the Dutch East Indies

In August 1916, David Petrie, the newly appointed Special Officer for dealing with Indian sedition and German intrigues in the Far East, wrote that the British government had ample and "conclusive proof of the existence of... hostile intrigues" by enemy agents all over the region. Not only that, he argued they were being aided by "a number of revolutionary Indians who are still at large." Most important, in his view, was "[t]he places which have served as the main bases for the prosecution of these conspiracies have been such neutral territories as America, Manila, the Dutch East Indies and Siam which, with the exception of the last, have afforded a safe asylum for the plotters. Certain places in China, notably Shanghai, have been similarly used."[1]

For all of the violence and drama surrounding the events of the Singapore mutiny in 1915, it was only one manifestation of the ways the war made itself felt in the region. When we zoom out to explore the rest of the region between 1914 and 1918, it is clear that the circumstances of the war influenced not only all of the colonies associated with a belligerent state but also those states and colonies that chose to remain neutral. In fact, as Petrie argued, much of the activity surrounding the attempts by Germany and its allies to disrupt colonial rule in the region took place on neutral territory, just outside Allied reach. From these neutral territories, individuals working on behalf of Germans and their anticolonial allies produced and distributed propaganda, arranged shipments of arms, incited unrest in enemy territory, and aided German ships in the area. At the same time, representatives of the Allied powers fought back by strengthening their networks of communication and information in order to foil those who would use neutral territory as their base.

---

[1] David Petrie to Sir John Jordan, Ambassador to China, August 16, 1916. Report 50898, Straits Settlements Original Correspondence: Foreign, 1916, CO 273/449. Petrie, about whom we will hear more below, eventually went on to become director of India's Department of Criminal Intelligence in 1924, and of MI5 in 1941.

This chapter and Chapters 4–6 demonstrate that neutral territories in Southeast and East Asia were critical to the struggle between Central and Allied powers in the region during the Great War. In this respect they explore mostly uncharted historiographical terrain. Although several important works have investigated schemes by the Central Powers to foment rebellion in Allied colonial territory, these have mostly focused on Central Asia, North America, or on the German–Ottoman relationship, either ignoring or glossing over East and Southeast Asia.[2] Some of the literature on the Ghadar party – notably Maia Ramnath's recent *Haj to Utopia* – devotes space to the "Batavia-Calcutta Scheme" discussed below, but the coverage is limited to a few pages.[3] Only Kees van Dijk explores such activity in depth, though his work focuses on the particular Dutch experience of the Great War in the East Indies rather than on Southeast Asia more generally.[4]

The neutral territories in Southeast Asia were not simply curious sideshows in the larger story of Central Power plans to foment rebellion in Allied colonies. Rather, they provided vital links in the global networks that sought to damage the Allies' ability to fight. The struggles between those who sought to use the neutral territories to further their ambitions against the Allies and those who sought to stop them meant that the war maintained a looming presence even in officially nonaligned areas.

This chapter and Chapter 4 focus on just one of the neutral territories vital to anti-Allied schemes by the Central Powers and their partners: the Dutch East Indies. The East Indies deserves extended attention because of the sheer amount of war-related activity that occurred in its territories, both by enemies and supporters of the Allies – the latter in this case represented mainly by Britain. The reasons for this flurry of activity were several. For one thing, the East Indies was geographically close to British territories in the Malayan peninsula and the island of Singapore, making it a convenient base from which to launch subversive attacks of many varieties. In addition, the East Indies was home to a large German population that grew even larger once British and French territories in the region expelled many of their German residents after the start of

[2] Sean McMeekin, *The Berlin-Baghdad Express: The Ottoman Empire and Germany's Bid for World Power* (Cambridge, MA: the Belknap Press of Harvard University Press, 2010); Peter Hopkirk, *Like Hidden Fire: The Plot to Bring Down the British Empire* (New York: Kodansha, 1997), on Central Asia; Tilman Lüdke, *Jihad Made in Germany: Ottoman and German Propaganda and Intelligence Operations in the First World War* (Münster; London: Lit; Global [distributor], 2005).
[3] Ramnath, *Haj to Utopia*.
[4] van Dijk, *The Netherlands Indies and the Great War 1914–1918*.

hostilities. Some of these Germans were wealthy, well-connected, patriotic, and openly hostile to the Allies. Such individuals, in conjunction with the German consulate, took advantage of Dutch neutrality to coordinate and finance covert operations designed to undermine British colonial rule and economic interests in Southeast Asia and beyond. Finally, the East Indies provided a strategic way station for various groups who hoped to undermine Allied rule around the world. These included, in particular, German-financed Indian revolutionaries traveling between the United States and India who, once in the East Indies, sought access to weapons, money, and anticolonial propaganda before proceeding to their intended destination on the subcontinent. They also included Ottoman–German–Indian efforts to use the Indies as a base for producing and distributing pan-Islamic, anti-British propaganda, which they sought to spread among Muslims in British Malaya and India.

Yet the Dutch East Indies was not simply a passive background against which these wartime struggles took place. On the contrary, the Dutch government and civilian populations in the East Indies were deeply engaged in responding to them, reacting against them, and sometimes in collaborating with them. For Dutch authorities, neutrality during the war did not reflect an ideological commitment to pacifism or isolationism: it was a deliberate strategy of survival. The government of the East Indies was well aware it did not possess the means to prevent military occupation by much more powerful belligerent forces on both sides. As such, its representatives believed their best hope for retaining the East Indies – by far the largest and most profitable Dutch colony – was to scrupulously maintain Dutch neutrality to the letter of the (international) law.[5] Because of this, Dutch authorities were forced to spend a vast amount of time and energy responding to British and German complaints about breaches of neutrality in Dutch territory, and in demonstrating to both sides their adherence to strict neutrality.

Dutch colonial subjects also engaged with the wartime machinations of the Central and Allied powers. The region's long engagement with Ottomans and the pro-Muslim policy of Germany meant that many of the majority-Muslim Dutch colonial subjects favored the Central Powers. And some of these subjects easily applied the anticolonial, pan-Islamic propaganda of Indian and Ottoman activists intended for Allied territory to themselves. Others saw in the growing power of the Japanese – now fighting as equals on the side of the Allies – an inspiration for anticolonial activism. Indeed, Dutch authorities repeatedly and consistently

---

[5] The only other Dutch territories in 1914 were in the Americas, including Surinam and six islands in the Antilles. All were quite small compared with the East Indies.

expressed fear about both pan-Islamic and Japanese influences on anti-colonial activists for most of the war.[6]

This chapter begins by demonstrating the war's massive impact on the Dutch East Indies in spite of its neutrality, not only in terms of politics but also in terms of economics and communications. Its focus, however, is on the ways Germans – both civilian and military – used Dutch territory to further German war aims both on their own and in collaboration with anticolonial activists, and on how Dutch authorities and, to a lesser extent, colonial subjects responded to such schemes. These schemes included the use of German merchant ships moored in Dutch East Indies ports for providing supplies and information to the German warship *Emden* in the early months of the war. They also included German-Ottoman plans to spread propaganda to British Muslim populations in Malaya and India. Even more importantly, they included German-Indian plans to use the East Indies as an entrepôt between North America and India. The effect of these plans, though generally unsuccessful, had wide-ranging repercussions in the East Indies, British Malaya, North America, India, and Europe. Chapter 4 traces these repercussions and their connections to actors in the East Indies by following the chain of evidence revealed by the detention of an American ship in Dutch waters in 1915 – the *S.S. Maverick*. Taken together, Chapters 3 and 4 demonstrate the central role of the East Indies in wartime schemes that sought to undermine Allied colonial rule in Southeast Asia. Viewed in this way, the Singapore mutiny of February 1915 needs to be understood as a local expression of a much larger phenomenon.

The War in the East Indies

Unfortunately for the East Indies, neutrality in the war did not constitute an exemption to measures the belligerent powers thought necessary to protect their interests, including restrictions on trade, communication, and travel. Neutral status could also change rapidly to belligerent if neutral powers were not vigilant about abiding by international conventions. Moreover, neutral status was no guarantee that civilian populations in neutral territories would remain aloof from the larger issues brought about by the war. The Dutch East Indies faced all of these inconveniences and uncertainties associated with neutrality. As a result, and even though the Dutch did their best to stay out of the war, it nevertheless came in multiple ways to the East Indies.

---

[6] Shiraishi, *An Age in Motion: Popular Radicalism in Java, 1912–1926*, 92.

One of the Allied strategies in the war was to form an economic blockade around Germany and Austria. Both British and French ships operated to ensure that neither power would be supplied with food, clothing,
and other trade items from the North Sea.[7] These restrictions applied to
neutral ports through which restricted items might be moved to enemy
territory, including those in the Netherlands. Neutral Dutch ships were
repeatedly stopped and searched to ascertain whether they were carrying
contraband cargo, and were often forced to call at British or French ports
instead of their intended destination. Cargos travelling on neutral ships
were subject to seizure or, if they were not seized, to long and expensive
delays.[8] And controls on shipping were not limited to European ports
and waters: since Allied ships controlled the world's oceans, they also
maintained a tight control over Dutch shipping to and from the East
Indies. The Allies restricted export items such as copra, rubber, and
sugar, resulting in an immediate and drastic drop in the trade of major
commodities from the East Indies beginning in August 1914.[9] One of
the duties of the British consul general in Batavia, in fact, was to monitor
Dutch trade and to help determine which trade goods should be banned.
By 1915, many items had been added to the list of contraband goods,
including lead, hides, jute, and cotton. To ensure these bans, Kees van
Dijk argues that nearly all neutral ships leaving or entering from Dutch
East Indies ports were stopped by British, Australian, or Japanese ships
in search of contraband.[10]

These trade restrictions, not surprisingly, were deeply damaging for
the Dutch East Indies economy during the war. Falling revenues, bans
on exports, shortages on imports, and higher unemployment, in turn,
led to conditions of greater social instability, dissatisfaction with colonial

---

[7] For a treatment of blockades in World War I, see Strachan, *The First World War*,
chapter 7.

[8] For a full account of the effects of neutrality on the Netherlands, see Maartje Abbenhuis,
Art of Staying Neutral: The Netherlands in the First World War, 1914–1918 (Amsterdam:
Amsterdam University Press, 2006).

[9] van Dijk, *The Netherlands Indies and the Great War 1914–1918*, 137. van Dijk demonstrates that between July and August 1914 trade in key commodities plummeted. For
example, trade in copra dropped from 7,62,000 kilograms in July 1914 to 1,727,000 kg
in August, while sugar fell from 233,33,000 kg to 126,541,000 kg in the same period.
Abbenhuis argues that the Germans believed Dutch neutrality was actually a benefit to
the German ability to survive the blockade, since some of the raw materials from the
East Indies managed to reach Europe in spite of the blockade. Abbenhuis, *Art of Staying
Neutral*, 29. Several of the essays in H. Brugmans' compilation explore the economic
consequences of the war for the Dutch East Indies. See H. Brugmans, ed., *Nederland
in den Oorlogstijd: de Geschiedenis van Nederland en van Nederlandsch-Indië Tijdens den
Oorlog van 1914 tot 1919, Voor Zoover Zij met dien Oorlog Verband Houdt* (Amsterdam:
Elsevier, 1920).

[10] van Dijk, *The Netherlands Indies and the Great War 1914–1918*, 357, 356, 353.

rule, and unrest among Dutch colonial subjects – an issue about which the East Indies government was deeply concerned.[11] Indeed, given the meteoric growth of the nationalist *Sarekat Islam* party since its founding in 1912 – itself established in response to economic competition by the Chinese – Dutch authorities worried that a wartime downturn would add fuel to the nationalist fire.[12]

It was not only trade that was affected by Allied interventions: travel and communications also suffered. In addition to searching for contraband trade items, Allied warships also stopped neutral ships in search of enemy passengers and mail. In the East Indies, they were particularly concerned with Germans passing themselves off as Dutch, and with communications between Germans in the Indies and Germany. If found, letters and packages to or from Germany on neutral ships were seized, resulting – according to the German consul in Batavia – in the loss of about 90% of mail in the early months of the war. Dutch mail, if not seized, was frequently subject to significant delays if ships were directed to make calls at Allied ports before proceeding. As an extreme example, no mail from the East Indies reached the Netherlands in the month of August 1914, including official mail directed to the Colonial Ministry.[13]

Telegraph lines were also vulnerable. After having been dependent on British telegraph lines for years, in 1905 the Dutch finally gained an independent line via a German cable company. Yet when the war started that line was subject to repeated attack by Allied ships, making telegraphic service sporadic at best. In the absence of the German line, the Dutch could revert to using British lines, but British wartime regulations required all telegrams to be unenciphered and in English or French in order to pass through the censor.[14] This made private government business between the Indies and the Netherlands difficult at best, and

---

[11] Takashi Shiraishi, *An Age in Motion*, 92–93.

[12] Ruth McVey argues that this is precisely what happened, in *The Rise of Indonesian Communism*, 1st Equinox ed. (Jakarta: Equinox Pub, 2006), 20. For more on the development of Sarekat Islam, see Deliar Noer, *The Modernist Muslim Movement in Indonesia, 1900–1942* (Kuala Lumpur; New York: Oxford University Press, 1973); Chiara Formichi, *Islam and the Making of the Nation: Kartosuwiryo and Political Islam in Twentieth-Century Indonesia* (Leiden: KITLV Press, 2012); and Shiraishi, *An Age in Motion: Popular Radicalism in Java, 1912–1926*. The authorities were worried about more than just an economic downturn in fueling nationalism. Hans van Miert argues that Indonesian nationalists were quick to see the hypocrisy between the massive destruction of the war and the western colonial civilizing mission. *Een Keol Hoofd en Een Warm Hart: Nationalisme, Javanisme, en Jeugdbeweging in Nederlands-Indië* (Amsterdam: De Bataafsche Leeuw, 1995), 47.

[13] van Dijk, *The Netherlands Indies and the Great War 1914–1918*, 138.

[14] van Dijk, *The Netherlands Indies and the Great War 1914–1918*, 138.

was a source of continual irritation to the Dutch government in both places.

As damaging, difficult, and frustrating as these disruptions in trade and communications were, they formed only a portion of Dutch anxieties about the war. The biggest worry by far was that the Netherlands would be dragged into the war on one side or the other. From the Dutch perspective, this was a lose-lose scenario. If, for example, the Netherlands were forced to join the Allies, the metropole itself would be vulnerable to occupation by the Germans.[15] In the East Indies, Germany might utilize the large German population there to engineer an attack on the islands, while the Ottoman Empire might wage a full-scale pan-Islamic campaign for revolution among the Indies' colonial subjects. If, however, the Netherlands had to join the Central Powers, not only would Dutch ports on the North Sea be open to attack, but the East Indies would be doubly threatened by both British and Japanese invasion.[16]

The first scenario, of fighting against the Central Powers, was frightening not only because of its potential for occupation but also for raising the specter of Dutch colonial subjects in revolt. When hostilities broke out, Dutch colonial subjects in the Indies – of whom the majority were Muslim – tended to side with the Germans because of their alleged pro-Muslim policies and support for pan-Islamic identities. This tendency grew even stronger once the Ottoman Empire entered the war.[17] Malay-language newspapers in Java and Sumatra cheered Allied defeats, offered prayers for Ottoman success, and proclaimed the Ottoman sultan as the caliph of Islam.[18] In addition, the mobile, international, and highly influential Arab communities of the Dutch East Indies were also generally pro-Ottoman and pro-German, and were not kindly disposed either to Dutch or British colonial rule.[19] In the event of hostilities with the Central Powers, Dutch authorities feared it would be a small step for Indonesian and Arab Muslims to focus the anticolonial sentiments of pan-Islam directly on the Dutch.

As worrisome as pan-Islamic ideology might be in the event of war with the Central Powers, the possibility of fighting against the Allies

[15] Maartje Abbenhuis, *Art of Staying Neutral*, 27.

[16] In a report about the various military changes made in the East Indies since the outbreak of war, the introduction rehearses the uncertainty about whether or not (and by whom) either the "Moederland" would be dragged into the war, and whether or not the Indies would be attacked. Verslag Omtrent de Belangrijke Militaire Maatregelen Sinds 31 Juli, P, January 8, 1915. Ministerie van Kolonien: Geheim Archief, 2.10.36.51, box 173, Nationaal Archief.

[17] van Dijk, *The Netherlands Indies and the Great War 1914–1918*, 310.

[18] van Dijk, *The Netherlands Indies and the Great War 1914–1918*, 311.

[19] van Dijk, *The Netherlands Indies and the Great War 1914–1918*, 313.

was even more alarming. Dutch relations with the British in Southeast Asia were historically tense. Both powers had competed for territory and influence as they consolidated their colonial states in the region over the course of the nineteenth century.[20] The Dutch feared and disparaged British naval superiority, which they believed made the British arrogant, domineering, and expansionist. At the turn of the twentieth century, the South African War inflamed anti-British sentiment among the Dutch in the East Indies to new heights, because the war seemed to be yet another example of international British heavy-handedness – in this case against a population descended from the Dutch.[21] When the Great War broke out, then, Dutch attitudes toward the British were far from friendly, and were not improved by the hardships imposed by Allied restrictions on trade and communications. From the Dutch point of view, the British were simply waiting for an opportunity to find fault with Dutch actions in order to take the Indies for themselves.[22]

Yet for all the Dutch feared British aggression once the war broke out, nothing outpaced their anxieties about the threat posed by the Japanese. At the end of the nineteenth century, Japanese modernization and the creation of a strong, well-equipped navy caused Dutch authorities to re-evaluate their perceptions of Japanese power. This reevaluation was hastened by British recognition of the Japanese as a great power in the Anglo-Japanese alliance of 1902.[23] Then, during the Russo-Japanese War (1904–1905), the Japanese made it quite clear to Dutch authorities that it would regard aid to Russian warships in Indies ports as a breach of neutrality that could justify retaliation. From that point forward, Dutch authorities grew increasingly preoccupied with the idea that the Japanese were searching for an opportunity to usurp Dutch control in the Indies.[24]

[20] Eric Tagliacozzo, "The Indies and the World: State Building, Promise, and Decay at a Transnational Moment, 1910," *Bijdragen Tot de Taal-, Land-, En Volkenkunde* 166 (2010), 273.

[21] Maarten Kuitenbrouwer, *The Netherlands and the Rise of Modern Imperialism: Colonies and Foreign Policy, 1870–1902* (New York and Oxford: Berg Press, 1991), 305. A few Dutch subjects, like the radical and nationalist Douwes Dekker, were so incensed by British actions in South Africa that they went to fight for the Afrikaners. See Paul W. Van der Veur, *The Lion and the Gadfly: Dutch Colonialism and the Spirit of E.F.E. Douwes Dekker*, Verhandelingen van Het Koninklijk Instituut Voor Taal-, Land- En Volkenkunde 228 (Leiden: KITLV Press, 2006).

[22] van Dijk, *The Netherlands Indies and the Great War 1914–1918*, 203.

[23] For the international effects of the Anglo-Japanese alliance, see Phillips Payson O'Brien, *The Anglo-Japanese Alliance, 1902–1922* (London; New York: RoutledgeCurzon, 2004).

[24] A.C. Tjepkema, "Strategic Dilemmas of a Small Power With a Colonial Empire: The Netherlands East Indies, 1936–1941," in Herman Amersfoort and Wim Klinkert, eds., *History of Warfare, Volume 65: Small Powers in an Age of Total War, 1900–1940* (Leiden: Brill Press, 2011), 323.

Part of the reason this was so alarming to the Dutch was that a variety of anticolonial activists in the Indies had begun to look to the Japanese as potential liberators from Dutch colonial rule. Particularly after Japan's victory in the Russo-Japanese War, some Muslim elites directly petitioned the Japanese government to interfere in the Indies on their behalf.[25] Added to these "pull" factors was an apprehension of explicit Japanese designs for further colonial expansion, given the state's recent annexation of Formosa and Korea. The Dutch ambassador in Japan kept a close watch on the Japanese press to gauge public support for such an expansionary program, while colonial authorities in the Indies closely monitored the activities of the Japanese consul, land purchases made by Japanese companies or individuals, and the numbers of Japanese people living in or emigrating to the East Indies.[26] Of paramount concern was the possibility of espionage by Japanese individuals, who were believed to be investigating Dutch military and commercial strength on behalf of the Japanese government.[27] Dutch suspicions of the Japanese were in fact so strong that authorities sometimes caused diplomatic incidents by their tendency to treat Japanese people as hostile enemies.[28] When war broke out, the Dutch lived in constant apprehension that the Japanese would take any opportunity to find fault with Dutch neutrality in order to justify occupying the Indies for themselves.[29] This apprehension was not lost

[25] For example, in 1908 the Sultan of Aceh had his minister petition the Japanese government to rescue his people from the Dutch, because he understood that the Japanese were going to take over the East Indies in any case. Panislamistiche Woelingen, 1904–1915, Ministerie van Buitenlandse Zaken, 2.05.03, Box 452, Nationaal Archief. Barbara Andaya also documents a similar phenomenon by the sultans in the Riau Islands in "From Rūm to Tokyo: The Search for Anticolonial Allies by the Rulers of Riau, 1899–1914," *Indonesia*, no. 24 (October 1, 1977), 148–152.

[26] For the monitoring of the Japanese press and economic activity, see for example the diplomatic papers between 1910 and 1918 in Ministerie van Buitenlandse Zaken: Gezantschap te Japan (Tokio), 1910–1930s, 2.05.115, box 173, Nationaal Archief; also Report L11, Ministerie van Koloniën: Geheim Archief, 1915, 2.10.36.51, box 177.

[27] A report about the political and economic expansion of the Japanese in the Indies began, in a section on espionage, by saying "It is often said that every Japanese is a spy, and that it is an honor to spy for the fatherland." It went on to say that although this was an exaggeration, there was nevertheless some truth in the claim. De Economische en Politieke Expansie van Japan naar Nederlandsche-Indie, Report S1, January 22, 1915. Ministerie van Koloniën: Geheim Archief, 2.10.36.51, box 174, Nationaal Archief.

[28] For example, an incident occurred at Landak in 1915 in which two Japanese merchants were arrested as spies and roughed up by the Dutch. This caused the Japanese consul to make a full investigation of the incident, with diplomatic repercussions on both sides. Report E13, Ministerie van Koloniën: Geheim Archief, 2.10.36.51, box 179, Nationaal Archief.

[29] This point is well made by Magda van Gestel, "Japanse Spionage in Nederlands-Indië: de Oprichting van de Politieke Inlichtingen Dienst (PID) in 1916," and José Mulders, "De Ambitie van Japan: Nederlands-Indië en Japan Tijdens de Eerste Wereldoorlog,

on colonial subjects: in 1916 a Chinese Malay newspaper scoffed that no people were as fearful as the Dutch, and that if a Japanese warship were to turn up in the port of Tanjung Priok "the government would certainly be afflicted by diarrhoea."[30]

All of this is to point out the multiple ways that the Great War was not only relevant to the Dutch East Indies but was an ever-present reality in spite of the fact that it remained neutral for the duration of the conflict. The economy suffered, communications suffered, and individuals no longer enjoyed freedom of movement. Just as important, throughout the conflict the Dutch clung to their neutral status as a matter of survival, for authorities believed that joining either side would mean the end of the Dutch colonial state in the Indies. As such, maintaining their neutral status was of primary importance. Given that they were so worried about the threat posed by the British and the Japanese, it is somewhat ironic that the greatest threat to Dutch neutrality in the East Indies turned out to come from the combined actions of German residents in the Indies and revolutionary Indians.

The Problem of the *Emden* and the Dutch East Indies

Almost as soon as the war began, British authorities became convinced that activities originating from Dutch territory were aiding the German war effort. Dutch authorities were equally convinced (at least until it was too late) that British complaints were unreasonable. They believed they had done all they could to protect Dutch neutrality by ensuring that no belligerent power could use the East Indies as a base for war-related activities. At immediate issue were the activities of the German cruiser *Emden* between September and November 1914 – the same ship whose captured crew later helped foment the Singapore mutiny in 1915.[31] But the pattern of diplomatic relations between the British and the Dutch that developed around the *Emden* was emblematic for how they would remain for the duration of the war. On one side, the British were deeply frustrated by what they saw as Dutch reluctance to prevent anti-Allied intrigues on Dutch territory, while on the other the Dutch found themselves in an

een Bronnenonderzoek," both in Elspeth Locher-Scholten *Beelden van Japan in Het Vooroorlogse Nederlands Indië* (Leiden: Werkgroep Europese Expansie, 1987).

[30] van Dijk, *The Netherlands Indies and the Great War 1914–1918*, 208.

[31] The *Emden* has been the subject of popular history for some time, including Edwin P. Hoyt, *The Last Cruise of the Emden: The Amazing True World War I Story of a German Light Cruiser and Her Courageous Crew* (Guilford, CT: Lyons Press, 2001); Dan Van Der Vat, *Gentlemen of War: The Amazing Story of Commander Karl von Muller and the SMS Emden* (New York: Book Sales, 1984).

expensive and time-consuming cycle of investigation, the outcome of which at any moment could threaten their neutral status.

The activities of the *Emden* were important to the Allies because for over two months it almost single-handedly disrupted Allied trade and travel in the South China Sea and the Indian Ocean. During this time, the *Emden* either sank or took possession of twenty-three ships over a vast swath of ocean. When the war broke out its captain – Karl von Muller – had taken his ship out of port at Tsingtao, the German concession in China, with the intention of doing as much damage as possible to Allied shipping in the region. In this he was quite successful. The *Emden's* activities caused panic from Indochina to India, shutting down shipping between Singapore and India and disrupting communications between Allied territories and Europe.[32] Among its more daring exploits was a raid on the port of Madras, India on September 22, 1914, when it fired on the shore and exploded the tanks of the Burma Oil Company.[33] Another occurred, as we saw in Chapter 2, in Penang Harbor on the coast of Malaya, when the *Emden* sank both the Russian *Zhemchug* and the French *Mousquet* on October 2. The dangers and disruptions caused by the *Emden* made it a target of primary importance for all Allied warships plying the waters of the region.

In order to carry out its mission, the *Emden* needed supplies of coal, food, and information about the location of Allied ships.[34] This is where the Dutch East Indies came in. In early September 1914, British authorities received intelligence that the Dutch were supplying the *Emden* with just such necessities. The news immediately inflamed anti-Dutch sentiment in Allied territories from Singapore to Saigon, as the press in both places printed rumors that Dutch sympathies lay with the Germans.[35]

---

[32] The disruptions caused by the *Emden* were not limited to the British. French sources in Indochina also noted problems communicating with France in a report included in Situation Politique, Administrative, Economique, Financière et Militaire de l'Indochine Depuis Août 1916, Indo/nf/29, CAOM. A report from January 21, 1915, "Sur les Mesures Intervenues en Indochine en Raison de l'Etat de Guerre" also noted that individuals were too afraid to leave Indochina during September and October 1914. Internements et Expulsions, 1914–1918, Indo/nf/36, CAOM.

[33] "Madras Bombarded: Raid of the German Cruiser Emden," *Straits Times* October 5, 1914, 12. Heike Liebau reports that stories about the *Emden* inspired fear and panic even in the remote Indian region of Chota Nagpur. See Heike Liebau, "Kaiser kī jay (Long Live the Kaiser): Perceptions of World War I and the Socio-Religious Movement among the Oraons in Chota Nagpur 1914–1916," in Heike Liebau, ed., *The World in World Wars Experiences, Perceptions and Perspectives from Africa and Asia* (Leiden, the Netherlands; Boston: Brill, 2010), 265.

[34] The *Emden* tried to mitigate its need for continued supplies of coal by capturing three colliers during the three months of its activity in the region. World War I Naval Combat, SMS Emden, http://www.worldwar1.co.uk/emden.html.

[35] In Saigon, one company fired its Dutch employees in order to avoid anti-Dutch riots. See van Dijk, *The Netherlands Indies and the Great War*, 184. An example of Dutch

Given Dutch intentions of remaining neutral, this was deeply alarming. In the face of such rumors, Dutch authorities began a diplomatic campaign to ensure all belligerent parties that they were committed to maintaining and enforcing strict neutrality.[36]

In hindsight, it seems clear that Dutch authorities were not intentionally aiding the German war effort. When the war began they took immediate steps to ensure they were in compliance with the rules of international law with respect to neutrality in the Indies. By mid-August the Dutch naval commander, Vice Admiral F. Pinke, had deployed the Dutch squadron to patrol the far-flung waters of the Indies with the express goal of making sure foreign warships did not violate Dutch neutrality.[37] To inhibit the use of merchant ships for coaling warships, Governor General Idenburg also decreed that foreign ships could not carry more coal than needed to move to the next port.[38] Additionally, Idenburg sought to prevent merchant ships from communicating with belligerent warships from Dutch ports by wireless radio. To accomplish this, he ordered that all radio antennae on merchant ships be dismantled and sealed for the duration of the war.[39] To illustrate their seriousness about these regulations, Dutch ships intercepted and detained several ships suspected of carrying cargoes destined for German warships during the month of September 1914.[40]

By that time, efforts by East Indies authorities to demonstrate their commitment to Dutch neutrality had convinced British civil and military authorities that the Dutch were not deliberately aiding the German war effort. Nevertheless, the British were not satisfied, because they were certain that Dutch efforts to prevent German merchant ships from using the East Indies as a base for aiding the *Emden* were inadequate. Beginning in mid-September, T.F. Carlisle, the interim British consul in Batavia, and Alan Johnstone, the British ambassador at the Hague, lodged a series of complaints alleging that German ships docked in East Indies harbors were communicating vital information to the *Emden* via wireless radio. From Singapore, Admiral Jerram repeatedly asked Carlisle to bring these intercepted messages to the attention of the Dutch authorities, and to let

---

residents defending themselves appeared in the *Straits Times* on September 3, 1914, 10. A letter to the editor by "Dutchman" sought to clear up "misapprehension as to the attitude of the Dutch in connection with the present war."

[36] van Dijk, *The Netherlands Indies and the Great War*, 185.

[37] Pinke's diary of this period was also published in 1986 by G. Teitler. See Teitler, *Dagboekaantekeningen van Vice-Admiral F. Pinke, Commandant Zeemacht in Nederlandse-Indië, 1914–1916* ('S-Gravenhage: Nijhoff, 1986).

[38] van Dijk, *The Netherlands Indies and the Great War*, 180, 181, 190.

[39] Telegram from Idenburg, November 30, 1914, Report T39, Ministerie van Kolonien: Geheim Archief, 1914, 2.10.36.51, box 172, Nationaal Archief.

[40] van Dijk, *The Netherlands Indies and the Great War 1914–1918*, 187–188.

them know they believed they were coming from German merchant ships anchored in East Indies ports.[41] Meanwhile Alan Johnstone did the same at the Hague on behalf of Sir Edward Grey, the British Foreign Secretary.

From the British perspective, there was little doubt about the origin of the wireless transmissions. They were intercepted by British warships in the vicinity, which were often able to identify both a sending station and a call sign. For example, on October 13 Alan Johnstone complained that British ships intercepted a signal "sent by a Telefunken station to the German cruiser "Emden" using her confidential call sign, and . . . one of the operators intercepting the message has come to the conclusion that the station sending it was Sitlyebondo in Java."[42] But until early November, both Idenburg and Pinke refused to believe that German merchantmen in East Indies ports could be communicating with the *Emden*. Both were certain that the measures they had taken to seal radio stations and take down antennae made it impossible that such communications could be taking place. When presented with the contents of enciphered messages intercepted by the British and the Australians in the region, Pinke offered various explanations, including that the enciphered messages were likely between Dutch warships, or that the *Emden* was too far away from the Indies to be within radio contact with any ship anchored in the East Indies.[43]

Given the delicate situation with regard to Dutch neutrality, however, Pinke and Idenburg were obligated to demonstrate a good faith effort to investigate each complaint. For example, on October 26 Pinke acknowledged that the British consul reported on behalf of Admiral Jerram that "a [German] ship believed to be [the] *Roon* sent two wireless messages to German man of war night of October 19 and repeated them night of October 20."[44] Alan Johnstone also complained about the same incident to the Dutch government at the Hague, threatening that it indicated a "failure to fulfill duties of neutrality" by the Indies government. This was enough to spur prompt action by the Minister of the Colonies, who told Idenburg that no effort must be spared in the conduct of a prompt and thorough investigation.[45] Pinke accordingly launched the investigation but remained convinced that the *Roon* could not have sent the messages. Nevertheless, as a sop to the British, he announced that he would

---

[41] Much of this correspondence can be found in Ministerie van Kolonien: Geheim Archief, 1914, 2.10.36.51, box 170 and 172, Nationaal Archief.

[42] Telefunken was a German company, so the insinuation here may have been deliberate. Report Y21, October 15, Ministerie van Kolonien: Geheim Archief, 1914, 2.10.36.51, box 170.

[43] Pinke to Idenburg, Ibid.   [44] Pinke to Idenburg, Ibid.

[45] van Dijk, *The Netherlands Indies and the Great War*, 193.

now ensure nightly rounds to keep watch on the ship. Additionally, he launched an investigation about whether or not such a signal could have been sent from other ships at the port of Cilacap. This, he thought, would facilitate later investigations in the likely event of still more British complaints.[46]

During this time, Idenburg and Pinke grew increasingly irritated by repeated British complaints about the use of wireless radio signals from the Dutch East Indies. From their point of view, they had taken the necessary precautions and were now caught in a never-ending cycle of investigating claims that seemed to have little validity. On October 23 Pinke expressed his growing exasperation over "how lightly the British naval authorities draw their conclusions about the misuse of wireless telegraphy," adding that there was probably little reason to attach too much value to most complaints.[47] Adding to their frustrations were frequent reports by Dutch naval and merchant ships that British warships – in their vigilant efforts to keep an eye on German merchantmen – were regularly breaching Dutch neutrality by entering the territorial waters of the East Indies. However, because authorities learned of these reports only after the fact, there was little that could be done besides lodge formal complaints of their own.

But at the end of October, new discoveries put the preceding months of British complaints in a fresh light. During the nights of the 27th and 28th, the Dutch wireless radio station at the port of Sabang (in Northern Sumatra) intercepted several messages believed to be coming from the *Emden* and directed to a German ship in the harbor.[48] When local Dutch officials investigated, they "discovered on board the German steamer *Preussen* along the ropeladder a skillfully constructed [,] from the outside [,] invisible antenne [sic] and a clandestine receiver station in the cabin of a subaltern officer."[49] Idenburg and Pinke were certain that the *Preussen* had not arrived with an antenna, which meant it had been constructed since its arrival in Sabang on August 3. Faced with such a clear violation of Dutch neutrality, Dutch authorities confiscated the ship, and the captain and an officer were sentenced to a year in prison.[50] By October 29 Pinke admitted that the case of the *Preussen* clearly pointed

---

[46] Pinke to Idenburg, October 20, U24, Ministerie van Kolonien: Geheim Archief, 1914, 2.10.36.51, box 172.

[47] Pinke to R. de Kat, Ibid.

[48] Idenburg to the Hague, November 30, U24, Ministerie van Kolonien: Geheim Archief, 1914, 2.10.36.51, box 172. The messages were immediately suspected to be coming from the *Emden* because the sender was using fictitious call names.

[49] Idenburg to the Hague, Ibid.

[50] van Dijk, *The Netherlands Indies and the Great War*, 185–186.

to the fact that Germans were misusing the protections they enjoyed in East Indies ports.[51]

Even more damning were Dutch discoveries in the port of Cilacap, on the southern coast of Java. After repeated British complaints about wireless messages being sent by the *Roon* from that location, Pinke sent a wireless expert to investigate in early November. It revealed that the sealing of wireless radios in port had been done clumsily and by amateurs, making it easy for anyone with knowledge of wireless technology to send and receive messages. What this meant, of course, was that it was likely the *Roon* had been sending messages to the *Emden* all along, and also that other German ships in East Indies ports had been doing the same thing. So incriminating was the evidence that Idenburg was afraid it would be enough for the British to declare war, were they to discover the depth of Dutch ineptitude in inhibiting wireless communication. For this reason, and with the blessing of his superiors in the Netherlands, Idenburg decided not to reveal the findings of the report.[52] In any case, tensions between Dutch and British authorities over the use of wireless communications eased shortly thereafter, because the *Emden* was sunk on 9 November.[53] With the *Emden's* demise the last real German naval threat to Allied shipping in the region disappeared, and Dutch authorities believed they could breathe a sigh of relief at having avoided being dragged into the war by the actions of German merchant ships.

The Dutch East Indies and the German-Indian Conspiracy

In fact, however, the crises over the *Emden* were just the beginning. In the months immediately following the sinking of the *Emden*, it became clear that the Dutch East Indies formed a vital link in the global plans of Germans, Indians, and Ottomans to foment unrest and revolution in Allied – particularly British – colonial possessions. These plans involved using the East Indies as a distribution point for anticolonial, often pan-Islamic propaganda; as a halfway point for the shipment of arms from North America to India; and as a meeting place for Germans and Indian revolutionaries to exchange ideas and money. From the beginning of 1915 through 1917, British authorities used all their available intelligence networks to expose the global and the local nature of these schemes, to make arrests when

---

[51] Pinke to de Graeff, November 29, U24, Ministerie van Kolonien: Geheim Archief, 1914, 2.10.36.51, box 172.

[52] van Dijk, *The Netherlands Indies and the Great War 1914–1918*, 196.

[53] F. Bauduin, *Het Nederlandsch Eskader in Oost-Indië* ('S-Gravenhage: Martinus Nijhoff, 1920), 66.

suspects entered British territory, and to bring them to the attention of the Dutch. And although the Dutch were genuinely concerned about the potential for anticolonial German-Indian plans to bleed over to emerging nationalist movements in the East Indies, they had to walk a fine line between placating the British and angering the influential German community in their midst. The results satisfied neither the British nor the Dutch but did allow Germans and Indian revolutionaries the space to develop and put into action several elaborate plans designed to wreak havoc on British India and Malaya.

We saw in Chapter 1 how Ghadar Party emissaries and propaganda, financed by the Berlin India Committee, contributed to the mutiny of the 5th Light Infantry in Singapore on February 15, 1915. But the mutiny was only the most dramatic episode that resulted from a much wider field of action involving people and places in multiple locations in Southeast Asia – including the Dutch East Indies.

This was because the Berlin India Committee, chaired by Virendranath Chattopadhyaya, envisioned three main routes to import revolutionary propaganda, weapons, and people into India: one overland through Persia and Afghanistan from Europe, a second across Siam and Burma from San Francisco, and a third through the Dutch East Indies, also from San Francisco.[54] Both routes to India from San Francisco involved travel through East and Southeast Asia. And while India was the ultimate target, the Berlin India Committee also saw the Far East as a strategic region in itself. A variety of locations around the region hosted sizeable Indian populations of either soldiers and police or laborers (or both), including Shanghai, Hong Kong, Malaya, the Philippines, and Sumatra. The Committee sought to utilize these diasporic populations to establish "subsidiary bases" for propaganda work, recruiting, and the creation of safe contacts to ease the passage of revolutionaries between North America and India. By the end of 1914 Ghadar activists were already in places like Shanghai, Java, Singapore, and Sumatra with the aim of recruiting new members, making contacts with other anti-Allied groups, and scouting for likely places to land weapons en route to India.

---

[54] Chattophadyaya was aided by several prominent Indian revolutionaries in Berlin, including Har Dayal, who arrived in Germany in 1914. Kris Manjapra, "The Illusions of Encounter: Muslim 'Minds' and Hindu Revolutionaries in First World War Germany and After," *Journal of Global History* 1 (2006), 372; Maia Ramnath, "Two Revolutions: The Ghadar Movement and India's Radical Diaspora, 1913–1918," *Radical History Review*, no. 92 (2005), 14. The Committee also established a secondary headquarters in Istanbul in 1915, in order to organize rebellions in Egypt, Mesopotamia, and Persia. Ramnath, *Haj to Utopia*, 74.

Neutral territories in the United States, the Philippines, China, the East Indies, and Siam were vital to the success of Committee plans to utilize the sea routes from California to India.[55] As long as they maintained their neutrality, these territories allowed Germans and Indians reasonable scope to come and go, as authorities generally refrained from involving themselves too deeply in their affairs. Each of the neutral territories also maintained a German consulate from which Indian revolutionaries could draw funds and receive information. And each provided a base into which propaganda and arms could be smuggled for redistribution to India or other Allied territories.

By early 1915, British authorities had pieced together the outlines of all three routes the Committee planned to use for the purpose of exporting revolution into India. It was already clear that locations in Southeast Asia were vital to the functioning of these routes, and that in order to expose the Committee's plans British authorities had to think not only locally but also globally. It is important to note, however, that the instruments by which they were able to piece these networks together were neither sophisticated nor particularly well-coordinated. In North America, London and British India had hitherto maintained separate intelligence networks that had very few points of connection, and it was only as a result of German-Indian conspiracy that they began to work together in a more coordinated fashion.[56] Even once coordination between London and India improved during the war, much British intelligence about German-Indian schemes originating in North America came from British consuls who had been instructed to keep an eye on the Germans and Indians within their jurisdiction.[57] What this meant, of course, was that intelligence varied according to the competence and ability of individual consuls, who were not trained for intelligence work.

---

[55] A.C. Bose, "Activities of Indian Revolutionaries Abroad, 1914–1918," in Amitabha Mukherjee, ed., *Militant Nationalism in India, 1876–1947* (Calcutta: Institute of Historical Studies, 1995), 313.

[56] Christopher Andrew, "Introduction: Intelligence and International Relations 1900–1945," in Christopher Andrew and Jeremy Noakes, eds., *Intelligence and International Relations, 1900–1945*, Exeter Studies in History (Liverpool: Liverpool University Press, 1987). As Richard Popplewell argues, most of the intelligence work on Indians in North America prior to (and even during) the war was done by a Canadian immigration officer, who was not even formally attached to a British intelligence service. Where India was involved (through the Department of Criminal Defense), the work was mostly carried out on the Pacific coast, while London focused mostly on the east coast. See Richard Popplewell, "The Surveillance of Indian 'Seditionists' in North America, 1905–1915," in Christopher Andrew and Jeremy Noakes, eds., *Intelligence And International Relations*, 55.

[57] Richard J. Popplewell, *Intelligence and Imperial Defence: British Intelligence and the Defence of the Indian Empire, 1904–1924*, Cass Series–Studies in Intelligence (London; Portland, OR: Frank Cass, 1995), 261.

The intelligence network in Southeast Asia was a similarly blunt instrument, at least until India's Department of Criminal Intelligence (DCI) created a Far Eastern Intelligence Office for East and Southeast Asia in 1916.[58] As in North America, British consuls stationed around the region were vital to obtaining relevant intelligence and for communicating it to the proper authorities throughout the war. Until 1916 they received very little help from the DCI for these efforts, which insisted they conduct and finance their own intelligence work, even when the intelligence concerned plots against India.[59] To make up for the initial absence of a formal intelligence network in the Far East, the new commander of the forces in Singapore in 1915 – Dudley Ridout of Singapore Mutiny fame – made the island city an informal center of British intelligence in the region.[60] Ridout was determined to improve British intelligence in the region because of the mutiny of the 5th Light Infantry, which occurred only weeks after he arrived at his post in January 1915. For Ridout, the apparent connection between the mutiny and anti-British, pan-Islamic propaganda spread by Ghadar agents necessitated gaining a better handle on who was moving through the region, how they were doing so, and what materials they were carrying with them. To accomplish this, Ridout maintained regular correspondence with the consuls in the region as well as with London, authorized the expenditure of government funds for intelligence, employed two Indian secret agents, and coordinated intelligence reports from various consuls.

British intelligence in North America and Southeast Asia during the Great War was thus makeshift, relied heavily on consular positions, and was only loosely connected at the highest levels of communication.[61] Nevertheless, it was coordinated enough for individual consuls as well as civil and military officials to work out an understanding of the global nature of the plans that aimed to threaten British colonial interests. And by mid-1915, thanks in large part to Dudley Ridout in Singapore and the consul general in Batavia (now W.R.D. Beckett), it had become clear that Britain's enemies were taking advantage of the neutrality of the Dutch East Indies in order to harm British colonial interests in Malaya and India.[62]

Until the end of June 1915, both Beckett and Ridout believed the main threat from the East Indies stemmed from Indian revolutionaries using it as a base to spread pan-Islamic, pro-Ottoman, and anti-British

---

[58] This will be discussed further in Chapter 6.
[59] Popplewell, *Intelligence and Imperial Defence*, 265–256.
[60] Popplewell, *Intelligence and Imperial Defence*, 261.
[61] The use of the term "makeshift" is in Popplewell, *Intelligence and Imperial Defence*, 261.
[62] W.R.D. Beckett replaced the acting consul Carlisle at the beginning of 1915.

propaganda. Beckett was already engaged in a public war of words with the German and Turkish consuls in Batavia, since the two latter individuals continually published statements in the press about Britain's anti-Muslim orientation, as evidenced by the fact that they were at war against the Ottoman caliph. In response, Beckett published statements indicating that the British were forced into a war against the Ottoman Empire, but that the war was not about Islam.[63] More worrisome to the British than these public duels was their belief that Indian revolutionaries were using the East Indies as a base from which to mass produce – and then distribute – printed calls to arms against the British.

Physical proof of such schemes emerged at the end of 1914, when Ridout forwarded to Beckett a pamphlet postmarked from the Dutch East Indies, dated December 3, 1914. The pamphlet was addressed to an Indian living in the Federated Malay States, and was called "Mis-statement by the English and our Duty Toward the Turks." It urged readers to "Read it yourself; read it to your friends; and send it other places."[64] Its contents condemned British duplicity with regard to the Ottoman Empire, and denied British claims to being friendly to Indian and other Muslims around the world. It ends by asking, "Now what should the Indians do?" The answer is to convince the British to treat the Ottoman Empire fairly. Should this be impossible, it exhorted readers that "then Oh Hindus, and Oh Mohamedans, draw your swords and drive the English out of India."[65]

Pamphlet in hand, in early 1915 Beckett brought it to the attention to the Dutch authorities. This was not the kind of material the Dutch were happy to see in the East Indies, even though it was directed toward the British rather than themselves. Dutch authorities had a long and deep-seated fear of pan-Islamism and its potential for inspiring anticolonial sentiments among the majority-Muslim population.[66] Accordingly, they

---

[63] van Dijk, *The Netherlands Indies and the Great War 1914–1918*, 307.

[64] Translation of "Mis-statement by the English and our Duty Toward the Turks," Report 36925, Straits Settlements Original Correspondence: Foreign, 1915, CO 273/431.

[65] Translation of "Mis-statement by the English and our Duty Toward the Turks," Report 36925, Straits Settlements Original Correspondence: Foreign, 1915, CO 273/431.

[66] van Dijk notes the Dutch were so fearful of the anti-Dutch pan-Islamism of Arabs in the East Indies that in 1917 the army commander recommended immediate internment of all Arab males in the event the Dutch should be dragged into the war, p. 14. There is an extensive literature on pan-Islam in the East Indies, including Michael Francis Laffan, *Islamic Nationhood and Colonial Indonesia: The Umma Below the Winds* (London; New York: RoutledgeCurzon, 2003); Chiara Formichi, "Pan-Islam and Religious National-ism: The Case of Kartosuwiryo and Negara Islam Indonesia," *Indonesia* no. 90 (October 2010); Anthony Reid, "Nineteenth Century Pan-Islam in Indonesia and Malaysia," *The Journal of Asian Studies* 26, no. 2 (1967): 278. Prior to the war, the Ministry of Foreign Affairs compiled large files relating to pan-Islamic turbulence in the East Indies and

made an effort to track down the postmark from the envelope, and eventually traced the pamphlet to a Kashmiri named Abdul Selam (called Silam in Dutch sources).[67] In addition to locating Selam, Dutch authorities discovered that he had engaged "a native Printing Press at Batavia" to produce six Urdu-language pamphlets advocating violence against the British in the name of Islam.[68] The printing press, to the dismay of the Dutch, was owned by a Sarekat Islam newspaper – the economic and political organization that increasingly aligned itself against Dutch colonial rule since its founding in 1912. To make matters more complicated, Selam had also been seen going in and out of the German consulate in Batavia. Given the evidence, Dutch authorities thought Selam was enough of a threat that they arrested him.

Beckett received word of Selam's arrest on March 24, 1915. At that point, Selam had successfully collected and distributed five of the six sets of pamphlets he had printed but had been detained before he could collect the final set. According to the Dutch, Selam confessed outright that "he came to Java with the intention of commencing propaganda from that country for the obtaining of self-government for British India."[69] Not only that, Beckett argued that the pamphlets contained "strong evidence of being manufactured in conjunction with German and Turkish intriguers."[70]

Given the inflammatory nature of the material, Beckett was anxious to keep Selam from being released and to prevent other Indians from following in his footsteps. But three weeks after informing Beckett of Selam's temporary arrest, the Dutch released him. They could not, they said, hold Selam any longer, "since no proof existed of an attempt to distribute these pamphlets in the Netherlands East Indies."[71] Under Dutch law, Selam could certainly be held if he were trying to spread propaganda within the East Indies, but not if he were using it for distribution elsewhere. Simply put, it was not a crime to plan the overthrow of a foreign government from Dutch territory. The Dutch Attorney General pointed out to Idenburg that Selam also could not be convicted of breaching Dutch

---

beyond. See Ministerie van Buitenlandse Zaken, Panislamistische Woelingen, Nationaal Archief, Den Haag, 2.05.03, Boxes 450 and 452.

[67] Tim Harper notes that Selam had lived and traveled in Burma before ending up in the Dutch East Indies, in "Singapore, 1915, and the Birth of the Asian Underground," *Modern Asian Studies* 47, no. 06 (2013), 1805.

[68] Beckett to Foreign Office, July 2, 1915, Report 36925, Straits Settlements Original Correspondence: Foreign, 1915, CO 273/431.

[69] Beckett to Foreign Office, July 2, 1915, Report 36925.

[70] Beckett to Foreign Office, July 2, 1915, Report 36925.

[71] Beckett to Foreign Office, July 2, 1915, Report 36925.

neutrality, unless he took concrete actions to materially help one of the belligerent powers.[72]

This infuriated Beckett, who wrote in disgust about the ability of people like Selam to print "and distribute through the post to different parts of the Indian Empire pamphlets of the most incendiary character but commit no offence."[73] In an effort to convince the Dutch authorities to enact legislation that would "prevent the territory of the Netherlands East Indies being used as a medium for such manufacture and dissemination," Becket wrote a detailed memorandum with the aim of showing that Selam's case was hardly isolated.[74] As part of his case, he argued that "large numbers of copies of the seditious newspaper "Gader" [sic] and of seditious posters in various Indian languages are being transmitted through the Post from the United States and elsewhere to persons residing in the Netherlands Indies."[75] To back up his claim, he enclosed ten names and addresses of Indians in the East Indies to whom these materials were addressed.[76] Finally, he shared a rumor that German agents in the United States were preparing to send two Indian journalists to Dutch territory in order to "publish newspapers under German control, and to disseminate German news in British India."[77]

Although Dutch law did not allow for Selam to be arrested or even expelled, in the end the Dutch Attorney General convinced Idenburg that the danger of not doing something could have disastrous effects on the East Indies, since he was sure the British would not "stand idly by" if they simply let him go free. After considering various options, in August 1915 Idenburg decided to intern Selam on the island of Timor because his freedom posed an immediate threat to Dutch security.[78]

If this were not evidence enough that the Dutch could at times be persuaded to contravene their own laws in order to placate the British, another case that occurred shortly thereafter in Sumatra should. In this instance, an Indian Sikh living in Medan, Sumatra, alerted the Dutch

---

[72] van Dijk, *The Netherlands Indies and the Great War 1914–1918*, 330–331.

[73] Beckett to Foreign Office, July 2, 1915, Report 36925. This indignation was rather disingenuous, given that the British had often used the same logic about extradition of Dutch political exiles who operated out of Singapore.

[74] Memorandum of facts which have been brought to the knowledge of His Britannic Majesty's Consul General which tend to show that serious attempts are being made to disseminate sedition in British India through agents in the Netherlands East Indies, Report 36925.

[75] Memorandum of facts, Report 36925.

[76] Memorandum of facts, Report 36925. Of the ten names, eight were Sikh, and nine of the ten addresses were in Sumatra.

[77] Memorandum of facts, Report 36925.

[78] van Dijk, *The Netherlands Indies and the Great War 1914–1918*, 331.

controller there about anti-British activity among his fellow Sikhs. Specifically, two Sikh priests new to the area – Wir Singh and Sewah Sing – had brought attention to themselves by attempting to raise money for a new temple that many suspected was fictitious.[79] When Dutch authorities investigated the matter, they did not find evidence of widespread anti-British discontent, but they did find sixty-three packages containing copies of *Ghadar* at various Sikh establishments and homes in the area.[80] However, as far as the Dutch authorities could tell, most of the Sikhs who had been sent copies of *Ghadar* had not requested them – and some had even turned them over to local authorities or sent them back to the United States. The Dutch controller surmised that the addresses – the same addresses found in Abdul Selam's possession – had been provided without consent by Wir Singh and his accomplice, Sewah Singh.[81] As a consequence, the controller expelled both men from the East Indies. The men were put on a ship to British Malaya after notifying the authorities there, and both were arrested immediately upon arriving in British territory.[82]

As it turned out, Wir Singh was a highly valuable catch because he had apparently been involved in planning the Singapore mutiny several months earlier. According to evidence the British compiled against him, Wir Singh had been in Singapore from December 1914 through January 1915, during which time he was alleged to have taken part in the organizational meetings that led to the mutiny. In January he went to Penang, and then – after someone alerted British authorities that he was collecting money for anti-British causes – fled to Dutch territory in Medan.[83]

The cases of Wir Singh, Sewah Singh, and Abdul Selam highlight several features about the Dutch East Indies in particular, and about Southeast Asia more generally, during the war. Although the sources do not allow us to hear the men's voices directly, their actions point to the existence of a mobile group of anticolonial activists who used colonial and state borders to their own advantage – producing material in one place that would have been illegal in another, moving items and people through territories just out of reach of their enemies, and crossing borders to escape punishment when the necessity arose. Anticolonial activists in

---

[79] van Dijk, *The Netherlands Indies and the Great War 1914–1918*, 332.

[80] Beckett to Government of India Home Department, September 29, 1915, Report 53464; also Controller Obdeijn to British Vice Consul Medan, September 1, 1915, Report 49548. Straits Settlements Original Correspondence: Foreign, 1915, CO 273/432.

[81] Beckett to Government of India Home Department, September 29, 1915, Report 53464.

[82] V. Obdeijn to Vice-consul Medan, September 14, 1915, Report 53464.

[83] V. Obdeijn to Vice-consul Medan, September 14, 1915, Report 53464.

Southeast Asia had used these techniques for decades prior to the war and would continue to use them after its conclusion. What was unique about the war years, however, was that they knowingly took the opportunities provided by official declarations of neutrality to protect themselves from prosecution under international law. Unfortunately for them, the circumstances of the war also meant that Dutch fears about angering the British – especially when combined with Dutch apprehensions about the ricochet effect of anticolonial propaganda in the Indies themselves – sometimes trumped strict interpretations of the law.

Conclusion

As we have seen thus far, the war had an enormous impact on the Dutch East Indies in spite of its official neutrality. Economically, the war was deeply damaging to trade between the Indies and the Netherlands, and contributed to unrest and volatility in the islands. Communications were at times nearly severed between the colony and the metropole, leaving the Indies government essentially alone in governing. Politically, the dance between placating both the Allies and the Central Powers enough to maintain Dutch neutrality was both time-consuming and expensive, not to mention exhausting. Dutch authorities worried constantly about the designs of the British, the Germans, and the Japanese on the archipelago. As it turned out, even though Dutch East Indies authorities insisted they were scrupulously following international law as it pertained to neutrality, they had plenty to worry about. German citizens and consular authorities did in fact aid German warships from East Indian territory until the *Emden* was sunk. In addition, Germans and Indians used the East Indies as a safe haven and way station in their schemes to undermine British colonial rule in Malaya and India. When viewed cumulatively, these plots and schemes demonstrate the multiple ways the war made itself felt in Southeast Asia, and the critical importance of the neutral Dutch East Indies in allowing this to happen. And as we shall see in Chapter 4, the fates of an American-made ship that ended up in Dutch East Indies waters expose in detail not only the German and Indian networks active in the colony but also their global connections.

4   The *S.S. Maverick* and the Unraveling of a Global Conspiracy

On June 28, 1915, the British consul general in Batavia, W.R.D. Beckett, received a telegram from Admiral Martyn Jerram in Singapore with the urgent news that the *Maverick*, an American-made steamship, was headed for the Dutch territory of Anjer (Anyer) near the Sunda Strait in west Java. The *Maverick*, Jerram believed, was loaded with arms and ammunition, which were intended for transshipment to India to fuel the revolutionary movement. Beckett immediately notified all of the British vice consuls in Dutch territory to keep a sharp eye out for the vessel or any information pertaining to it. The next day, he wrote a letter to the Dutch General Secretary in the East Indies, notifying him of the ship's expected arrival and adding that the ship had been chartered in San Francisco by a German and was owned by a German firm. Most important, he wrote, "she is believed to have on board large quantities of rifles and ammunition which she shipped from an American schooner off the coast of Mexico." Beckett requested that the Dutch place a strict watch on its ports and asked authorities to keep him informed regarding its whereabouts.[1]

The Dutch authorities acted immediately on this threat. Governor General A.F.W. Idenburg and Vice Admiral F. Pinke were both concerned about the implications such a plan would have on Dutch neutrality if weapons of war were exchanged in its territories. Not only that, following on the heels of a May 31 letter from Beckett conveying a rumor that Germans in the East Indies were attempting to arm the German merchant ship *Roon* for an unspecified purpose, Idenburg could not completely dismiss the idea that the weapons supposedly aboard the *Maverick* were intended to arm Germans living in the colony for an eventual takeover of the Indies rather than for Indian revolutionaries.[2]

---

[1] Beckett to General Secretary, June 29, 1915, F11, Ministerie van Kolonien: Geheim Archief. 2.10.36.51, Box 177.

[2] Idenburg to Minister of Colonies, July 7, 1915, Beckett to General Secretary, May 31, 1915, F11, Ministerie van Kolonien: Geheim Archief. 2.10.36.51, Box 177. In his letter to the Minister of Colonies, Idenburg acknowledged that despite some doubt on his part,

Idenburg and Pinke instructed authorities in all Dutch ports to keep a close eye on moored German ships and then sent Dutch ships out to search for the *Maverick*.

After a series of misadventures, the *Maverick* did indeed end up in the Dutch East Indies port of Tanjung Priok, where it was detained for the duration of the war. And although the *Maverick* failed in its assigned task, its story is significant because it exposed not only critical details of the global nature of the German-Indian conspiracy but also provided clear evidence that Germans (and Indians) in the Dutch East Indies were central to its execution. Between July 1915 and May 1916, individuals with intimate knowledge about the *Maverick* and its related business helped British authorities uncover a network of highly placed German businessmen, working in consultation with the German consul at Batavia, whom were involved in various schemes to transport weapons and revolutionaries from North America and other locations into India from the East Indies. These Germans were in frequent contact with, and gave money to, a number of revolutionary Indians and other pro-German supporters who moved between North America and India via the East Indies, often with subsidiary visits to Siam, China, and the Philippines. In short, the failed journey of the *Maverick* led to the complete exposure of how one of the key prongs in the German-Indian conspiracy functioned. At the same time, the intelligence made possible by the *Maverick* and the people who understood its mission also highlighted the limits of Dutch willingness to cooperate with British demands. Even when presented with copious and damning evidence about German schemes to undermine Allied rule from Dutch territory, Dutch fears about angering the German community in its midst led the government to deny both its significance and its relevance. This refusal to intervene, in turn, meant that the East Indies remained a central locus for German-Indian anticolonial plots for much of the war.

This chapter begins with the story of the *Maverick* and sets it in the context of related schemes to funnel arms through the East Indies to India. It then moves to the revelations provided by a series of people connected to the *Maverick's* mission, particularly two double agents and four men arrested as a result of intelligence the agents provided to British authorities. Finally, it explores British attempts to convince Dutch authorities to take action against the Germans involved in the *Maverick* scheme, as well as Dutch unwillingness to risk their neutrality by angering the large community of Germans in the Indies. Even in spite of the

the weapons were probably not intended for use inside the Dutch East Indies, but rather for transshipment to British India or even East Africa.

Dutch unwillingness to act, however, the detention of the *Maverick* – and the information provided by crucial actors connected with it – allowed British authorities to unravel many of the threads in German-Indian schemes to undermine Allied colonial rule.

The Journey of the *Maverick*

The summer of 1915 was a difficult one for the Dutch East Indies government, which as we know was highly invested in maintaining Dutch neutrality. This was because in spite of its desire to stay out of the war, events originating thousands of miles away repeatedly threatened to drag the Indies into the melee. As it turned out, it soon became clear that the *Maverick* was not an isolated threat but rather was only one in a series of plans to ship armaments through the East Indies and on to India.

In mid-July the Dutch government discovered that the British ambassador in Washington, D.C., Cecil Spring-Rice, had alerted his government that a Dutch officer was rumored to be in San Francisco trying to buy $1.5 million in "rifles, machine guns, aeroplane parts and powder," presumably for the purpose of sending the lot to India.[3] United States authorities had also recently foiled plans by the German firm Schenker & Company to purchase weapons in New York and San Francisco for transport to Java in Dutch merchant ships.[4] Then, only two weeks after writing to the Dutch about the *Maverick*, Beckett alerted Dutch authorities that another American ship, the *Henry S.*, was sailing under the direction of two German men from Manila toward the Dutch port of Pontianak in western Borneo. Like the *Maverick*, the *Henry S.* was believed to be carrying a large cargo of arms and ammunition intended for India. As a result of these threats, all British consuls in East and Southeast Asia were put on high alert, and on Beckett's warning the Dutch authorities added yet another ship to their watch list.[5]

The Dutch navy was fully occupied with responding to these threats during the month of July. To intercept the *Maverick* before its expected arrival on about July 18 at Anjer, Pinke sent a cruiser and torpedo boat to patrol the Sunda Strait. He also sent a ship each to Makassar (south Sulawesi), Cilacap (southwest Java), and Emmahaven (west Sumatra). Once it became clear that the *Henry S.* was also on its way, Pinke sent a

---

[3] Telegram from Spring-Rice, July 15, 1915, Report 33122, July 19, 1915. Straits Settlements Original Correspondence: Foreign, 1915. CO 273/431, TNA.

[4] van Dijk, 334. The plan was foiled when a Dutch captain, who did not approve of carrying the cargo, alerted U.S. authorities.

[5] See the series of telegrams in Report 33122, July 19, 1915. Straits Settlements Original Correspondence: Foreign, 1915. CO 273/431, TNA.

ship to Pontianak as well.[6] On July 19, the Dutch ship *Scylla* made contact with the *Maverick* when the latter anchored at Merak, at the western tip of Java.[7] However, on searching the ship Dutch authorities could find no evidence of weapons or contraband on board. The next day, therefore, they let it proceed to the port of Tanjung Priok, near Batavia, where it was to remain for the rest of the war.[8] A few weeks later, on August 7, Dutch authorities at Paleleh (north Sulawesi) reported that the *Henry S.* had come to anchor off the coast after having troubles with its engines. Pinke sent the *Tromp* to investigate, but once again a search revealed no evidence of weapons.[9] In any case, the *Henry S.* could not continue on its journey without engine repairs, especially since both the *Tromp* and the Japanese ship *Akashi*, which also made contact, refused to give it a tow.[10] Like the *Maverick*, then, the journey of the *Henry S.* came to an unexpected halt in Dutch colonial territory.

Although all of the foiled attempts to ship arms through the Indies during the summer of 1915 helped British authorities piece together the larger networks of the German-Indian conspiracy, it was the information connected to the *Maverick* that yielded the jackpot. But before we explore the nature of this information, let us take a more detailed look at what reportedly happened on the *Maverick's* ill-fated journey.[11]

In early 1915, the German shipping firm F. Jebson & Company commissioned the *Maverick* – an oil tanker – from the American-owned Maverick Steamship Company. The ship's crew consisted of a Captain Nelson, a young German-American purser named J.B. Starr-Hunt, twenty-three other crew, and five men posing as "Persian waiters" but who were in fact Indian revolutionaries active in the Ghadar party. The *Maverick*

---

[6] Pinke to Idenburg, August 18, 1915, H12, Ministerie van Kolonien: Geheim Archief. 2.10.36.51, Box 178.

[7] Bauduin, *Het Nederlandsch Eskader in Oost-Indië, 1914–1918*, 93.

[8] Pinke to Idenburg, August 18, 1915, H12.

[9] Pinke to Idenburg, August 18, 1915, H12. What the authorities in the Indies did not yet know was that the *Henry S.* had indeed tried to load a cargo of arms and ammunition in Manila, but that U.S. customs officials forced the crew to remove it before the ship was allowed to proceed to Pontianak.

[10] Pinke to Idenburg, August 18, 1915, H12; F. Bauduin, *Het Nederlansch Eskader*, 94–95. van Dijk indicates that the *Henry S.* finally left Dutch waters in October 1915, 336.

[11] Although British authorities had already worked out the broad outlines of the Maverick's ill-fated journey, the details were provided by the 1916 arrest of the purser, J.B. Starr-Hunt, in Singapore. Starr-Hunt later became a crucial witness for the prosecution in the San Francisco Conspiracy Case against Ghadar leaders. Statement by Starr-Hunt, September 14, 1916, Report 43873. Straits Settlements Original Correspondence: Foreign, 1916. CO 273/449. Various accounts of the *Maverick's* journey have been published elsewhere (also relying on Starr-Hunt's testimony), including French Strother, *Fighting Germany's Spies* (Garden City, NY: Doubleday Page & Company, 1918), chapter 10.

set sail with its crew at the end of April 1915 from San Pedro, California. After stopping at San Jose del Cabo and getting clearance for Anjer, Java, the ship set sail for Socorro Island, 600 miles west of Acapulco, on April 28. Once the ship arrived in Socorro, it was supposed to have met with another American ship, the *Annie Larsen*, which was carrying an estimated 30,000 rifles and revolvers.[12] At that remote location the crew of the *Annie Larsen* was to transfer its cargo to the *Maverick*, and the *Maverick* was to sail on to Java. The purser, Starr-Hunt, was supposed to then take charge of the *Annie Larsen* and use it to conduct trade in Mexico, while the captain of the *Annie Larsen* was to come aboard the *Maverick*. Starr-Hunt was carrying secret instructions about the ship's mission that he was supposed to hand over to *Annie Larsen's* captain when he came aboard.

But when the *Maverick* arrived at Socorro, the *Annie Larsen* was not there. Its crew had left a message (in a bottle buried in the sand, no less) that it had been waiting for the *Maverick* for a month, that it had to leave to get water and supplies, but that it would return. The *Maverick* then waited twenty-nine days at Socorro, during which time its crew was visited by an American collier, Mexican customs agents, and two British naval ships. The British ships each searched the *Maverick* for suspicious cargo but found nothing. Before British officers could board the *Maverick*, however, the leader of the "Persian waiters" (who went by the name Jehangir but was really Hari Singh) became very agitated because he said he had six suitcases of printed material that "he was very anxious to hide" from the British.[13] Both Nelson and Starr-Hunt persuaded Singh to burn the material, which he did.

When the *Annie Larsen* did not appear after twenty-nine days, the *Maverick* sailed to Hilo, Hawaii, where it received instructions to go to Johnson Island and wait for the *Annie Larsen* there. But the *Maverick's* captain, Nelson, had been loose-lipped in Hawaii and disclosed to the press where the ship was headed. Once news about the indiscretion had gotten out, a German merchant ship gave the *Maverick* news that its mission was to be abandoned because too much was known about it. It was now to proceed to Anjer, via Johnson Island, without its intended cargo. From Anjer, it was to proceed to Batavia, where the captain and Starr-Hunt were to report to the manager of the German firm called Behn, Meyer & Company.[14]

---

12 Van Dijk, 334.
13 Statement by Starr-Hunt, September 14, 1916, Report 43873. Straits Settlements Original Correspondence: Foreign, 1916. CO 273/449.
14 Statement by Starr-Hunt, September 14, 1916.

Thus from Hilo, the *Maverick* sailed on to Anjer without its cargo of weapons and without its anti-British propaganda into Dutch waters, where Dutch ships – having been made aware of its every move by Beckett – were waiting for it. The plan had been a grand one, involving German money, Indian revolutionaries, and secret rendezvous. But in the end the *Maverick* never made it to India and never distributed its propaganda or weapons. What it did do, however, was provide concrete evidence of the global nature of German-Indian plans to undermine British colonial rule. It had also – along with the *Henry S.* – activated nearly the entire Dutch navy, not to mention the British diplomatic and consular network in Southeast Asia and around the world.

Unraveling the German-Indian Conspiracy Via the *Maverick*

Although the journey of the *Maverick* appeared to constitute physical proof of a German-Indian conspiracy against British colonial rule, the absence of weapons on board made it impossible for the British or Dutch to demonstrate that the ship had a covert and violent purpose. But it turned out that the most important consequence of the *Maverick* lay not so much in the events of the journey or the ship's cargo, but in the information individuals with knowledge of the ship and its purpose revealed. On the very same day consul general Beckett received word from Ridout about the impending arrival of the *Maverick*, June 29, 1915, he also received an anonymous tip in the mail offering inside information about the same thing. That tip was the beginning of a relationship with a secret source who was critical in helping the British piece together the full extent of German-Indian plans to facilitate a revolution in India via connections through the neutral East Indies. The information provided by this source, in turn, led Ridout to detain several people who had been participants in the *Maverick* affair as they passed through Singapore, and to extract incriminating testament from them. These sources, combined with Ridout's success in turning a German secret agent into a British collaborator in the summer of 1915, allowed British authorities to gain a detailed understanding about the complexity of the plot, the main characters involved, and their specific plans.

On June 29, just hours after getting the news from Ridout about the *Maverick*, a letter postmarked from Bandung, Java arrived in the mail for Beckett. Inside was an unsigned note that asked, "Is a steamer loaded with rifles and ammunitionis [sic] worth fl. 500.000 (five honderdthousand) [sic] for you to pay to me?... If yes put in Wednesdays Nieuws van den Dag [Daily News] for a long experienced rubber planter for Perak."[15]

Beckett did not place an ad in the *Nieuws van den Dag* that Wednesday, partially because the Dutch authorities were opposed to the idea. In any case, he believed he had the information he needed about what could only have been the *Maverick*. But on July 16, Beckett received another note – this time a request for a meeting regarding "a secret concerning the war which must be of utmost interest to your Government."[16] The two met at Beckett's house on July 19. During his interview with the half-German, half-Swedish man who became known to the British only by his code name "Oren," Beckett became convinced that his informant really did have access to intelligence concerning German plots. Although Oren was disappointed to learn that Beckett already knew about the *Maverick* (and thus that he had no need to pay for the information), Beckett sought to preserve the connection for future use. After ensuring permission from Admiral Jerram at Singapore and the War Office in London, Beckett entered into a formal contract with Oren for information in exchange for money. The agreement, which was signed on July 28, stated "I, the informer, hereby agree to divulge ... all information that I now do or may hereafter possess in connection with this plot [the *Maverick*] or design to introduce arms or material of war from the United States ... to the destination which I shall divulge." In return, Beckett agreed to pay Oren a sum equal to the value of one-third of the cargo of whatever was found or, if no cargo were found, one-sixth of its estimated value if the perpetrators of the scheme were convicted.[17]

In the interval between Beckett's receipt of Oren's second letter and the conclusion of their agreement, Beckett also received a letter forwarded from his vice-consul at Medan about a German spy in the Dutch East Indies. The letter, which was from an anonymous "friend" of the spy, tipped the British off about how they could discover his identity. When Beckett received the letter, he followed its instructions and discovered that the man in question was C.F. Vincent Kraft, born in Batavia to a Dutch father. According to the tip, Kraft had fought in the Great War on the German side and then entered the German secret service after being wounded. He had subsequently been "sent out to the Netherlands

---

[15] Copy of unsigned note to Consul General Becket, F11, Ministerie van Kolonien: Geheim Archief. 2.10.36.51, Box 177.

[16] Beckett to Sir Edward Grey, German Activities in the Far East, Report 42428. Straits Settlements Original Correspondence: Foreign,1915, CO 273/432, 2.

[17] "Agreement," Report 42428. Straits Settlements Original Correspondence: Foreign,1915, CO 273/432, 5.

East Indies for the 'revolution business'."[18] On July 29 Beckett had the opportunity to meet Kraft in person, as he had traveled from Medan to Batavia and now sought a visa to travel to Singapore, Hong Kong, and Shanghai. Since Kraft had a Netherlands East Indies passport and his papers were all in order, Beckett issued the visa. However, he was convinced that "Kraft is one of the most active and dangerous of the band of workers which are in this country," and therefore reported his intended stay in Singapore to the authorities there, who were waiting to arrest him when he arrived on August 3.[19] Almost immediately after being arrested in Singapore, Kraft turned into a double agent for the British.

Between July and October, Beckett and Ridout learned – through Oren and Kraft – a growing number of details about the people and places involved in German-Indian plans to finance revolution in India. For one thing, their information confirmed the deep involvement of Emil and Theodor Helfferich – German businessmen and brothers in Batavia – in anti-British networks. Beckett had been suspicious of the pair for months, but only now was he able to put more of the pieces together. Oren likewise provided information about the Indians in Batavia with whom the Helfferichs were working. As proof of the reliability of his information, Oren had told Beckett in one of their earliest meetings that an Indian man calling himself C.A. Martin had traveled to Batavia from India in the spring of 1915 to meet with Emil Helfferich. When Beckett checked the information by making inquiries at the hotel where Martin supposedly stayed, he discovered that Oren's information had been correct.[20]

Kraft's arrest also led to the arrest, in Singapore, of the exiled nationalist leader of the Javanese Indische party – Ernest Douwes Dekker.[21] Douwes Dekker, who came from mixed European and Javanese parentage, had long been a thorn in the side of the Dutch East Indies government because of his anti-Dutch, pro-Indonesian sympathies, and the use of his skills as a journalist and editor to publish them. The two newspapers he founded just before the war featured articles written by radical

---

[18]   Beckett to Sir Edward Grey, German Activities in the Far East, Report 42428, 1.
[19]   Beckett to Sir Edward Grey, German Activities in the Far East, Report 42428, 2; Popplewell, "British Intelligence in the Far East, 1914–1918," 263. Popplewell indicates that Kraft had intended betraying the Germans from the very beginning. Alun Jones also discusses Kraft briefly in his dissertation entitled Internal Security in British Malaya, 1895–1942 (Ph.D., Yale University, 1970), 84.
[20]   Beckett to Sir Edward Grey, German Activities in the Far East, Report 42428, 3.
[21]   Douwes Dekker was the nephew of the famous Eduoard Douwes Dekker, known as Multatuli, who had written *Max Havelaar* in 1860, a book that excoriated the Dutch for their exploitive colonial practices.

anticolonial thinkers from around the world – including future leaders of the Ghadar party – whom he had come to know during his earlier travels in Europe.[22] When the war began, Douwes Dekker had been in exile in Europe for his political beliefs for about a year. While there, he was courted by Indian nationalists like Har Dayal, and even went to Berlin in 1915 to discuss ways to contribute to the German-Indian conspiracy. In the same year, he helped several revolutionary Indians obtain passports so they could travel to the East Indies and, fatefully, he arranged the passport of Vincent Kraft – the soon-to-be British double agent – as well.[23]

British authorities were familiar with Douwes Dekker's activities on behalf of Indian revolutionaries, so when Vincent Kraft alerted them to his plans to return to the East Indies in the fall of 1915, they monitored his every move. Douwes Dekker fell ill in Hong Kong on his way to Batavia and, when he recovered, the British put him on a ship to Singapore, where they arrested him as "a German spy and propagandist" on arrival.[24] While Douwes Dekker did not play a leading role in the German-Indian conspiracy, his involvement indicates that at least some anticolonial activists in the Dutch East Indies were attracted to the violent message of the Ghadar Party. Consul general Beckett was well aware of this and repeatedly sought to use the Douwes Dekker case to convince the Dutch that the security threat posed by the German-Indian conspiracy was not only relevant to British colonies but to the East Indies as well. While the Dutch did not respond to these admonitions to the satisfaction of Beckett, they were nevertheless happy to let the British keep Douwes Dekker away from Batavia by interning him in Tanglin Barracks, Singapore, for the rest of the war.

Yet the arrest of Douwes Dekker was not the most important detention that resulted from the information given by Oren and Kraft in the wake of the *Maverick* incident. Now that Beckett was armed with reliable information about who to watch and where individuals were going, between mid-October and December 1915 he was able to help facilitate the arrests of four men who, when interrogated by Singapore police, provided astonishingly detailed statements that exposed not only the details of the *Maverick's* journey but also how the German-Indian conspiracy functioned in Southeast Asia more generally.

---

[22] These newspapers were *Het Tijdschrift* and *De Expres*. van Dijk, *The Netherlands Indies and the Great War 1914–1918*, 47.

[23] van Dijk, *The Netherlands Indies and the Great War 1914–1918*, 346–347.

[24] Beckett to Earl Grey, November 18, 1915, Report 53464. Straits Settlements Original Correspondence: Foreign," 1915, CO 273/432; van Dijk, *The Netherlands Indies and the Great War 1914–1918*, 350.

The testimony of the four men demonstrated that the Helfferich brothers, about whom Beckett had been suspicious for months, were the key to the whole system. The Helfferich brothers were well placed to work on behalf of German government schemes to undermine British colonial rule from Batavia. Both men were wealthy and successful businessmen who had ties to most of the German community in the Dutch East Indies and beyond. Emil Helfferich, the elder of the two, had begun his career in Southeast Asia with Behn, Meyer & Company in 1899. Prior to the outbreak of the war he became director of the *Straits und Sunda Syndikat*, which was a company founded in 1910 to manage agricultural estates in Java and Sumatra, and which maintained – in his own words – "friendly" relations with Behn, Meyer & Company.[25] When the war broke out, he was stationed in Singapore. Two days after Britain entered the war, he and a group of other Germans tried to leave the island on a Dutch ship but were not allowed to sail. Instead, as we saw in Chapter 1, German citizens were required to remain in Singapore under a liberal interpretation of house arrest, as long as each signed a declaration promising not to engage in hostile activities. Helfferich did this and was allowed to continue his business until the exploits of the *Emden* inspired the government to intern German men at the Tanglin Barracks in November 1914. At some point shortly thereafter and prior to the mutiny that occurred in February 1915, Helfferich apparently escaped from Tanglin and made his way to Batavia to join his brother Theodor.[26]

The younger Theodor was director of Behn, Meyer & Company in Batavia, which had been turned into an independent company at the outbreak of war so its assets could be separated from its Singapore headquarters. Theodor was also commercial councilor to the German consul general in Batavia, which meant not only that he was next in line for the position but also that he had access to German cipher codes during the war.[27] Both brothers were also directly connected to the German government in Berlin. Their older brother, Karl, became Minister of Finance in 1915 and then from 1916–1917 was Minister of the Interior and Vice Chancellor.

In Batavia together by late 1914, Emil and Theodor used their wealth and connections in both Germany and Southeast Asia to aid the German war effort. They readily understood the strategic value of the neutral East Indies and sought to create there an organized center of communication and site for the distribution of arms, money, and propaganda. Their

[25] Quoted in van Dijk, *The Netherlands Indies and the Great War 1914–1918*, 325.
[26] van Dijk, *The Netherlands Indies and the Great War 1914–1918*, 325–326.
[27] van Dijk, *The Netherlands Indies and the Great War 1914–1918*, 326.

ability to shape German efforts in this regard was dramatically enhanced by the fact that the German consul general had just gone home on leave as the war was breaking out, leaving the inexperienced vice consul, Dr. Erich Winkels, in his place. The result, according to a German national in the East Indies, was that Helfferich "has succeeded in gaining virtual control, not only over the actual working of the Consulate, but also over German interests in general."[28] This was not an isolated opinion, but was corroborated by other Germans in the East Indies who were opposed to the Helfferichs' methods. Dr. Karl Gehrman, whose letter to the German government about the situation was intercepted by the British, believed the Helfferichs were motivated by economic gain. Regardless, Gehrman argued that "the personality of [Winkels] is so bound up with that of the brothers Helfferich – especially Mr. Emil H. – as to be considerably overshadowed by the latter."[29] As proof, Gehrman pointed to the fact that Winkels had recently gone to live with the Helfferich brothers.

Beckett had been deeply suspicious that the Helfferichs played an important and influential role in the German 'intrigues' taking place in the East Indies prior to the *Maverick* and *Henry S.* incidents. The problem had been a lack of concrete evidence. With the information provided by Oren, Kraft, and the four detainees captured in Singapore, both Beckett and his superiors believed they now had such evidence. Their information indicated that the Helfferichs were acting on behalf of the German government through the German consulate in Shanghai, that they were using German government funds to pay for anti-Allied activities, that they were in collaboration with Indian revolutionaries and other pro-German activists, that they were deeply involved in trying to ship arms from North America to India via the *Maverick* and other vessels, and that they were involved in a variety of plans to undermine British rule.

The first three arrests British authorities made in Singapore led to confessions that allowed them a detailed understanding about the geographical scope of the German-Indian conspiracy, several of the key individuals involved, and the nature of its links with already existing Indian

---

[28] Statement by Karl Freundlich, Report 43873. Straits Settlements Original Correspondence: Foreign, 1916. CO 273/449, 44. This was not exactly a "statement": it was an intercepted letter from Freundlich to the German government, which was included in the evidence against the Helfferich brothers. Freundlich was a critic of the Helfferichs, arguing that their bombastic behavior in Batavia had done serious damage to German reputations in the East Indies and also unnecessarily increased British surveillance there. Freundlich hoped to persuade the German government to appoint a new consul in January 1916.

[29] Statement by Karl Gehrman, Report 43873. Straits Settlements Original Correspondence: Foreign, 1916. CO 273/449, 41.

revolutionary movements. Let us take each in order, so that we can get a sense of the manner in which intelligence about the conspiracy unfolded.

The first to be arrested was Kumod Nath Mukerjie, a forty-two year old Brahmin lawyer from Calcutta. Mukerjie had arrived in Singapore from Batavia on his way back to Bangkok, where he lived and worked, on October 15, 1915. British authorities arrested him a few days later, and on October 23 he made a detailed confession.[30] As with all confessions made under duress, Mukerjie's – and the others who followed him – must be read carefully. There is no doubt that Mukerjie would have been afraid for his future and even his life, since he was a British colonial subject arrested for aiding an enemy in time of war. The charges were serious, and as a lawyer Mukerjie would have known this. This is no doubt why Mukerjie sought to portray himself as an innocent purveyor of information, unconnected to Indian revolutionary activity except through the acquaintances who ultimately landed him in a Singapore prison. Nevertheless, Mukerjie's statement corroborated information provided originally by Oren and Kraft, and was later substantiated in multiple ways by the other three detainees who themselves made confessions to the British authorities.

Mukerjie told British authorities that he had first come into contact with Indian revolutionaries by happenstance, while living in Bangkok. In March 1915, a friend of a friend – a Punjabi named Atma Ram – came to Bangkok, introduced himself, and the two struck up a friendship. Ram began to bring his own friends to see Mukerjie, who were mostly Punjabi and had recently come from the United States and Shanghai. Eventually, Ram told Mukerjie he was in Bangkok to see the German consul about getting a shipment of arms to India. Mukerjie was given to understand that one of Ram's fellow revolutionaries had already extracted a promise of arms from the German consul in Shanghai.[31] The consul in Bangkok assured Ram that arms and money were on their way, and that they should arrive in India on July 13, 1915 in a ship called the *Maverick*.[32] Atma Ram supposedly told Mukerjie that he needed to convey this information to his

---

[30]   Alan Johnstone, British Ambassador at the Hague, to Loudon, October 17, 1915, L16. Ministerie van Kolonien: Geheim Archief 1916, 2.10.36.51, Box 189, Nationaal Archief.

[31]   According to Uma Mukherjee, Virendranath Chattopadya of the Berlin Indian Independence Committee had communicated to revolutionaries in early 1915 that the Germans would support them in their revolutionary work during the war, though the decision had been made in Berlin at the start of the war. See her "Revolutionary Movement in Eastern India, 1914–1918," in Amitabha Mukherjee, ed., *Militant Nationalism in India, 1876–1947* (Calcutta: Institute of Historical Studies, 1995), 236.

[32]   Statement by Kumod Nath Mukerjie, Report 43873. Straits Settlements Original Correspondence: Foreign, 1916. CO 273/449, 46.

compatriots in Calcutta but was too afraid to go back to India because he was being watched. Ram then asked Mukerjie to take the message, since the British did not suspect him of revolutionary activity. In his confession, Mukerjie insisted that he agreed to make the trip only because he was in debt, and Atma Ram gave him enough money not only to travel but to pay off all his debts.

Mukerjie traveled to Calcutta sometime during the spring of 1915, found the contact to whom he had been directed, and delivered his message about the *Maverick* and its shipment of arms. This contact was fairly open about the revolutionary organization to which he belonged. He told Mukerjie that he was one of about 10,000 members, mostly young men, committed to ending British rule, and that they were divided by district and led by five or six men. As Mukerjie got ready to return to Bangkok, he received a message that one of the leaders wanted to meet him. Although Mukerjie did not learn the man's name at the time of the meeting, he later discovered that he went by the alias Martin, and that he was attended by a younger man who went by the name Payne.[33] Martin asked Mukerjie if he would go to Batavia before returning to Bangkok to deliver yet another message. Once again, they promised to pay, and Mukerjie agreed.

In Batavia, Mukerjie recalled, "I was to see in Batavia an Indian whose name they gave me as Silam [Abdul Selam], and to ask him to take me to a German named Helfferich.... I was to tell Helfferich that arms, ammunition and money promised to them by the Germans was not enough, and that they wanted more according to the promise made to them previously."[34] In addition, Mukerjie was to request an additional 300,000 rupees and 500 Germans who could train Indians in the use of the weapons.

Mukerjie finally arrived in Batavia on August 8, 1915. As we know, by that time the *Maverick* had already arrived, empty, and it was clear that the mission had failed. Nevertheless, Mukerjie made contact with both Helfferich and Selam. He learned that Selam (the same Abdul Selam who had been arrested for printing anti-British pamphlets in Chapter 3) was in the process of making plans to travel to India with money and instructions for an altogether new conspiracy, which would be financed with German funds through the Helfferichs.[35] However, the Dutch interned Selam

---

[33] Statement by Kumod Nath Mukerjie, Report 43873, 48. The man, Martin, was the future M.N. Roy, and the party to which he referred was the revolutionary Yugantar Party, which had recently united under the leadership of Jatindranath Mukherjee. Mukherjee, "Revolutionary Movement in Eastern India," 236.

[34] Statement by Kumod Nath Mukerjie, Report 43873, 48.

[35] Statement by Kumod Nath Mukerjie, Report 43873, 49.

shortly after Mukerjie's arrival, which obviously meant that he could not travel to India. Selam and the Helfferichs tried to salvage the situation by asking Mukerjie to bring the instructions for the conspiracy back to Calcutta. The necessary money, meanwhile, would be carried by a Chinese companion in the form of a bank draft tucked under a hat band.[36]

This last request was too much for Mukerjie, who thought the chances of being discovered were too great. According to his testimony, he refused. Shortly thereafter, the revolutionary leader he had met in Calcutta – who went by the name Martin – appeared in Batavia with his companion Payne. Martin was visibly irritated at Mukerjie's refusal to return to Calcutta but was not able to change his mind.[37] It was shortly after this, in mid-October, that Mukerjie left Batavia for Bangkok via Singapore. Beckett, having received a tip from Oren, warned the Singapore authorities, who in turn arrested Mukerjie after his arrival. Mukerjie ended his confession with a physical description of Martin, Payne, Atma Ram, and every other Indian with whom he had worked.

Just days after Mukerjie was arrested, on October 22, British authorities in Singapore also arrested Ong Sin Kwie, a Chinese merchant from Batavia. His brief confession, given on October 27, substantiated Mukerjie's claim that Helfferich was involved in the transfer of money for arms and demonstrated that Mukerjie's testimony about using a Chinese man as a carrier was accurate. According to Ong, he knew Helfferich in connection with the pepper trade. At some time in early October, Ong said that Helfferich asked him to call at his house. When Ong called that evening, Helfferich asked him if he would convey money to Singapore. When Ong objected that he did not speak English, Helfferich assured him that he would only need to transfer it by hand signal to a waiting Bengali. Helfferich also assured him that in the context of the war it was easier for Chinese people to travel without suspicion than for Indians.[38] As Ong prepared to make the journey, Helfferich told him that he also needed to take a letter along with the money, and also that Ong might need to convey both all the way to Calcutta. According to Ong, he and Helfferich negotiated for several days over the details, since Ong felt that carrying a letter and the money was extremely risky. Helfferich insisted that it was necessary, or else the man waiting for the message would not "know where and on what date he was to expect six ships."[39] Although

---

[36] Statement by Kumod Nath Mukerjie, Report 43873, 50–51.
[37] Statement by Kumod Nath Mukerjie, Report 43873, 51.
[38] Statement by Ong Sin Kwie, Report 43873, 38–39.
[39] Statement by Ong Sin Kwie, Report 43873, 39.

Ong insisted to the British that he did not know what was going to be on the ships, he admitted he thought it must be for a "bad purpose."[40] At the end of his confession, Ong also gave a physical description of an Indian man who had been at one of his meetings with Helfferich. From his description of a small, thin, clean-shaven, dark man with a long, thin face, the man matched Mukerjie's recent description of Martin.[41]

Taken together, Mukerjie and Ong's testimony seemed to confirm reports that the Helfferich brothers were directly involved in financing schemes to provide arms to revolutionary Indians. Mukerjie's longer confession also pointed to a network of German-Indian connections that stretched between North America and Shanghai, Bangkok, Batavia, and Calcutta – with the German consulate at each location functioning as the key node of communication, information, and financial remuneration.

But the arrest in November of Fanindra Kamur Chakravarti, alias William Arthur Payne, was even more illuminating. Chakravarti, who was arrested in Shanghai on November 24 and then brought to Singapore, made a confession on December 19. He was an especially important detainee because he had been the personal companion of Martin – one of the leaders of the Indian revolutionary movement with which Mukerjie had been acquainted. Chakravarti's statement not only confirmed the earlier confessions in terms of the involvement of the Helfferichs but also provided detailed and deeply incriminating evidence about the Indian revolutionaries – including Martin – involved in the scheme. Like Mukerjie, Chakravarti insisted that he himself was not a revolutionary, but rather that he was selected to convey information because he was innocent of any crimes against the British Raj. However, Chakravarti's own testimony seems to belie this claim, as his contacts from his early school years until his arrest read like a "who's who" of Indian revolutionaries in Bengal. For example, while living for a short time in Darjeeling in 1908 Chakravarti attended the moral lectures given by Jotindra Nath Mukerjie [Jatindranath Mukherjee] – who became one of the leaders of the revolutionary and vehemently anti-British Yugantar party in Bengal.[42] Later, when attending school in Calcutta, he joined the *Anusilan Samiti* with two of his cousins, which was one of dozens of cultural organizations (*samitis*) that had sprung up in Bengal in the early twentieth century to

---

[40] Statement by Ong Sin Kwie, Report 43873, 39.

[41] Statement by Ong Sin Kwie, Report 43873, 40. Mukerjie's description is on page 52.

[42] For more on the Yugantar party, see A.C. Bose, "Activities of Indian Revolutionaries Abroad, 1914–1918," and Uma Mukherjee, "Revolutionary Movement in Eastern India, 1914–1918," in Amitabha Mukherjee, ed., *Militant Nationalism in India, 1876–1947* (Calcutta: Institute of Historical Studies, 1995); also Hiren Chakrabarti, *Political Protest in Bengal: Boycott and Terrorism, 1905–1918* (Calcutta: Papyrus, 1992).

inculcate physical and mental self-help among Bengali men. Some of the *samitis* were also connected to secret revolutionary cells whose members were involved in bombings, assassinations, and robberies. The *Anusilan Samiti* was among the most notorious of these militant *samitis*, and in fact produced several militants who would go on to play important roles in the Ghadar movement.[43] In his statement, Chakravarti insisted that he only joined the *Anusilan Samiti* in order to take part in its physical education activities, but given his previous and future radical associations this assertion is open to question. In any case, Chakravarti did admit to becoming interested in politics beginning in 1912 in Calcutta. He and his friends used to gather together at a shop run by Saileswar Bose – another revolutionary and close associate of Jatindranath Mukerjie – to discuss various issues, and it was at this shop that he reconnected with a high-school acquaintance named Nornendra Nath Battacharji, who Chakravarti called Noren – better known in his later years as M.N. Roy.[44]

It is clear from Chakravarti's confession that he knew Noren was a proponent of political violence, or dacoities, as such acts were called in India. In fact, by the start of the war Noren had been working closely with Jatindranath Mukerjie – who Chakravarti called Jotin – for seven years already and had taken part in numerous dacoities, from shootings to robberies.[45] Chakravarti also knew about the close connection between Noren and Jotin, as he describes visiting Jotin in the company of Noren and coming to the realization that both men were revolutionaries.

Although Chakravarti knew about his friends' revolutionary beliefs, he maintained that he did not agree with them. Rather, he said he believed that the Indian people needed to be won over to the fight for independence, and that dacoities would simply alienate them. That, however, did not stop him from becoming a go-between for communications between revolutionaries associated with Jotin in early 1914, including especially Atul Ghose, who was being watched by the Indian police.[46]

---

[43] Maia Ramnath, "Two Revolutions: The Ghadar Movement and India's Radical Diaspora, 1913–1918," *Radical History Review*, no. 92 (2005), 19; see also Peter Heehs, *The Bomb in Bengal: The Rise of Revolutionary Terrorism in India, 1900–1910* (Delhi; New York: Oxford University Press, 1993); Dalia Ray, *The Bengal Revolutionaries and Freedom Movement* (New Delhi: Cosmo Publications, 1990).

[44] Statement by Fanindra Kumath Chakravarti, Report 43873, 31. Battacharji was also an active member of the *Anusilan Samiti*. See Samaren Roy, *M.N. Roy: A Political Biography* (Calcutta: Orient Longman Limited, 1997), 4.

[45] Samaren Roy, *M.N. Roy*, 5–6; Mukherjee, "Revolutionary Movement in Eastern India," 246.

[46] Statement by Fanindra Kumath Chakravarti, Report 43873, 32.

By early 1915, Chakravarti and Noren saw each other almost daily.[47] In March, Chakravarti recalled that Joti sent for him and, in the company of Noren, asked him to go to Batavia to see the German consul. According to Chakravarti, Jotin indicated that "the idea of getting money and arms [from] the Germans was the result of a message brought by some Indians from America . . . The man who brought the message said that someone from India should go to Batavia to see the German consul there, as that was the nearest place we could get in touch with the German authorities."[48] Chakravarti refused the request the first time, and thus Noren himself made the trip in April. While there, Noren made contact with the Helfferich brothers and arranged for the shipment of arms to Bengal on the *Maverick*.[49] At that point, Noren began to call himself by the alias C.A. Martin, which is the name by which the Helfferichs knew him.

Noren returned to Calcutta and made ready to receive the promised arms. When the *Maverick* failed to turn up, Noren returned to Batavia to find out why. This time he convinced Chakravarti to go with him under the alias William Arthur Payne, ostensibly because Chakravarti was still able to obtain a passport without arousing suspicion. The two men left India via Madras, where no one checked their papers, and proceeded to the city of Penang in British Malaya. From there they boarded a Chinese boat to Deli, Sumatra in the Dutch East Indies; and from Deli they sailed to Batavia.[50]

Once in Batavia, Chakravarti reported that Noren, or "Martin," met with the Helfferichs several times as they tried to arrange a new plan for shipping money and arms to India. During that time, Chakravarti confirmed having met with Kumod Nath Mukerji – who was arrested in Singapore in October – and to meeting an Indian man from New York who called himself Mohamed Ali who was also involved in the scheme. Throughout his journey with Noren, Chakravarti maintained that he was deeply skeptical about the chances such schemes had for success, and that he believed "Indians [from] outside promised things which the Indians

---

[47] This contact was interrupted in mid-February when Noren took part in the audacious Garden Reach dacoity – a robbery in broad daylight – and had to go underground for a while. See Prakash Chandra, *Political Philosophy of M.N. Roy* (New Delhi: Sarup & Sons, 1992), 21.

[48] Statement by Fanindra Kumath Chakravarti, Report 43873, 35. Virendranath Chattopadya had apparently sent the message from Berlin. Mukherjee, "Revolutionary Movement in Eastern India," 245.

[49] This visit is confirmed by all the other testimony collected by the British government, and also in Roy's biographies. See Kris Manjapra, *M.N. Roy: Marxism and Colonial Cosmopolitanism* (New Delhi: Routledge, 2010), 8–9.

[50] Statement by Fanindra Kumath Chakravarti, Report 43873, 35.

in India cannot perform."[51] Eventually, Chakravarti said his lack of faith in the enterprise led him to ask Noren for permission to leave Batavia and the whole arms-shipping business. Chakravarti testified that Noren assented only on the condition that he first travel to Shanghai to meet with the German consul. Whether Chakravarti intended abandoning the scheme after that or not was moot – he never made it to the German consul and was picked up instead by the French police in Shanghai and turned over to the British.[52]

Clearly, Mukerjie, Ong, and Chakravarti each hoped to portray themselves in the most innocent light possible, as mere bearers of messages or money, and as reluctant participants. In spite of this, their testimony sheds light on the structure of connections between Indians and Germans involved in conspiring against British rule during the war. Each of their statements corroborate the involvement of the Helfferichs and Martin in what was obviously an attempt to ship arms, money, and ammunition to India from North America via the Dutch East Indies. The testimony is also revealing about how information and individuals traveled between the East Indies and India itself. For one thing, we are able to get a sense for how slow and unreliable communications among the various parties had to be in a wartime environment in which telegrams and letters were subject to being intercepted at any point along the way. While the various parties involved could (and did) use the telegraph for urgent messages, this was normally only considered worth the risk when communicating with German consulates in cipher. If Indian revolutionaries wanted to be sure of their communications, they needed to send individuals who could bring messages back and forth in person. Such a system was, by its nature, extremely slow and subject to all kinds of delays and problems. This was all the more true for Indian revolutionaries who sought to leave or reenter India, since British authorities kept a close eye on many Indian ports, and the various British consuls around the world reported the movement of Indians who came to their attention. This was no doubt the reason that Mukerjie, Noren, and Chakravarti all left India via Madras, where surveillance was much more relaxed than in northern

---

[51] Statement by Fanindra Kumath Chakravarti, Report 43873, 36. In fact, many Ghadarites encountered this kind of skepticism when they arrived in India in late 1914 and 1915, and frequently experienced a cool – even hostile – reception from Indians who had remained in India. Maya Gupta, "Revolutionary Movement in Northern India, 1914–1918," in Amitabha Mukherjee, ed., *Militant Nationalism in India, 1876–1947* (Calcutta: Institute of Historical Studies, 1995), 275.

[52] Alan Johnstone, British Ambassador at the Hague, to Loudon, October 17, 1915, L16. Ministerie van Kolonien: Geheim Archief 1916, 2.10.36.51, Box 189, Nationaal Archief.

ports like Calcutta.[53] Even after they successfully left India, their routes had to be carefully planned for avoiding suspicion, as when Noren and Chakravarti had to first travel to Penang before proceeding indirectly to Batavia in neutral Chinese and Dutch ships. Given the obstacles to efficient communication and the enormous geographical areas involved in these anticolonial plans, it is surprising they were able to move forward as far as they did. And in fact, we know from the testimony collected in Singapore and in numerous other sources that Indians from North America had gone to India to encourage collaboration with the Germans. We also know that Indians traveling from both North America and India made contact with one another in a variety of locations around the world, including Manila, Bangkok, Shanghai, and of course, the Dutch East Indies.

Equally revealing in the testimony of Mukerjie and Chakravarti was that the Indian revolutionaries who were engaged in working with the Helfferichs were not neophytes who came to their ideas via German inspiration. Rather, the men who were trying to coordinate the shipment of arms to India – especially Jatindranath Mukerjie and Nornendra Nath Battacharji – were seasoned leaders of organized revolutionary groups that had been active years before the war began.[54] Chakravarti in particular exposed the involvement of his mentors and friends from the Yugantar Party and *Anusilan Samitra*, which advocated overthrowing the British by violent means. It could even be said that Noren, alias Martin, was already a hardened revolutionary by the time he went to Batavia to meet with the Helfferichs for the first time, having already taken part in numerous armed robberies and even assassinations. As such, it is important to keep in mind that the Indians involved in conspiracies with the Germans were hardly puppets. Rather, they saw the German desire to undermine colonial rule in India as an opportunity to gain the funds and the equipment necessary for a goal they had been pursuing for the last decade.[55]

In addition to Mukerjie, Ong, and Chakravarti, Singapore authorities made one other critical arrest in connection with the *Maverick*. This was John B. Starr-Hunt, the ship's purser, a twenty-three-year-old American who worked for the German-owned American firm (F. Jebson & Company) that had hired the ship. Starr-Hunt was originally detained

---

[53] Popplewell, *Intelligence and Imperial Defence*, 170.

[54] For the internationalism of these revolutionary groups, see Kris Manjapra, *Age of Entanglement: German and Indian Intellectuals Across Empire* (Cambridge: Harvard University Press, 2013), chapter 2.

[55] Heehs, *The Bomb in Bengal*, 248.

on November 27, 1916 as he was passing through Singapore on his way
back to the United States. The conditions of his initial detention were
liberal, no doubt owing to his social status and racial privilege, as he was
allowed to stay at the well-appointed Raffles Hotel as long as he promised
not to get in touch with enemy contacts.[56] However, he broke this condition on December 2 and 3, 1915 by writing letters of warning to Emil
Helfferich, and when Singapore authorities got wind of it they held him
under close arrest. Starr-Hunt finally made a full and detailed statement
about his role in the affair in May 1916.[57] His testimony clearly outlined
the German and Indian interests that led to the failed *Maverick* and *Annie
Larsen* affair in the United States and corroborated previous testimony
implicating the role of the Helfferichs and a variety of other Germans
and Indians in Batavia. In fact, Starr-Hunt later became a key witness
for the prosecution in the San Francisco Hindu-German conspiracy trial
against the Ghadar party in 1917–1918, which convicted the Helfferichs
in absentia.

Starr-Hunt gave his statement to the investigator in Singapore, Hector
Kothavala, over a period of eight days.[58] For most of the first four days,
Starr-Hunt related his experience on board the *Maverick* in great detail,
from the time he was given the job as purser until the ship was finally
moored at Tanjung Priok near Batavia. At the start of the journey in
the United States Starr-Hunt's German boss, Mr. Jebson, gave him a
sealed envelope addressed to the captain of the *Annie Larsen*, who was
supposed to take Starr-Hunt's place on board when the two ships made
their rendezvous at Socorro Island.[59] As we know, the ships never met,
and eventually the *Maverick* went to Java without any cargo. When the
Maverick neared Anjer, Starr-Hunt decided to finally read the secret
letter so he would know what to do once he arrived. The letter gave
instructions for how to store the cargo of rifles – once transshipped from
the *Annie Larsen* – in the large, empty oil tanks on the *Maverick*. It also
indicated that the *Maverick* should not try to avoid contact with British
warships, but that if the cargo were discovered and the ship about to be
captured, the captain was to sink the ship. Finally, the letter indicated

---

[56] Starr-Hunt's father was a leading American lawyer in Mexico. Statement by John B.
Starr-Hunt, Report 43873, 12.

[57] Alan Johnstone, British Ambassador at the Hague, to Loudon, October 17, 1915,
L16. Ministerie van Kolonien: Geheim Archief 1916, 2.10.36.51, Box 189, Nationaal
Archief.

[58] Kothavala was a highly skilled interrogator and was able to handle both Starr-Hunt and
also Vincent Kraft, the informant. Kothavala was a Parsi who had been a police officer
in Bombay but was seconded to Singapore at the request of General Ridout in April
1915. Popplewell, *Intelligence and Imperial Defence*, 263.

[59] Statement by John B. Starr-Hunt, Report 43873, 13.

that the *Maverick* would be met at Anjer by a friendly boat, whose crew would give them further instructions.[60]

When Starr-Hunt had been in Hawaii en route with the *Maverick*, the German captain who told the crew that the mission was to be abandoned instructed him that, once the ship arrived in Batavia, he was to seek out a man named Helfferich at Behn Meyer & Company and deliver a sealed package. Once the *Maverick* arrived at Tanjung Priok, Starr-Hunt had no difficulty finding the Helfferichs. As instructed, he gave Theodore the package, which contained an enciphered letter.[61] After that, Starr-Hunt remained in Batavia for about four months, and during that time he saw the Helfferich brothers repeatedly. Emil told him that he had waited for the *Maverick* in the Sunda Strait near Anjer for three weeks and had been mightily displeased when it did not show up. Emil also took control of the finances for the *Maverick* and its crew through Starr-Hunt, paying for the crew's wages, fees for the ship, and anything Starr-Hunt asked for. In total, Emil Helfferich paid out about 24,000 guilders to the young purser for expenses related to the *Maverick*. Helfferich also told Starr-Hunt of his repeated telegrams with the German consul at Shanghai over the fate of the *Maverick*, since it could not be moved out of Tanjung Priok without fear of being captured by British warships.[62]

Among the many incidents Starr-Hunt observed in and around the Helfferichs' house was an intense set of meetings toward the end of October 1915 between the Helfferichs and other prominent Germans in the East Indies. The meetings were secret and thus Starr-Hunt was not present for them, but according to his testimony Emil Helfferich let him know that "they had not despaired of success yet."[63] Starr-Hunt gathered that another voyage was in preparation, involving yet more German money, which seemed to be confirmed by the fact that two of the Germans disappeared from Batavia soon afterwards. Among those present at the meetings was August Diehn, whom we know from Chapter 1 as the manager of Behn, Meyer & Company in Singapore and as an escapee from Tanglin barracks during the mutiny of the 5th Light Infantry. In conversation, Diehn told Starr-Hunt about his difficult journey from Singapore to Batavia in the aftermath of the mutiny.

Starr-Hunt's testimony also corroborated and added to the testimony about "Martin" given by Mukerjie and Chakravarti. British authorities had not been able to discover the whereabouts of Martin, whom they

---

[60] Statement by John B. Starr-Hunt, Report 43873, 21.
[61] Statement by John B. Starr-Hunt, Report 43873, 22.
[62] Statement by John B. Starr-Hunt, Report 43873, 23–24.
[63] Statement by John B. Starr-Hunt, Report 43873, 25.

very much wanted to detain for questioning. Not only did Starr-Hunt confirm Martin's involvement with the Helfferichs, but Starr-Hunt himself assisted in an exchange of identities between Hari Singh – one of the Ghadar party members who had traveled with Starr-Hunt from the United States – and Martin. Having exchanged passports, Martin traveled on to Manila with a message to the German consul there and then eventually made his way to the United States.[64]

When we step back and consider the testimony of all four detained men together with the information provided by Oren and Kraft, the role of the Dutch East Indies in the German-Indian conspiracy comes into sharper focus. All of the sources locate the Helfferich brothers as central figures in coordinating anti-British plans between North America and India. Their strong managerial interest in Behn, Meyer & Company lends credibility to British suspicions that the Singapore branch was being used to provide aid to the *Emden* in the fall of 1914, as does their continuing connection with August Diehn. Their association with Abdul Selam [Silam], as noted by two of the detainees, points to the involvement of the Helfferichs and the German government in facilitating the spread of anti-British, pan-Islamic propaganda from the neutral East Indies. And all of the sources except Ong indicate that the Helfferichs were deeply connected with the German consular network in the United States, Manila, and Shanghai. Further, they indicate that the Helfferichs had access to German government money to pay for arms, ammunition, travel expenses, and propaganda in the effort to undermine British colonial rule.

The Problems of Neutrality and the Dutch Response

By November 1915 consul general Beckett, General Ridout, and their superiors believed they had all the evidence they needed to prove, beyond a shadow of a doubt, that Germans acting on behalf of their government were violating Dutch neutrality by conspiring to commit hostile acts from the East Indies. Their confidence was due in large part to the *Maverick* and the subsequent arrests associated with it. In addition, during the time Singapore authorities were interrogating Mukerjie, Ong, and Chakravarti, new information continued to come to light in both Singapore and the Dutch East Indies that pointed to a much larger conspiracy. Yet in spite of this growing mountain of evidence, Dutch authorities in the East Indies refused to bring charges against powerful Germans like

---

[64] Statement by John B. Starr-Hunt, Report 43873, 28.

the Helfferichs. Whereas the Dutch understood that the sacrifice of individual Indians could improve Anglo-Dutch relations while also working in favor of Dutch interests, the same could not be said about the sacrifice of Germans. When Germans were directly involved, Dutch authorities feared that any action against them might threaten Dutch neutrality. As we shall see, this situation allowed influential Germans in the East Indies – and those with whom they were closely associated – the freedom to continue plotting against the Allies. Ironically, one result of this was that the war from which Dutch authorities wanted so desperately to remain aloof continued to intrude on the life of the colony for much of the war.

The revelations about the role of the Indies in the German-Indian conspiracy provided by those arrested in conjunction with the *Maverick* were enhanced and deepened by related intelligence over the course of 1915 and 1916. In September 1915, for example, Consul General Beckett discovered that one of the German passengers who had been aboard the ill-fated *Henry S.*, G.P. Boehm, had made his way to Batavia. By keeping track of his movements, Beckett knew of his intention to proceed to Singapore and, as he had done with Vincent Kraft, alerted the authorities there. When Boehm arrived in Singapore on September 25, he was detained and interrogated. His statement indicated that he was a former German soldier who had naturalized to the United States at the beginning of the century. In early 1915 he had become friendly with Indians in Chicago and then San Francisco, and these men had hired Boehm "to train men for the campaign against India."[65] From San Francisco, he had gone to Manila with the leader of the *Henry S.* expedition, A. Wehde, and had gotten stuck with the ship when it developed engine trouble. Although nothing came of the expedition, Boehm's statement nevertheless added depth to British assertions that simultaneous plans via both the *Henry S.* and the *Maverick* to send armaments and people to India had only recently been foiled.

Also in September, Beckett employed two Indian agents to uncover information about the involvement of Indians "and others" involved in producing anti-British propaganda and sentiment in the East Indies. The first, Mathura Das, had already traveled around Java and had visited Abdul Selam at his internment camp on the island of Timor. According to Beckett, Selam had provided Das with significant information regarding such anti-British activities. The second agent, Rahim Baksh, had been sent by the British ambassador at Tokyo. In late October, Baksh

---

[65] Beckett to Sir Edward Grey, October 28, 1915, Report 57320. Straits Settlements Original Correspondence: Foreign and India, 1915, 2.

was on a mission to uncover information from the Turkish and German consuls, and also from the head of the very large Arab community in Batavia. According to Beckett, the latter "was an open adherent of German designs and plots." Beckett hoped that Baksh's information not only would expose anti-British activity but also would help convince the Dutch to take an interest in Arab activity since he believed they were "wholly bent on revolution not only against Great Britain, but against the Netherlands government here."[66] And it wasn't just Indians and Arabs that were of concern. In early November, Beckett wrote that his informers had been able to ascertain:

as an unquestionable fact, that in the three largest islands of the Netherlands East Indies . . . each residency or district has at least one German . . . whose duties are to collect funds for the prosecution of the conspiracy, to distribute and keep an account of these funds and of the moneys devoted to the purpose by the German Government which . . . represent a very large sum, to assist in the distribution of arms which the Netherlands East Indies Government are with complacency allowing.[67]

To substantiate these claims, Beckett included a list of sixteen of "the most active conspirators," many of whom were German and Austrian businessmen from places like Surabaya and Bandung whom he had not mentioned in previous reports. Of those who had been mentioned before, August Diehn came in for particular condemnation. This man, "the dangerous escapee" who had been manager of Behn, Meyer & Company at Singapore, was now an "arch-conspirator." According to Beckett's sources, not only was Diehn a member of the Helfferichs' inner circle, but he also "openly takes with him on his travels throughout the Netherlands East Indies a chest containing a wireless instrument" capable at least of receiving, and some believed of transmitting, wireless messages.[68]

To cap off the seemingly endless supply of information regarding anti-British plots from Dutch territory, Beckett's secret informer Oren reappeared after a two-month absence to inform him of a new plan to foment an armed uprising against British colonial interests. Before Oren would hand over the information, he negotiated a new "contract" with Beckett – with the assent of the Singapore authorities – that would entitle him to an advance payment of 50,000 guilders, and then an eventual

---

[66] Beckett to Sir Edward Grey, October 28, 1915, Report 57320. Straits Settlements Original Correspondence: Foreign and India, 1915, 4.

[67] Beckett to Sir Edward Grey, November 8, 1915, Report 58774. Straits Settlements Original Correspondence: Foreign and India, 1915, 1.

[68] Beckett to Sir Edward Grey, November 8, 1915, Report 58774, 1.

reward of either 200,000 or 300,000 guilders.[69] Once Oren had received his advance, he handed Beckett a letter detailing plans for a rebellion of prisoners in a British prison colony in the Nicobar Islands. According to Oren's sources, a ship laden with arms had already been landed somewhere in the Nicobar Islands, its cargo unloaded and ready for retrieval. On Christmas Day 1915, a German ship sailing from the Dutch port of Sabang (Sumatra) with about 200 soldiers would land at the prison colony, liberate the approximately 250 Indian soldiers there, load the waiting arms, and then proceed to Rangoon, Burma to act against the British government there.[70] The plot did not succeed. It did, however, demonstrate yet again to British authorities that Germans and Indians continued to foment active plans to undermine British rule from neutral Dutch territory.[71]

Yet Beckett's repeated attempts to convince the Dutch East Indies government to bring charges against the Helfferichs and the other alleged German conspirators during the fall of 1915 were in vain. On November 8 he confided in Grey that Idenburg was rumored – even by well-known Dutch residents in the Indies – to have pro-German sympathies. Beckett was careful not to endorse such a view wholeheartedly. Rather, he said, "whatever his sentiments, neither he nor his council are disposed to do more than to assert their neutrality and, at the same time, to shut their eyes firmly against any attempts on my part to prove that Germans are abusing that neutrality."[72]

Beckett's frustration with the Dutch authorities was echoed by his superiors in Singapore and London. But a few months later, after Starr-Hunt gave his detailed statement to the Singapore authorities in May 1916, General Ridout thought they finally had an airtight case with which to convince the Dutch authorities to bring charges against the Helfferichs. Ridout composed a long memorandum of allegations against both Theodore and Emil Helfferich, liberally interspersed with quotations by a wide range of informants. To this Becket added several of his previous memoranda from late 1915, a letter written by the Governor General of Singapore in January 1916, the full statements of Mukerjie, Ong, Chakravarti, and Starr-Hunt, and the two intercepted letters from K.W. Freundlich and K. Gehrmann. Beckett then sent the whole thing to the head of the newly created *Politieke Inlichtingendienst* (Political

---

[69] Agreement between W.R.D. Beckett and 'Oren,' Report 58774. Straits Settlements Original Correspondence: Foreign and India, 1915, 3.

[70] Letter from 'Oren,' Report 58774, 3–4.

[71] Manjapra, "The Ilusions of Encounter,"363–82.

[72] Beckett to Edward Grey, November 8, 1915, Report 58774, 2. Kees van Dijk argues that Idenburg was not, in fact, pro-German.

Intelligence Department), Captain W. Muurling, whose job was to investigate threats to Dutch neutrality.[73]

On June 6 Muurling, having read the material, came to see Beckett in his Batavia office. Beckett described his surprise when Muurling told him that he didn't think there was enough evidence to convict the Helfferich brothers. So deep was his surprise that "I could not conceal from him a certain amount of indignation at his taking this view in face of what appeared to me the most complete and convincing proof of facts and intentions ever recorded against two individuals in time of war."[74] Beckett also told Muurling, who was on his way to see the new Governor General of the Dutch East Indies, Count von Limburg Stirum, that the British government was not going to be happy if this evidence were rejected by the Dutch without very good reason. He also reminded Muurling that this was a prime opportunity for the Dutch "to rid themselves once and for all" of two men who were not only a threat to the British, but to the East Indies as well.

Beckett's admonitions didn't seem to have much of an effect, however, because when he met with Limburg Stirum three days later, the Governor General said he thought "the case was a weak one, and in his opinion would not succeed."[75] Beckett then asked Limburg Stirum to read the whole memorandum he had prepared, and outlined some if its main features. At the end of the interview the Governor General assured Beckett that "it was his duty, and one which he would strictly perform, to prevent any person from using this country as a base of operations against Great Britain."[76] He went on to say, however, that if charges were filed against the Helfferichs, he was certain that the German government would demand to review the evidence on which the charges were

---

[73] The PID was launched in May 1916 ostensibly to guard against threats to Dutch neutrality, but also to monitor Japanese activity in the East Indies. Takashi Shiraishi, "A New Regime of Order: The Origin of Modern Surveillance Politics in Indonesia," in James Siegel and Audrey Kahin, eds., *Southeast Asia Over Three Generations: Essays Presented to Benedict R. O'G. Anderson* (Ithaca: Cornell Southeast Asia Program Publications), 54. See also Harry Poeze, "Political Intelligence in the Netherlands Indies," in Robert Cribb, ed., *The Late Colonial State in Indonesia: Political and Economic Foundations of the Netherlands Indies, 1880–1942* (Leiden: KITLV Press, 1994). Magda van Gestel makes the point that the PID was originally created to counter potential Japanese espionage during the war, in "Japanse Spionage in Nederlands-Indië: de Oprichting van de Politieke Inlichtingen Dienst (PID) in 1916," in Elspeth Locher-Scholten, *Beelden van Japan in Het Vooroorlogse Nederlands Indië* (Leiden: Werkgroep Europese Expansie, 1987).

[74] Beckett to Edward Grey, June 14, 1916, Report 43873. Straits Settlements Original Correspondence: Foreign, 1916. CO 273/449, 1.

[75] Beckett to Edward Grey, June 14, 1916, Report 43873, 2.

[76] Beckett to Edward Grey, June 14, 1916, Report 43873, 2.

based. Nevertheless, Limburg Stirum promised to read the documents carefully.

Nothing happened. Having received no satisfaction on the matter in the East Indies, in September 1916 the Foreign Office instructed its ambassador at the Hague, Alan Johnstone, to refer the material directly to the Dutch government. To underscore the seriousness of the matter, Johnstone was instructed to say that "His Majesty's government must hold the Netherlands government responsible for any prejudice caused to British interests by the machinations disclosed."[77] Johnstone duly sent a strongly worded letter on October 17, which not only included the warning but also stated that the materials provided "afford conclusive proof, if any be still needed, of the fact that the brothers Helfferich and other Germans have been using the Netherland East Indies as a base for the promotion of a revolution in India."[78] A month later, the Dutch foreign minister replied that they were still awaiting a response from Limburg Stirum about the materials, but added that the Dutch government had no reason to presume that the East Indies government would not have been diligent in preventing any attacks directed toward British India within its jurisdiction.[79] Loudon's confidence, however, was only partly for show. On the same day he wrote to Johnstone, he also confided to the Dutch colonial minister that although he could not be certain of the trustworthiness of the evidence provided by the British ambassador, "I cannot deny that the statements, especially the one by Starr-Hunt, strike me as reliable."[80]

The East Indian government finally initiated a formal inquiry of the affair in 1917. The inquiry concluded that it could find nothing illegal in the actions of the Helfferichs or any other Germans. Theodore Helfferich and the German consul general, Windels, had refused to give up their correspondence about the *Maverick* to the inquiry, because they argued that doing so would reveal secret German codes. They insisted that since no arms had ever been found, they could not be prosecuted. The Dutch agreed. They also convinced the Dutch attorney-general that Ong Sin Kwee had traveled to Singapore on legitimate business, and that Emil Helfferich had only gone to meet the *Maverick* to warn it.[81] Instead of being disciplined and interned like the British wanted, Emil Helfferich

---

[77] Cover letter, September 12, 1916, Report 43873.
[78] Alan Johnstone, British Ambassador at the Hague, to Loudon, October 17, 1915, L16. Ministerie van Kolonien: Geheim Archief 1916, 2.10.36.51, Box 189, Nationaal Archief.
[79] Loudon to Johnstone, November 20, 1916, L16.
[80] Loudon to Pleyte, November 20, 1916, L16.
[81] Van Dijk, *The Netherlands Indies and the Great War 1914–1918*, 337.

remained an influential figure in the German community in the East Indies for another eleven years before returning to Germany as a wealthy man.

The Dutch response to the case against the Helfferichs was similar in many respects to their approach throughout the war. The main concern, right from the beginning, was to avoid getting pulled into the war. Were they to be pulled in on the Allied side, they risked German aggression in the Netherlands themselves and also in the East Indies. Were they to be pulled in on the side of the Central Powers, they risked attack in the Indies not only by the British but also by the Japanese. The geographical location of the East Indies was unfortunate for a state that wished to remain neutral during the Great War, because the islands were both strategically close to Singapore and British Malaya and were also a natural stopping point between North America and India. Add to its strategic location an already large and influential German population living in the Indies themselves, and maintaining the peace became a delicate and difficult balancing act. Dutch authorities no doubt worried that it would have been extremely difficult to prosecute and intern Germans as influential and well-connected as the Helfferichs and their compatriots without bringing down the ire of the German government on the East Indies. Politically, they could afford to cooperate with the British when it came to revolutionary Indians like Abdul Selam or their own part-Javanese Ernest Douwes Dekker, but not when it came to German nationals.

But while the British were never impressed with Dutch management of anti-Allied activity in its territories, it is entirely inaccurate to say they did nothing at all. Rather, in nearly every situation the Dutch responded to British complaints by sending warships, conducting investigations, and carrying out prosecutions where the evidence was clear. In fact, the management of war-related matters consumed an inordinate amount of time and energy for the Dutch authorities, particularly when they threatened to add to internal unrest. And at the end of 1916, the Dutch finally agreed to an all-out ban of shipments of arms to the East Indies – a measure the British had been requesting for nearly two years.[82]

We should also remember that the Dutch hardly had reason to do more for the British than the minimum required to maintain their neutrality. As we saw in Chapter 3, the Allied blockade of Germany and the trade restrictions imposed on the East Indies significantly damaged the East Indian economy. Not only that, Allied attempts to curtail communications among its enemies involved deeply invasive procedures with regard to the supervision of mail, telegrams, and individual travel. From the

---

[82] Van Dijk, *The Netherlands Indies and the Great War 1914–1918*, 334.

Dutch perspective, the British were at once begging for fair treatment under the terms of international neutrality laws, while at the same time restricting a wide variety of Dutch liberties. This situation, combined with their strong distrust of the Japanese, did not lend itself to an abundance of sympathy for the Allies.

British concerns over the use of the Dutch East Indies by Germans and Indians did not decrease in 1917, even though the number of crises diminished significantly. In hindsight, we now know that German-financed plans to foment revolution in India that had once seemed so hopeful were increasingly seen, by both Germans and Indians, as impractical. Early divisions between Germans and Indians that had once seemed possible to paper over now seemed insoluble, and German interest began to focus elsewhere.[83] But at the time, British authorities in Southeast Asia continued to worry about enemy plans to foment unrest in its territories. Even the entry of the United States into the war and its sudden about-face with regard to the Ghadar Party did not change this. Despite the fact that United States authorities immediately arrested the leaders of the Ghadar Party for conspiracy to breach U.S. neutrality in May 1917, British authorities in Southeast Asia anticipated continuing problems from an influx of conspirators who would now move to the East Indies from North America and the Philippines. Once in the East Indies, the British feared they would redouble their efforts to produce and disseminate anti-British propaganda. These worries had very real effects on the Indies: in mid-1917 the British government declared that Dutch ships could no longer carry any letters at all, unless they were official or commercial and had received prior permission. Now, all Dutch letters from the Indies had to be sent on British or French ships from Singapore after having been processed by the censor, which meant that Dutch ships had to transport all of its ordinary post to Singapore before it could be moved to its intended destination.[84]

While British authorities were never able to get satisfaction for what they believed were clear violations of Dutch neutrality during wartime, they were eventually vindicated by the proceedings of an American court in San Francisco thousands of miles away. Between November 1917 and April 1918, the U.S. government brought thirty-five Germans and Indians to trial in San Francisco in what became known as the Hindu German Conspiracy Trial. The trial was the longest-running and most expensive in the history of the United States to that point and involved

---

[83] Manjapra, "The Ilusions of Encounter," 373. Manjapra argues that German interest began to wane as early as the autumn of 1915.
[84] Van Dijk, *The Netherlands Indies and the Great War 1914–1918*, 408.

the release of abundant evidence – including the testimony of J.B. Starr-Hunt himself – documenting the multiple ways Germans and Indians had tried to undermine British colonial rule via schemes that involved actors from North America to India.[85] The Dutch East Indies featured largely in this evidence, as did the Helfferich brothers who were indicted, along with many others around the world, *in absentia*. At the end of the trial, on April 30, 1918, all of the defendants were found guilty of "being members of a conspiracy to commit a breach of American neutrality by setting on foot a military enterprise against the British administration in India."[86] And while British authorities were not pleased at what they believed were light sentences for the guilty, they were satisfied that the evidence "proved clearly that Batavia was one of the principal scenes of the conspiracy."[87] In fact, they were not above rubbing the noses of the Dutch in it by sending the Minister of Foreign Affairs a copy of the memorandum stating exactly that, accompanied by a snarky cover letter by the British ambassador. On August 28, 1918, just a few months before the end of the war, the ambassador wrote the Minister that he had been instructed:

to remind you of the correspondence exchanged in 1916 between Your Excellency and my predecessor on the subject of the use of the Netherland East Indies as a base for German intrigues against India and to transmit to you the enclosed copy of a Memorandum of the evidence produced at the "Ghadr" trial at San Francisco which establishes the use of Dutch colonial territory for this purpose.[88]

After perusing the memorandum, the Dutch Foreign Minister wrote the Colonial Minister to say that he could not deny that the actions of the Helfferich brothers in the East Indies had been "very suspicious."[89] Even taking into account British tendencies to be overzealous in their pursuit of conspirators, the weight of all the evidence clearly indicates that the Dutch East Indies had been crucial to the design and execution of the German-Indian conspiracy. The fact that very few of these schemes were successful is not the point: rather, the point is the sheer scale of war-related activity that occurred in this Southeast Asian colony that was not even belligerent. The point, in other words, is that even though the East Indies never formally took part in the war, the war certainly played a very big role in the East Indies.

---

[85] Ramnath, *Haj to Utopia*, 78 passim.
[86] Report F9, Ministerie van Kolonien: Geheim Archief, 1918, 2.10.36.51, Box 201, Nationaal Archief.
[87] Report F9, Ministerie van Kolonien: Geheim Archief, 1918, 2.10.36.51.
[88] Report F9, Ministerie van Kolonien: Geheim Archief, 1918, 2.10.36.51.
[89] September 9, 1918, Report F9, Ministerie van Kolonien: Geheim Archief, 1918, 2.10.36.51.

Conclusion

The journey of the *Maverick*, combined with the corroborating evidence about other schemes provided by Oren and other informers, was crucial in exposing both the truly global nature of the German-Indian conspiracy and the central role of the Dutch East Indies within it. At the same time, British demands that Dutch authorities take action against the Germans implicated in the *Maverick's* mission and in other anti-Allied activities highlighted Dutch reluctance to prosecute German nationals in the Indies even in the face of compelling evidence. When push came to shove, the Dutch were not willing to risk their neutrality by angering powerful Germans in their midst. Taken in isolation, we can see how this situation ensured the continuing centrality of the Dutch East Indies to German-Indian plans to disrupt colonial rule in Malaya and India, and also how the war continually intruded on the East Indies themselves. Taken together with German schemes in Siam and China, which are the subjects of Chapters 5 and 6, we are able to grasp the scale and scope of the multiple ways the war came to Southeast Asia.

5   Siam and the Anti-Allied Conspiracies

Twelve days after the Singapore Mutiny, on February 27, 1915, the consul-general in Bangkok – T.H. Lyle – wrote the Foreign and Political Department in India that "there may be some intimate connection between the efforts of Indian political agitators [in Siam] and the recent outbreak of Indian troops in Singapore."[1] According to Lyle, a credible source indicated that a "well-educated leader of the Indian revolutionary movement" had been in Bangkok in January 1915 and had then gone to Singapore "to cause a rising among the Indian troops."[2] Moreover, he added, the General Advisor to the Siamese Government had recently told Lyle that Germans in Siam were anxiously anticipating a general Indian uprising that was supposed to occur in late February or early March.[3]

Whether or not Lyle's information was accurate, its importance for our purposes is in the way it linked Indian revolutionaries in Siam not only with disturbances in Singapore but also with hostile Germans seeking to disrupt British colonial rule. As it turned out, the route between North America, the East Indies, and India discussed in Chapters 3 and 4 was only one of the paths through which Indian revolutionaries and Germans sought to smuggle arms and insurgents to India through Southeast Asia. A second route was through Siam – an independent state sandwiched between British Burma to the west, British Malaya to the south, and French Indochina to the east.[4] Like its northern neighbor China, Siam remained neutral during the war until summer 1917. As in all neutral

---

[1] Letter from Consul-General T.H. Lyle to the Secretary to the Government in India in the Foreign and Political Department, February 27, 1915. Report 20829, Straits Settlements Original Correspondence: Foreign, CO 273/430.

[2] The source was a German correspondent, who had reported this tale in the *Bangkok Times* on February 24, 1915. Report 20829.

[3] T.H. Lyle to the Secretary to the Government in India in the Foreign and Political Department, February 27, 1915. Report 20829. The General Advisor at this time was Wolcott Pitkin, a Harvard-educated American.

[4] There was to be a third, northern, route as well, through Afghanistan, though this route is outside the scope of this book. A.C. Bose, "Activities of Indian Revolutionaries Abroad,

countries or colonies, Siamese neutrality meant that the diplomatic and business interests of both the Central Powers and the Allies continued to operate there after hostilities commenced. As a result, Siam provided – at least initially – a staging ground from which anti-Allied colonial activists and representatives of the Central Powers could operate with relative impunity.

Siam was strategically important to those who sought to undermine Allied colonial rule because of its unique geography. To its east lay Indochina, the most important French colony in Asia, while to its west lay Burma, which not only was a British colony but also allowed overland access to Britain's largest and richest colony: India. Siam's proximity to both Indochina and India also meant that substantial numbers of Vietnamese and Indians already lived and worked in the state prior to the outbreak of war. And while only a small number of these individuals were anticolonial revolutionaries, Siam's independent status made it a place of refuge for those seeking to avoid persecution by either the French or the British colonial authorities. For all these reasons, Siam became a focal point for anti-British and anti-French activity in Southeast Asia for the first two years of the war. Indeed, for a brief moment in 1915 Germans and Indians came as close to an actual invasion of British colonial territory that they were ever going to get during the war.[5]

Yet Siam's moment as a staging ground and refuge for enemies of the Allies was short lived. Unlike in the Dutch East Indies, where (as we have seen) the British consul tried in vain to convince Dutch authorities to take action against individuals involved in anti-British activity, in Siam the King and his ministers were quite willing to assist Allied representatives. By the middle of 1915, in fact, the King allowed his own police force to apprehend anticolonial activists acting against either the British or the French, and then allowed the captives to be extradited out of Siam to their various, and almost always unfortunate, fates. While this policy did not stop all war-related activity in Siam, by late 1915 it did make it much more dangerous for activists to operate there than in either the East Indies or, as we will see in Chapter 6, China. So much did the King invest in his close relationship with Britain that in July 1917 he declared war on the Central Powers. In 1918, the King made good on his declaration of

---

1914–1918," in Amitabha Mukherjee, ed., *Militant Nationalism in India, 1876–1947* (Calcutta: Institute of Historical Studies, 1995), 305.

[5] Thomas G. Fraser, "Germany and Indian Revolution, 1914–18," *Journal of Contemporary History* 12, no. 2 (April 1, 1977), 267. A.C. Bose argues that by January 1915 Bangkok had become the "advance base of the planned Ghadr attack on India." In "Activities of Indian Revolutionaries Abroad, 1914–1918," 315.

war by sending a small force of ambulance drivers, medics, and aviators to fight for the Allies in France.[6]

Despite Siam's complex entanglements in the war, virtually nothing has been written about it. Scholarly general histories of Thailand tend to mention the war only in passing, as part of the new nationalism under King Vajiravudh.[7] Works specifically about Vajiravudh's reign do at least discuss the war, but even then the material covers only a few pages.[8] This scholarly lack of attention is reinforced by the more or less accurate perception that the war did not matter very much to most ordinary people in Siam. Siam was not a democracy in 1914, and political decisions were ultimately in the hands of the King and a few of his ministers. But even if the war did not attract the interest of most ordinary people, the Siamese government had little choice but to devote a great deal of time and energy negotiating the fragile politics of neutrality between the Allies and the Central Powers before it finally declared war in 1917. Moreover, plenty of European, Indian, and Vietnamese foreigners living in and moving through Siam were deeply invested in the outcome of the war. This investment and its associated activity has been noted by scholars concerned with Indian or Vietnamese anticolonial movements but has been virtually ignored by historians concerned with the global impact of World War I.[9]

This chapter begins with a brief overview of Siam's relationship to Britain, France, and Germany by 1914 as a way of illuminating not only the calculated care with which Siamese kings had sought to maintain their independence, but also the strategic importance of Siam to the European powers even before the war. It then moves to the outbreak of the war and the various activities through which Germans, Indians, and Vietnamese sought to undermine colonial rule in neighboring Allied colonies. Although anticolonial revolutionaries and their German partners targeted both French Indochina and British Burma, this chapter will focus most closely on schemes involving Indian revolutionaries. There are two reasons for this. First, German-Indian conspiracies in

---

[6] Stephen Lyon Wakeman Greene, *Absolute Dreams: Thai Government under Rama VI, 1910–1925* (Bangkok: White Lotus Press, 1999), 110, 113.

[7] For example, Christopher John Baker and Pasuk Phongpaichit, *A History of Thailand*, 2nd ed. (Cambridge; New York: Cambridge University Press, 2009); also David Wyatt, *A Short History of Thailand*, 2nd ed. (New Haven: Yale University Press, 2003).

[8] Greene, *Absolute Dreams*, 102–113.

[9] Two scholars who have noted the connections between revolutionaries, Germans, and Siam are Maia Ramnath, *Haj to Utopia: How the Ghadar Movement Charted Global Radicalism and Attempted to Overthrow the British Empire* (Berkeley: University of California Press, 2011); and Christopher Goscha, *Thailand and the Southeast Asian Networks of the Vietnamese Revolution, 1885–1954* (Richmond, Surrey: Curzon Press, 1999).

Siam were on a greater scale, and were more complex and involved, than those involving Indochina. Second, because of the integral relationship between Vietnamese schemes, China, and Siam, I discuss German-Vietnamese schemes more thoroughly in Chapter 6. From there, the chapter explores the response of the Siamese government to the international crisis of the war, particularly the King's decision to cooperate with British and French requests for arresting and extraditing suspected revolutionaries. This decision offered a stark contrast to government actions in the East Indies and China, and had the effect of drastically curtailing anticolonial activity in Siam by early 1916. Finally, this chapter explores the short- and long-term consequences of anticolonial revolutionary activity in Siam – particularly in terms of the British response. The government of India was so concerned about the threat posed by this activity that it set in motion the creation of the first British coordinated security organization in the region: the Far Eastern Agency.[10] And while it turned out that Siam became less of a threat as a result of the king's actions, the agency was increasingly used to gather reliable intelligence about "seditious" activity all over Southeast and East Asia. This did not, of course, halt anticolonial activity in the region, but it did increase the ability of the British to track and thwart plots against it across a much wider geographical area than ever before. Taken together, this chapter demonstrates not only that the war had important effects on Siam, but that Siam was integral to schemes designed both to undermine and to uphold Allied rule in colonial Southeast Asia.

Siam and the European Powers in 1914

In 1914, King Vajiravudh had been on the throne for four years, having inherited it from his reform-minded and western-oriented father Chulalongkorn (r. 1873–1910). So important did Chulalongkorn believe an understanding of the west that he sent Vajiravudh to Britain for his education, making him the first Siamese crown prince to be educated abroad. Vajiravudh lived in Britain from the age of twelve to twenty-two, during which time he read history and law at Oxford, trained at Sandhurst Military Academy, and served briefly in the British army with the Royal Durham Light Infantry.[11] He was on friendly terms with King George V, spoke English fluently, and grew deeply familiar with British customs and culture. Perhaps not surprisingly given his upbringing, then, Vajiravudh

---

[10] Appointment of David Petrie as Special Officer for Dealing with Indian Sedition and German Intrigue, May 9, 1916. Report 23134. Straits Settlements Original Correspondence: Foreign, CO 273/448.

[11] Greene, *Absolute Dreams*, 32; Baker and Phongpaichit, *A History of Thailand*, 106.

was an unabashed Anglophile who was predisposed toward British government representatives once he became king.

The Siam that Vajiravudh presided over at the beginning of his reign was vastly different than the one his father had inherited at his own coronation in 1873. By 1910, the state capital at Bangkok had transformed from a modest port town dominated by Chinese business interests to a cosmopolitan and international city.[12]

Chulalongkorn had allowed the establishment of a wide variety of western business interests in his country – particularly in teak, rice, tin, and rubber – which drew large numbers of managers and employees from around Europe. The international diplomatic and consular system also grew to accommodate, protect, and serve these interests, and by 1910 all of the European powers had ministers and consuls-general in Bangkok, as well as consuls in outlying areas. Vajiravudh also continued his father's tradition of recruiting foreigners, particularly Europeans, to serve as advisors and employees to the Siamese government. In 1914, Vajiravudh's government employed 208 of these foreign advisors, of whom more than half (113) were Britons.[13] And it was not just Europeans who gave Siam – and especially Bangkok – its international flair. As Siam's economy opened up to western companies under Chulalongkorn, large numbers of workers and traders also came from Burma and India to support the industries.[14] Although many of these new (and often temporary) immigrants lived in the hinterlands where mining and logging enterprises were most active, some also settled in Bangkok. Beginning in the late nineteenth century, Siam also attracted groups of Vietnamese anticolonialists who relied on the state's independence to provide a safe haven from persecution in neighboring French Indochina.[15] By the start of Vajiravudh's reign, then, the capital at Bangkok and significant portions of the hinterland were host to a variety of peoples who had been drawn to Siam either for its economic opportunities or for the relative freedom it offered from the colonial powers in the region.

The westernization of Siam and its opening to European commercial and diplomatic interests so visible in Vajiravudh's reign had been part of Chulalongkorn's long-term strategy for maintaining Siamese independence in an era of intense European empire building. But no one, least of all Chulalongkorn himself, believed that reforms alone could convince

[12] Baker and Phongpaichit, *A History of Thailand*, 90, 91.

[13] Greene, *Absolute Dreams*, 104, 105.

[14] J. Chandran, "British Foreign Policy and the Extraterritorial Question in Siam 1891–1900," *Journal of the Malaysian Branch of the Royal Asiatic Society* 38, no. 2 (December 1965), 291.

[15] Goscha, *Thailand and the Southeast Asian Networks of the Vietnamese Revolution, 1885–1954*, 14, 21.

European powers to leave Siam untouched. For that, the King had to give up massive portions of Siamese territory to both British and French colonial interests in the east, south, and west. He also had to accept trade agreements that favored European companies as well as European rights of extraterritoriality on Siamese soil. Just as important, he had to rely on the larger regional and global context of Anglo-French diplomatic negotiations in the hopes that the two powers would limit not only each other's colonial designs in Siam but also the designs of other would-be colonizers. In this respect, Chulalongkorn was at the mercy of international Great Power politics. Indeed, one of the lessons of his reign – a lesson not lost on his less able son – was that the fate of Siam could not be isolated from international diplomacy and politics.

This lesson was brought home repeatedly in the last two decades of Chulalongkorn's reign. By that time, the King had already embarked on a series of reforms to modernize the Siamese state along western lines in order to stave off European encroachment, which included increasing government centralization and control as well as the westernization of government structures.[16] Notwithstanding these reforms (many of which were geared toward enhancing the King's claim to Siamese territory), both Britain and France continued to covet large swaths of land in areas the King claimed as part of the Siamese state. In 1893, the weakness of these claims were exposed when the French annexed a large piece of territory east of the Mekong River already claimed by Siam.[17] The Paknam Incident, as it came to be known, prompted Chulalongkorn to send a military force against the French, but in the end he was forced to concede the territory. Encouraged by their success and hungry for more territory, the French considered making all of Siam into a protectorate. Although it was perfectly clear that such a course would have been against Chulalongkorn's wishes, the plan was abandoned primarily because of British objections, as the British did not wish to see their own interests in the region usurped by the French.[18] In fact, the Paknam Incident led to one of the first bilateral Anglo-French Declarations about the status of Siam, for in 1896 both powers agreed that it was in their mutual interests to respect the integrity and independence of central Siam as a buffer between their respective interests in Burma, the Malayan peninsula, and Indochina.[19] In the wake of this Declaration, it was clear to Chulalongkorn that in spite of his efforts to modernize and thus to

---

[16] Baker and Phongpaichit, *A History of Thailand*, 56.

[17] Thongchai Winichakul, *Siam Mapped: A History of the Geo-Body of a Nation* (Honolulu: University of Hawaii Press, 1994), 110–111.

[18] Baker and Phongpaichit, *A History of Thailand*, 59, 61.

[19] Chandran, "British Foreign Policy and the Extraterritorial Question in Siam 1891–1900," 290.

convince Britain and France of the inviolability of Siam's borders, the independence he so strongly desired was guaranteed not because of his own actions, but rather because of an agreement reached by European powers regarding their strategic interests in the region.

That the 1896 agreement was mostly about Anglo-French strategic interests was evident by the fact that it did not eliminate the possibility of further British and French encroachments on Siamese territory in either the south or the northeast. It also did nothing to reform disadvantageous trade agreements or to revise existing European rights of extraterritoriality – two issues that caused the King deep concern.[20] And over the next decade, the situation did not improve. Instead, it became ever more clear to the King and his ministers that the British and French intended to determine Siam's fate between themselves. For example, one of the provisions of the Anglo-French *Entente Cordiale* of 1904 – which signaled the beginning of their mutual alliance against Germany – made provisions for the future of Siam. As in the 1896 Declaration, the 1904 agreement disclaimed "all idea of annexing Siamese territory or contravening the provisions of existing Treaties."[21] But the entente went on to specify that both the French and the British would respect each other's established "sphere of influence" in regions adjacent to their respective colonies. In those areas, "each Government shall have liberty of action so far as concerns the other."[22] According to the Siamese Foreign Minister, Prince Devawongse, this agreement – signed as it was without the participation of the Siamese government – was particularly problematic because it delineated foreign "spheres of interest" on Siamese sovereign territory. Moreover, it was all the more distasteful because the Siamese government remained deeply suspicious about French ambitions in Siam as a result of the Paknam Incident. As Prince Devawongse wrote to the British Ambassador in Bangkok, "His Majesty's Government cannot refrain from expressing regret that the French contention [about the existence of "spheres of influence"] has been finally accepted by His Britannic Majesty's Government."[23]

---

[20] For specifics about the nature of extraterritoriality in Siam, see J. Chandran, "British Foreign Policy and the Extraterritorial Question in Siam 1891–1900."

[21] Secretary to the Siamese Legation Sir Ralph Paget to Prince Devawongse, Foreign Minister, April 15, 1904. Report 21141. Straits Settlements Original Correspondence: Foreign. TNA CO 273/350.

[22] Secretary to the Siamese Legation Sir Ralph Paget to Prince Devawongse, Foreign Minister, April 15, 1904. Report 21141.

[23] Prince Devawongse, Foreign Minister to Secretary to Sir Ralph Paget, Siamese Legation, April 18, 1904. Report 21141. Straits Settlements Original Correspondence: Foreign. TNA CO 273/350.

In order to prevent continual losses of territory and to shore up Siamese sovereignty, the King and Devawongse spent the next five years negotiating agreements with both Britain and France that would establish permanent Siamese borders and eliminate European extraterritoriality within them. The negotiations came at a high price for Siam. In order to convince the French to renounce the extraterritorial rights of their subjects on Siamese soil and to recognize permanent Siamese boundaries, in 1907 the King agreed to give up still more of his territory – this time, the Khmer provinces of the northeast. And in order to achieve the same result from the British, in 1909 the Siamese gave up the four provinces of Kedah, Kelantan, Trengganu, and Perlis in the northern Malayan peninsula.[24]

While the treaties of 1907 and 1909 finally resolved irksome questions of sovereignty and borders while guaranteeing Siamese independence, European influence on Siamese affairs remained strong. This was particularly true for the British, who maintained a visible and sometimes dominant presence in the economic and political life of Siam. By 1914, for example, Siam's rice export economy was dominated by British shipping and by British-ruled clients, particularly Hong Kong and Singapore.[25] In the political and administrative spheres, we have already seen that British nationals made up the largest number of foreign advisers to the Siamese government, followed distantly by Germans, Danes, and others.[26] Moreover, Britons were represented in every department of the government rather than in one or more specific units.[27] In the same period, the British even made contingents of Indian units available to the Siamese government for police work, and in 1914 both the Commissioner and Deputy Commissioner for the Police in Siam were Britons.[28]

Britain's special position in early twentieth century Siam also made its representatives jealous of other competing interests in the country. Although Britain's decades-long competition with the French in the

---

[24] Baker and Phongpaichit, *A History of Thailand*, 64.

[25] Baker and Phongpaichit, *A History of Thailand*, 89.

[26] The numbers at the turn of the century were: 58 British, 22 Germans, 22 Danes, 9 Belgians, 8 Italians, and 20 "others." Baker and Phongpaichit, *A History of Thailand*, 68. The fact that there were not enough French nationals to count in the Siamese service was the result of the lack of trust on the part of the Siamese, according to William Archer of the British Legation. William J. Archer to the Marquess of Landsdowne, December 4, 1901. Report 2471. Straits Settlements Original Correspondence: Foreign. TNA CO 273/286.

[27] Greene, *Absolute Dreams*, 105.

[28] Archer remarked that the presence of British-Indian subjects in the Siamese police force was "a constant source of irritation both to the Russian and the French Minister as a sign of the covert protection of England over Siam." William J. Archer to the Marquess of Landsdowne, December 4, 1901. Report 2471.

region had more or less been settled by 1910, other European powers – particularly Germany and Russia – sought to expand their influence in Siam at this time. In fact, the British were aware of German ambitions in the area as early as 1885. In a report prepared at the request of the Foreign Office, the author urged the British to lay claim to the northern states of the Malay peninsula still claimed by Siam, because "annexation is becoming a rage in this part of the world, and any day these States might be annexed by Germany or France."[29] At the turn of the twentieth century, British officials even feared that the ongoing Anglo-French rivalry for influence in Siam might lead the Siamese government to the conclusion, as Sir Francis Bertie put it, "that their only chance of escaping from practical absorption or a state of protection and ultimate division by France and England would be an appeal to Russia and Germany who, nothing loath, would come forward with their good offices."[30] While Chulalongkorn did not end up appealing to either the Russians or the Germans for help, German political and business interests in particular nevertheless continued to grow in Siam in the first fifteen years of the twentieth century. By the turn of the twentieth century, German advisers to the Siamese government were second only to British advisers, and by 1914 German engineers positively dominated the Siamese railroad department – developments that British representatives in the country regarded with trepidation even before the war.[31]

The point of all this is that for decades prior to the war, the political situation in Siam had been marked both by the King's efforts to secure Siamese independence and also by the reality that this independence could not have been achieved without the convergence of this goal with larger British and French strategic interests in the region. Before his death in 1910, Chulalongkorn had to walk a fine line between asserting his sovereign control over Siam and the reality of British and French hegemony in mainland Southeast Asia. In attempting to preserve his independence, he pursued modernization along Western lines, invited foreign participation in his government and in his economy, and pragmatically conceded large territories to both the British and the French in exchange for the recognition of permanent boundaries. The state he left for his son in 1910 had thus been consciously shaped with the understanding that the integrity of the Siamese state could be achieved

---

[29] Report of Mr. Holt Hallett upon the Present State and Political Aspect of Indo-China, for the Information of the Foreign Office, April 1885. TNA FO 881/5110, 1.

[30] Chandran Jeshurun, "Lord Lansdowne and the 'Anti-German Clique' at the Foreign Office: Their Role in the Making of the Anglo-Siamese Agreement of 1902," *Journal of Southeast Asian Studies* 3, no. 2 (September 1, 1972), 238.

[31] Green, *Absolute Dreams*, 105.

only by paying scrupulous attention to regional and international politics – particularly as they applied to the strategic and economic interests of European powers. And although Vajiravudh has generally not been seen as the statesman his father was, both his upbringing in Britain and the lessons learned during his father's reign made him aware that ignoring international politics and diplomacy as a global war was unfolding could only be to the peril of Siam.

Siam and the War Against the Allies

Notwithstanding Vajiravudh's Anglophilia, when the European powers went to war in July 1914 the King and his ministers determined that Siamese interests would best be served by remaining neutral. There was never any question that Siam would declare war on the side of the Central Powers in any case, given Britain's dominant role in the Siamese economy and the nearness of its military presence in the form of the Indian army. But at the same time there seemed to be few compelling reasons to move hastily toward siding with the Allies. For one thing, the multiplicity of foreign business and political interests representing both the Allied and Central Powers meant that neutrality was the best option for allowing the Siamese economy and government to continue along its prewar course. In addition, given Siam's recent history with both Britain and France, Stephen Greene argues that "many Thai felt it would be a humiliating experience to come to the assistance of those nations that only a short time before had expropriated over one-third of the nation's territory."[32] Thus Siam committed itself to upholding the 1907 international conventions of neutrality and pledged that it would not assist either side or allow hostile activity to occur on Siamese soil.[33]

But the enemies of the Allies had very different plans for Siam. Nowhere else could representatives of the Central Powers hope to be in such close range to three Allied colonies, with French Indochina to the east, British Burma to the west, and British Malaya to the south. Not only that, Siam offered land access through Burma to India – an important feature given Allied naval dominance in the region by late 1914. Additionally, as we have seen Siam was already host to communities of Vietnamese and Indian revolutionaries who were using the state as a safe haven prior to the war. When the war broke out, then, it was relatively

[32] Greene, *Absolute Dreams*, 104.
[33] Rights and Duties of Neutral Powers and Persons in Case of War on Land (Hague V); October 18, 1907.

easy for these revolutionaries to find German and Austrian enemies of their enemies, and vice versa.

This was certainly the case for a group of Vietnamese revolutionaries under the leadership of Phan Bội Châu and Cuong De, who had been using Siam as a base from which to plan future operations since 1910.[34] Only a little more than a month after hostilities broke out, in September 1914, one of these revolutionaries, Tran Huu Luc (born Nguyen Thuc Duong), sought out the German and Austrian consuls in Bangkok with the intent of obtaining money for a border uprising in French Indochina. Tran, who was an integral member of Phan Bội Châu's Viet Nam Restoration Association, had gone to Siam two years earlier, in 1912, to raise an army of expatriate Vietnamese to fight against the French.[35] But in order to make his plans work, Tran needed both weapons and money. The outbreak of war gave him the opportunity he had been seeking, and he called on France's enemies to provide the needed supplies for his planned uprising. In response to Tran's request, the German and Austrian consuls gave the revolutionaries 10,000 piastres, which Tran then used to organize and fund a border attack at the French post of Tulang in northern Tonkin in March 1915. Unfortunately for Tran, the attack failed and its leaders – including Tran himself – were caught and executed. Prior to their execution Tran and his compatriots were brutally interrogated and revealed the source of their funding.[36]

In spite of Tran's failure, representatives of the Central Powers in Siam did not immediately give up on Vietnamese revolutionaries. On at least one other occasion, in late autumn 1915, the German and Austrian ministers approached members of the Viet Nam Restoration Association with an offer of money and supplies for bringing about "some kind of sensational incident within your country that would cause our governments to take notice."[37] When the ministers met with the Association's emissary, Nguyen Thuong Hien (alias Mai Son), they promised an initial sum for funding attacks on French Indochina as well as additional funds if Nguyen was successful. Nguyen accepted the money and brought it to China, where it was divided between revolutionary cells

---

[34] This story, and the story of Vietnamese revolutionaries more generally, will be fleshed out more fully in Chapter 6, because the German-Vietnamese schemes in Siam were also intricately connected with German-Vietnamese schemes in China. As it turned out, the German-Vietnamese schemes in Siam were far less substantial than those that originated in China.

[35] Phan Bội Châu, *Overturned Chariot: The Autobiography of Phan-Bội-Châu*, SHAPS Library of Translations (Honolulu, HI: University of Hawai'i Press, 1999), 154.

[36] Governor General Roume to Minister of Colonies, February 22, 1916, 26. Troubles et Complots en Indochine, Indo/nf/3, CAOM.

[37] Phan, *Overturned Chariot*, 225.

for a series of border attacks. However, these attacks also ended in failure, and many of the participants were caught. By early 1916 the French Governor-General of Indochina reported to his superiors that while these German-supported activities deserved attention, he did not believe that the schemes emanating from Siam continued to pose a significant threat to the security of French Indochinese borders.[38] For the rest of the war, German-Vietnamese schemes coming from Siam functioned as a sideshow to the much more involved schemes originating in China, which we will explore in Chapter 6.

In contrast to the German-Vietnamese schemes, German-Indian schemes originating in Siam were far more extensive because they involved the international machinery of the Ghadar network, which connected North America to many parts of East, Southeast, and South Asia. We have already seen, in Chapters 3 and 4, how Ghadar revolutionaries utilized the neutral Dutch East Indies as a major transit point and meeting place on the journey from North America to India. Yet the Batavia route was not the only one intended to bring expatriate Indians back to India. In October 1914 the Ghadar Party leadership – in conjunction with German officials in Berlin – determined to create a second major route through Siam and Burma.[39] Siam was ideal because, like the Dutch East Indies, it was neutral and thus allowed Germans, Austrians, and Indians relative freedom of movement. In addition, Siam's border with Burma offered the potential of reaching India via land, which was vital given the logistical difficulties of landing ships with revolutionaries and smuggled weapons in heavily guarded Indian ports.

The German-Indian plan involving Siam was complex and required the mobilization of people and resources from many different locations. The first goal was for Germans and Indians to take advantage of Siam's neutrality by setting up a military training camp in the remote Siamese jungles near the Burmese border. The camp's trainees were to be composed of Ghadar revolutionaries, who were to make their way to Siam from North America and other locations from around East and Southeast Asia. German military veterans, meanwhile, were to be transported to Siam in order to command the training camp, while arms and ammunition were to be shipped to Siam from China on the authority of the German consul in Shanghai. Once these arrangements were complete and the revolutionaries had been sufficiently trained, Ghadar revolutionaries were meant to slip across the Burmese border in an effort to turn the approximately 15,000 men of the Burma Military Police – most of whom

---

[38] Governor General Roume to Minister of Colonies, February 22, 1916, 25.
[39] Fraser, "Germany and Indian Revolution, 1914–18,", 266.

were Sikhs or Punjabi Muslims – against the British.[40] Finally, with the successful incorporation of these new recruits from the Burma Military Police, the much-enhanced and well-trained force was to conquer an unspecified portion of Burma and use it as a toe-hold for launching a general revolution in India.

British officials in Siam began to hear about suspicious activity related to the Ghadar party just a couple of months after its leaders made the decision to use Siam as a route to India. By late December 1914, acting Consul-General J. Crosby wrote that the Deputy Commissioner of Police in Bangkok, a Briton called Mr. Trotter, had found "a number of bundles of a newspaper printed in an Indian language" suspected to be "of seditious character" lying unclaimed in the Bangkok post office.[41] Upon further inquiry by the Commissioner of Police (also a Briton), it appeared that the papers had been sent from San Francisco via Hong Kong and were addressed to a Sikh who could not be located in Bangkok. The Commissioner did find another Sikh who had been seen reading a similar paper, and this Sikh said he had received the paper from one of the many Sikhs who were working for the Siamese Southern Railway Department at Bandon. And although British authorities could not locate that particular Sikh either, the British consul at Singora had obtained information that the head of the Siamese Southern Railway in Bandon was a German named Doering, who was "very bitter on the subject of the present war; he was said to be doing all he could to disseminate German news and to forward German interests and German trade."[42] Not only that, the consul from Singora reported that all of the Europeans working on that section of railroad were Germans, and that the weekly mail to Bandon "brought with it a newspaper in Indian characters, which was read with great attention by the Indians residing there" and was said to be published in California.[43] Crosby indicated that these reports were somewhat difficult for consuls to verify because local Indians were reluctant to talk to them, and recommended that if the Indian government thought the situation serious enough, they should send an Indian secret agent to make inquiries. He ended his report by adding that the situation in Bangkok did not offer much reassurance, since the Indian Muslim community in Bangkok were noted for their "disloyal sentiments," and that

[40] Fraser, "Germany and Indian Revolution, 1914–18," 266–267.
[41] Memorandum by J. Crosby, December 28, 1914. Report 7052. Straits Settlements Original Correspondence: Foreign, TNA CO 273/430.
[42] Memorandum by J. Crosby, December 28, 1914. Report 7052. Bandon and Singora are both to the south of Bangkok on the narrow isthmus that included part of Burma, Siam, and British Malaya.
[43] Memorandum by J. Crosby, December 28, 1914. Report 7052.

the German Legation in the city "is reported to be pursuing "an active anti-British propaganda among the local Indian community."[44] This propaganda was even supposed to have included "magic-lantern displays" that told the story of the war from the German point of view. In any case, by the end of 1914 it already seemed pretty clear to Britons in Siam that a strong connection had been forged between Ghadar literature coming in from the United States, Sikh and Muslim communities in Siam, and German citizens and diplomats engaged in negative propaganda against the Allies.

Just a few months later, in March 1915, the British Legation in Siam received information from British intelligence in North America and China "of a migratory movement of Sikhs and other Indians, from America via Chinese ports, to Siam with the object of crossing the frontier secretly into British territory."[45] At that point, the British government in India decided that the situation was serious enough to warrant further investigation by a secret agent. In coordination with the Singapore authorities, they therefore arranged for an Indian secret agent to travel from Singapore to Siam. His orders were to uncover the details of seditious Indian activity taking place in Siam and to provide evidence about the extent to which German consuls were involved.[46]

By late July 1915, the new British ambassador to Siam, Herbert Dering, felt confident enough in the evidence he had collected to present the full weight of it to Prince Devawongse, the Siamese Foreign Minister. According to Dering, information gathered by the Siamese police network, the Indian secret agent from Singapore, and reports from British consuls in North America and China confirmed that groups of revolutionary Indians had already arrived in Siam – and many more were expected – for the purpose of entering British territory in Burma. They were being coordinated, he said, by a group of at least twelve Indian men in Bangkok who had entered Siam from North America via Chinese ports. One of these men was "a person of influence and importance as a revolutionary leader" who claimed that he had "already organized a force of between six and seven hundred Indians."[47] In a follow-up memorandum written the next day, Dering added that "it has been established

---

[44] Memorandum by J. Crosby, December 28, 1914. Report 7052.
[45] Secret Memorandum from Herbert Dering to Prince Devawongse, August 6, 1915. Report 43512. Straits Correspondence Original Correspondence: Foreign. TNA CO 273/432.
[46] Fraser, "Germany and Indian Revolution, 1914–18," 267.
[47] Very Secret and Urgent Memorandum from Herbert Dering to Prince Devawongse, July 31, 1915. Report 43512. Straits Correspondence Original Correspondence: Foreign. TNA CO 273/432.

that these men are the adherents of the revolutionary party known as the Ghadr party, whose headquarters are at San Francisco and whose leader is the notorious Hardial [Har Dayal]."[48] He went on to say that there was also strong reason to suspect that Indians working for the Siamese Railway Department were being subjected to propaganda by the many German engineers under whom they served but acknowledged that conclusive proof was still lacking. He did, however, have it from a "private source" that "some one hundred Sikhs and Mohammedans of seditious character" were camped out near Paknampho (north of Bangkok) with two Germans and were in the process of manufacturing explosives. Moreover, Dering wrote that there were "centers of seditious activity at Bandon, Singora, and Renong" in southern Thailand that were responsible for sending seditious material across the Siamese border with Burma.[49]

If that information were not enough, Dering wrote, his combined intelligence revealed what he called "the following startling facts" which threatened "to assume very serious proportions." He told Devawongse that Ghadar party activists in Siam planned to organize an armed force – for which they claimed they had already recruited six or seven hundred men but hoped to raise as many as 10,000 – and use it to seize a portion of Burma. In order to achieve their goal, according to Dering, the German Legation in Bangkok intended to arm all of the recruits with weapons and ammunition. Moreover, the Ghadar recruits were expecting a German military officer "to drill the proposed raiding force."[50] That officer would determine precisely where the attack would be made along the Burmese frontier.

As far-fetched as these plans might seem in hindsight, the outlines of Dering's intelligence nevertheless were in fact fairly accurate. We know from the Indian secret agent, a variety of Indian and German memoirs, and from testimony in the long-running Hindu-German Conspiracy Trial in the United States that Ghadar activists – with the collusion of the German Foreign Office and German consuls in Bangkok, Shanghai, and Chicago – did in fact plan to raise a force in Siam for rebellion in Burma. It later became clear that the German Foreign Office had arranged for three German men living in Chicago to provide crucial assistance in the scheme. Albert Wehde, a Chicago art dealer, was to use his cover as a buyer of "oriental antiquities" to act as financier for the operation. In addition, two German army veterans living in Chicago were to arrange shipments of arms for transit to Siam and were then

---

[48] Secret Memorandum from Herbert Dering to Prince Devawongse, August 6, 1915.
[49] Secret Memorandum from Herbert Dering to Prince Devawongse, August 6, 1915.
[50] Secret Memorandum from Herbert Dering to Prince Devawongse, August 6, 1915.

themselves to proceed to Siam in order to train the Ghadar soldiers along the Burmese frontier.[51] It was also true that the German consul in Bangkok, Erwin Remy, had established a military base near the Burmese border where Ghadarites arriving from North America could train. The German ambassador in Shanghai, Knipping – about whom we will hear more in Chapter 6 – also contributed to the scheme by sending three men from the embassy guard in Peking to help with the training. Moreover, Knipping convinced a Norwegian ship's captain to smuggle arms for the Ghadar revolutionaries in Siam from the Chinese port of Amoy.

Only a year after the war began, then, German-Indian plans to foment revolution in India from Siam appeared well-developed, had utilized significant sums of money, and involved hundreds of people from North America to India, and from Europe to China. British authorities in Siam and India viewed these developments with particular alarm, for Siam had become a primary location from which British enemies were engaged in active collaboration to bring down the Raj. As Thomas Fraser has argued, by the end of July 1915, "with a sizeable group of armed Ghadarites near the Burmese border, the Germans were as close to achieving an uprising in the Indian empire as they ever would be."[52]

The Failure of the Siamese Schemes

But in the end the Siamese schemes were no more successful than those involving Singapore or Batavia. Multiple factors contributed to this failure. First, it appears that both the Germans and Indians involved woefully underestimated the ability of British intelligence to uncover the plot. For example, neither representatives of the Central Powers nor the Ghadar revolutionaries themselves seemed to have questioned the loyalties of the Indian secret agent sent from Singapore to investigate the situation. As a result, he found the conspirators perfectly willing to speak with him about their plans from his earliest arrival in Bangkok.[53] Moreover, neither Germans nor Indians had adequately taken into account the level of direct influence Britons had in the machinery of the Siamese government. We know, for example, that both the Commissioner and Deputy Commissioner of Police in Bangkok were British, and that because of this they had direct access to police networks in the rest of the state. We also

---

[51] Fraser, "Germany and Indian Revolution, 1914–18," 266. Also Ramnath, *Haj to Utopia*, 85; Donald M. McKale, *War by Revolution: Germany and Great Britain in the Middle East in the Era of World War I* (Kent, OH: Kent State University Press, 1998), 124.

[52] Fraser, "Germany and Indian Revolution, 1914–18," 267.

[53] Apparently the Austrian chargé d'affaires gave the agent most of the details of the plan the first time they met. Fraser, "Germany and Indian Revolution, 1914–18," 267.

know that Britons were well represented in every bureaucratic branch of the Siamese government, which allowed information to pass relatively freely – for example, from the Railway Department to the Police Department – when enquiries needed to be made. Moreover, Britons working for the Siamese government appeared perfectly willing to pass critical information on to the British Legation when it involved plots against Britain or British India.

A second reason the Siamese scheme failed was that neither the promised arms shipments nor the German officers ever arrived in Siam. Wehde and the two German veterans from Chicago, Boehm and Sterneck, did indeed start on their way to Siam from North America in the spring of 1915 aboard the *Henry S.* But when the Germans attempted to add a supply of arms to the ship's cargo when it made a scheduled stop in Manila, the American authorities refused to allow it. In the end, the Germans were forced to leave the weapons behind in Manila.[54] But still more ill fortune plagued the ship's journey. As we saw in Chapter 3, the *Henry S.* developed engine trouble on its way westward and was stranded in Sulawesi when neither the Dutch nor the Japanese navy would give it a tow to a port where it could be repaired. The end result of these misfortunes was that neither of the two German veterans ever made it to Siam, nor of course did the weapons they had planned to provide.

Yet the most important reason the Siam scheme failed was the result of Siamese cooperation with the British. Unlike in the Dutch East Indies (or, as we shall see in Chapter 6, in China), where state authorities were either unwilling or unable to work with British authorities to detain suspected anticolonial activists, in Siam the situation was quite different. Siam was far too dependent on British friendship to jeopardize relations over the protection of British Indian subjects. Moreover, even though the Siamese state was still neutral in 1915, the King himself was a known supporter of Great Britain even to the point of violating the rules of neutrality. In 1915, for example, Vajiravudh donated £1000 to the Royal Durham Light Infantry for widows and orphans of British officers who had fallen in the war. Also in 1915, Vajiravudh and King George V of Britain exchanged honorary military titles, giving Vajiravudh the odd distinction of serving as a "General" in the British army while the Siamese state was officially neutral.[55]

Thus when Dering approached Prince Devawongse with the evidence he had compiled of German-Indian schemes taking place within Siam, his expectations of a friendly and helpful response were far higher than those of Beckett, his colleague in Batavia. In fact, Dering's goal in compiling

---

[54] McKale, *War by Revolution*, 124.   [55] Greene, *Absolute Dreams*, 103.

the evidence was not simply to make a case to the Siamese government, but to demand – subtly and diplomatically – action. After compiling his secret memoranda with evidence of German-Indian conspiracies in Siam, Dering met Devawongse on July 31, 1915 to discuss the matter. What Dering wanted was the immediate arrest and extradition of "some dozen Indians," whose presence in Siam, he argued, was "likely to compromise the friendly relations existing between Siam and a neighboring State."[56] Much to Dering's satisfaction, Devawongse responded that he was prepared to take immediate steps to apprehend the suspects and have them deported directly to Singapore, where they could be dealt with by British authorities. Devawongse further assured Dering that he was certain the King would support such an action, because he knew "that the King's wish was to keep all revolutionary and dangerous persons out of the country and to have no trouble here."[57]

Despite Devawongse's apparent willingness to help, Dering drove the urgency of the matter home by saying that several Indians in the Bangkok area were known to be manufacturing explosives for their cause, and "there was no reason why they should not, under foreign instigation, even reserve a bomb or two" for Dering himself. Dering indicated that he was not particularly concerned about his own safety but asked Devawongse "whether it would be pleasant for the Siamese government to have an incident of the kind occur."[58] Dering was satisfied that "this argument appeared to impress Devawongse," who then repeated his assurances of help.

In fact, Devawongse authorized the arrests of the first three of the suspected Ghadar revolutionaries in Bangkok the very next day, on August 2, 1915. Among these men was the alleged leader, who had entered the country as a Persian under the name Hassan Zadé, but whose real name was Jodh Singh Mahajan.[59] Also among them was Thakur Singh, whose personal effects included a detailed set of instructions for making explosives and ammunition.[60] Two days later, three more suspected revolutionaries were arrested who were known to have recently arrived from San Francisco. According to Dering, interrogation of these men "proved beyond doubt that they are intimately connected with the Ghadr or revolutionary party in India and had come here with the definite object of fomenting disturbances in this country in Burma in the first instance,

---

[56] Dering to Earl Grey, Foreign Office, August 6, 1915. Report 43512. Straits Correspondence Original Correspondence: Foreign. TNA CO 273/432.
[57] Dering to Earl Grey, Foreign Office, August 6, 1915.
[58] Dering to Earl Grey, Foreign Office, August 6, 1915.
[59] Ramnath, *Haj to Utopia*, 83.
[60] Dering to Earl Grey, Foreign Office, August 6, 1915.

and eventually also against India."[61] The men were held in a Bangkok jail until a police escort from Singapore arrived to take them into British custody on September 14.[62] In addition to these first six men, thirteen more arrests and deportations were requested by David Petrie, who had arrived in Siam as a representative of India's Criminal Investigation Department (CID) in early September. The Siamese government also complied in the arrest of these men. Over the course of the remaining months of 1915, Siamese police succeeded in apprehending about fifty individuals in Bangkok and near the Siamese frontiers. Only six revolutionaries actually made it to Burma, where they were caught and later hanged for trying to incite revolution.[63] In the Mandalay Conspiracy Trial that convened in December 1915 to deal with the individuals detained in connection with the Siam-Burma scheme, nine of the men who had been arrested in Siam were hanged, and seven were transported for life.[64]

Given the Siamese government's close relationship with Britain, it is unsurprising that Prince Devawongse proved so willing to help Dering in his request for help in apprehending Indian suspects. As a result of this assistance, British authorities were able to put an end to the revolutionary activities of over fifty Ghadar party members, and thus to cut the Siam-Burma scheme off at its knees. That is not to say, however, that the scheme would have been successful without Siamese intervention. We know that there were significant logistical and strategic problems already within the Indian and German circle of conspirators. But by making it impossible for Indian revolutionaries to seek protection from apprehension from a neutral state, their plans to wreak havoc from Siam were over by the end of 1915 – thus allowing British authorities to focus most of their attention on places like Shanghai and Batavia, where the authorities were far less accommodating.

Fortunately for the French, the willingness of the Siamese government to support the British in their mission to apprehend Indian revolutionaries also extended to Vietnamese revolutionaries working against the French. The French Governor General noted with satisfaction that the King's government was going out of its way to be helpful in both the surveillance and apprehension of Vietnamese revolutionaries operating from within Siam. As of October 1915, he noted that Siamese efforts in

[61] Dering to Earl Grey, Foreign Office, September 8, 1915. Report 48374. Straits Correspondence Original Correspondence: Foreign. TNA CO 273/432.
[62] Cypher telegram from Herbert Dering, September 15, 1915. Report 43514. Straits Correspondence Original Correspondence: Foreign. TNA CO 273/432.
[63] Fraser, "Germany and Indian Revolution, 1914–18," 267.
[64] Maia Ramnath, *Haj to Utopia*, 88.

this regard had already resulted in approximately twelve arrests, and he was confident that "all of [the rest of] these individuals will end up falling into our hands."[65]

Yet it is also important to note that Siamese action in support of British and French requests was directed exclusively toward Indian and Vietnamese sedition rather than the German activity that funded and encouraged them. Perhaps wisely, given the relative weakness of Siam from an international perspective, and quite unlike Beckett in Batavia, at no time did Dering ask the Siamese government to arrest members of the German Legation, German members of the civil service, or German entrepreneurs suspected of supporting the Indian revolutionaries. From the British and Siamese perspective, it was far easier to demand control over the Allies' legal subjects than to spark an international incident – and perhaps trigger war – by targeting German nationals.

One consequence of this reluctance to implicate German diplomats and consuls in Siam was that their representatives continued to try to undermine Allied authority and prestige even after it was clear that German-Indian schemes to launch a revolution in India would not succeed. Most conspicuously, German diplomats in Siam targeted one of the King's half-brothers for a potential coup against Vajiravudh. In November 1915, Dering became aware of a rumor that the Germans planned on "overthrowing the dynasty, substituting for the King a Prince of German choice."[66] This "Prince of German choice" was Nahkon Sawan, who had gone to school in Germany and had returned to serve Siam as the Minister of Marine. Dering communicated the rumor to Devawongse, but by early 1916 these rumors had already spread all over Bangkok, clearly identifying Nakhon Sawan as the German choice to replace the Anglophile King. To eliminate the threat posed by such a plot, the King placed Nakhon Sawan under surveillance and imprisoned several sympathetic army officers.[67] While the situation was controlled without much drama, it did nothing to encourage friendly feelings by Vajiravudh for the Central Powers. Instead, the incident only pushed the King further

---

[65] Governor General Roume to Minister of Colonies, February 22, 1916, 27. Troubles et Complots en Indochine, Indo/nf/3, CAOM. In fact the arrangements between Siam and France for extradition were not exactly the same as those with Britain, as the Siamese government insisted on extraditing Vietnamese revolutionaries to Singapore, whereupon the British authorities could hand them over to the French if they desired. See Dering to Earl Grey, September 8, 1915. Report 48374. Straits Settlements Official Correspondence: Foreign. TNA CO 273/432.

[66] Dering to Earl Grey, Foreign Minister, November 7, 1915. Report 60260. Straits Correspondence Original Correspondence: Foreign. TNA CO 273/433.

[67] Greene, *Absolute Dreams*, 103–104.

toward the Allies, fueling his growing desire to declare war on the Central Powers, seize German assets in Siam, and dismiss the German nationals working in the Siamese government.

By early 1917 the King was actively looking for a pretext to declare war on Germany. He had hoped to use Woodrow Wilson's call, in February of that year, for neutral nations to break off relations with Germany because of its return to unrestricted submarine warfare, but his own ministers – including Devawongse – were much more cautious and insisted on discussing the matter until the end of May. Eventually, however, the King swayed his ministers in favor of war by arguing that if Thailand did not enter the war and the Allies won, Britain would emerge even stronger than before and would therefore be in an even more powerful position to dominate Siam. By entering the war on the side of the Allies, the King argued that Siam would ensure itself a place at the bargaining table when the war was over, from which it might be able to negotiate a more favorable international status for itself.[68]

After the King won his cabinet over, Siam officially declared war on the side of the Allies on July 22, 1917. According to a preset plan, the government immediately seized the nine German ships that had been trapped in Bangkok harbor and rounded up about three hundred Germans for eventual shipment to India, where they would remain interned for the duration of the war.[69] After three years during which the enemies of the Allies sought to undermine Allied territory and dominance from within Siam, the Vietnamese, Indian, and German intrigues were over.

Connections and Mobilities

Siam's experience during the war was deeply shaped by the mobilities and international connections of nearly all the involved parties. Even the Siamese government's predisposition toward Great Britain was enhanced by the fact that the King had physically gone there for education and training, and thus established strong personal connections with members of the British elite and with the physical geography of Britain.

But the internationalism of the Siamese war experience went far deeper than that. For starters, the Europeans who lived and worked in Siam bore a large part of the responsibility for the reason the war became such an issue there in the first place. When war broke out, patriotic Europeans in many locations were often eager to contribute to their home country's war

---

[68] Such a course of action, of course, was not unique to Siam: the government of China also made the same argument and was similarly successful in 1917.
[69] Greene, *Absolute Dreams*, 106–107.

effort in whatever way possible, whether by providing funds to the war effort, providing useful intelligence to their governments, or sabotaging the economic or political affairs of their enemies. The result in a place like Siam was a raft of German railway engineers suddenly willing to provide strategic intelligence about accessible border crossings into Burma, or British police officers and advisors working for the Siamese government who were willing to collect information about German activities for the use of the British government.

The presence of European diplomats and consuls in Siam added another layer to the international connections linking Siam with the rest of the world. As we saw in British Malaya and the Dutch East Indies, the consuls and diplomats in Siam not only interacted with the Siamese government and with one another, but they kept up a constant correspondence with their home governments and with other consuls and colonial officials in neighboring territories. Dering, for example, maintained regular contact with his Foreign Minister in London, who then often copied Dering's reports back to Singapore, Delhi, Batavia, Manila, Rangoon, San Francisco, and other relevant locations. Dering also maintained independent correspondence with the British governments in India, Burma, and Singapore. Information provided by Dering was also used by the Government at Singapore to work out the extradition of Vietnamese nationalists with the Government of Indochina. The French and German ministers also communicated regularly back to their home governments, both supplying and receiving information and instructions from their respective Foreign Offices; while the French minister was in regular contact also with the Government of Indochina and with French consuls in China and in Hong Kong.

This constant communication enabled representatives of each European state to maintain a network of information that could, when needed, either span the globe or else closely connect nearby areas. Moreover, each of these networks could be connected to one another either voluntarily – when diplomats from different states chose to exchange useful information, for example – or involuntarily, such as when telegrams and correspondence generated by enemies was intercepted.

These networks became that much more important in a strategic location like Siam, where consular intelligence was linked to the security of the colonies. For the British, Dering not only provided information about Ghadar revolutionaries that was considered vital to the security of Burma and India, but he also received information from a global network that aided him in knowing where to look for that information. For the Germans, Remy served not only as the eyes and ears of the German government in Siam but also as an on-the-ground organizer – in coordination with other German consuls in China, Manila, and the Dutch East Indies – of German policy to undermine Allied colonial rule. What all this meant was that European civil servants, diplomats, and consuls played an important role in bringing events like the First World War right into local politics halfway around the world.

The other actors responsible for bringing the war to Siam were, of course, the Vietnamese and Indian revolutionaries themselves, whose physical mobility allowed them to function as human links in a broad pattern of anticolonial resistance. In the case of Indochina, Vietnamese revolutionaries found it necessary to physically remove themselves to neutral territories like Siam in order to evade French persecution and gain the freedom to organize. By 1914, they had already created a regional anticolonial network that included activists working not only in Siam but also in China and, to a lesser extent, Japan. In this way the very physical mobility of these revolutionaries into territory outside French control helped bring the war to Siam.

Physical mobility also marked the Indian revolutionaries who became so central to war-related intrigue in Siam, and on a far larger scale than Vietnamese revolutionaries. Indeed, the global footprint of the Ghadar activists was truly remarkable during the war years, extending from North America to the Philippines, the Dutch East Indies, Japan, China, Siam, Burma, India, Afghanistan, and the Ottoman Empire. Individual Ghadar revolutionaries who became involved in Siamese intrigues illustrate the physical mobility that characterized many Ghadar activists. This is certainly the case with Jodh Singh Mahajan (alias Hasan Zade), one of the first Indians arrested by Siamese authorities at the request of the British in August 1915. Jodh Singh had been born in India, but in 1907 had sailed to North America to work as a laborer. Finding North America inhospitable because of racial prejudice, he next traveled to Britain, where he met Har Dayal at London's India House. He moved next to Berlin, where he made contact with radical anti-imperialist groups, and then in 1910 he sailed for Rio de Janeiro, where he worked among Indian emigrants until 1915.[70] Sikh emigrants in Rio introduced him to the *Ghadar* journal in early 1915, and shortly thereafter Jodh Singh became an individual subscriber. In February 1915 a Ghadar party activist asked Jodh Singh to assist in arranging the coordination between the German government and the Ghadar party in North America. After accepting, he first sailed back to Berlin for instructions – where he met Har Dayal again as well as the German Max von Oppenheim – and then crossed the Atlantic to New York. But his travels were far from over, for once

[70] Ramnath, *Haj to Utopia*, 83–84.

he reached New York Ghadar party members there persuaded him that his services were even more needed in Siam. In Siam, he was to work with the three Germans from Chicago who had been slated to provide money and arms to Indian revolutionaries there (Wehde, Boehm, and Sterneck). Although we know that Boehm and Sterneck never made it to Siam because of the ill-fated journey of the *Henry S.*, Jodh Singh did arrive in Bangkok on July 17, 1915 via Manila and Amoy, China.[71] Once in Siam, he took a leadership role in organizing the German-Ghadar strategy of invading Burma as a way to get to India. However, as a result of British intelligence and informers within the movement, Jodh Singh was arrested only a couple of months after his arrival. Nevertheless, his trajectory around India, the Americas, Europe, and Southeast Asia is representative of the many mobile individuals who had left India, developed revolutionary ideals in their self-imposed exile, and then attempted to return to India – with the help of German conspirators and financiers – through the neutral territory of Siam. Their plans, even though they did not succeed, played a large role not only in bringing the war to Siam but in connecting Siam to multiple places around the world.

Legacies

While Indian-German conspiracies failed in Siam, their legacies lived on in various ways – with consequences not only for Siam but for Southeast and East Asia more generally. For the Ghadar party, World War I was not the end. Rather, the revolutionaries of the war era were viewed as courageous and selfless warriors for the cause, and as inspirations for the future.[72] British repression of the movement had been so concerted that the efforts to eradicate Ghadar gave away just how threatening a movement it was. In the immediate postwar period, then, Ghadar activists did not give up but rather increasingly switched their allegiance to a new ideology that promised aid to anticolonial revolutionaries: international communism.

One of the legacies specific to Indian-German conspiracies in Siam was that they set in motion the organization of a new, and much more coherent, British security apparatus in the region. This new organization taught the British important lessons about cooperation between local intelligence agencies and about the importance of consuls in making this machinery function smoothly.[73] These lessons, in turn, would prove

---

[71] Ramnath, *Haj to Utopia*, 87–88.
[72] Maia Ramnath traces the development of the Ghadar party until its dissolution in *Haj to Utopia*.
[73] Popplewell, *Intelligence and Imperial Defence*, 328.

important in British efforts to counter both the threat posed by the Japanese and the threat of Bolshevism throughout the Far East in the interwar period.

In 1915, when Dering and others were becoming aware of the German-Indian scheme to send an invasion force from Siam through Burma, the government of India took the threat quite seriously. During the summer of that year, the Indian government sent David Petrie – a rising young star in the Indian Department of Criminal Intelligence – to assess the situation in Bangkok. Petrie arrived in Bangkok on August 24, 1915, just as the Siamese government was about to comply with Dering's request to apprehend and deport the first six Ghadar activists. When Jodh Singh and his compatriots were extradited to Singapore, Petrie traveled there in order to interrogate them. Based on his reports indicating a widespread German-Indian conspiracy to foment revolution in India, the Indian government asked Petrie to establish a new Far Eastern Intelligence Agency to combat such conspiracies.[74] Since the purpose of the new Agency was primarily to gather intelligence on threats to India, it was to be paid for and supervised by the government of India. Petrie's jurisdiction was to be wide, encompassing Siam, China, Japan, the Straits Settlements, Hong Kong, the Philippines, and the Dutch East Indies.[75]

Petrie's appointment was made official in May 1916, when he was announced as "Special Officer for Dealing with Indian Sedition and German Intrigue," whose duty "will be to collect and advise upon all information on that subject."[76] In commenting on the post, Petrie said that "one essential of the scheme is to provide officers in the Far East with specialized assistance on the question of Indian sedition."[77] In order to determine just what needed to be done in this regard from each of the places under his jurisdiction, between May and August 1916 Petrie toured Singapore, Hong Kong, China, Japan, and the Philippines. At the end of his tour, he concluded that his headquarters should be in

[74] Dering to Foreign Office, December 8, 1915. Report 56559. Straits Settlements Original Correspondence: Foreign and India Offices. TNA CO 273/433.

[75] March 6, 1916. Report 10900. Straits Settlements Original Correspondence: India Office and War Office. TNA CO 273/450. Originally the Indian Government wanted Petrie to have jurisdiction in North America as well, but the Interdepartmental Committee in London balked at the suggestion, arguing that Petrie's presence in North America could jeopardize existing intelligence there.

[76] May 9, 1916. Report 23134. Straits Settlements Original Correspondence: Foreign. TNA CO 273/448.

[77] Dudley Ridout to Governor, Straits Settlements, May 27, 1916. Report 25402. Report 10900. Straits Settlements Original Correspondence: India Office and War Office. TNA CO 273/450.

Shanghai rather than Singapore as originally intended, because it was there he believed the most dangerous – and unchecked – activity was taking place.[78]

From Shanghai, Petrie set up a network of Indian agents stationed around the areas of his jurisdiction. Because of the distances involved between each area, it was critical that the Indian agents work closely with each of the British consuls.[79] In Shanghai, Petrie himself worked closely with the British consul both to communicate intelligence and to act as an advisor. As a result of these arrangements, not only did Petrie's agency provide a model for how intelligence could be centralized and shared across various government agencies, but it also ensured that British consuls would henceforth have a large role to play in the collection and communication of intelligence themselves. Of course, we have seen already that the consuls in Batavia and Bangkok had voluntarily taken a leading role in acting as intelligence agents during the war. But as a combined result of the war and the demands placed by Petrie and his agents, what might have been a temporary response to wartime conditions in fact helped to transform the post of consul from its primarily economic and administrative functions to a deeply political post by the 1920s. And it would be this reformed version of the consular post that would be used in the fight against communism and Japanese expansion in the interwar period.

Conclusion

In spite of the fact that no battles erupted in Siam during World War I, for the first two years of the war Siam was an important theater for the various anti-Allied intrigues staged by the Central Powers and their revolutionary anticolonial conspirators from both Vietnam and India. By virtue both of its neutrality and its geography – situated as it was in the midst of three Allied colonies – anticolonial activists and representatives of the Central Powers sought to use Siam as a staging ground for launching attacks to both the east and the west. Siam's neutrality and geography had also contributed to the international nature of its temporary residents, from European advisors and diplomats to already established communities of subjects from nearby colonies. Finally, the conspiracies that originated in Siam had long-lasting effects on the region even after they failed, since they gave rise to a more coherent model of colonial security agency which,

---

[78] Popplewell, *Intelligence and Imperial Defence*, 268, 269.
[79] Popplewell, *Intelligence and Imperial Defence*, 266.

in the interwar period, would be used to combat the growing international communist movement. Thus even though the historiography on Siam during World War I is extremely limited, it is clear not only that the war came to Siam in multiple ways but also that Siam was integral to schemes designed both to undermine and to uphold Allied rule in colonial Southeast Asia.

On December 14, 1914, a British detective with the Hong Kong police
arrested a Vietnamese man who was staying at a local boarding house.
Initially the man pretended to be Chinese, but once detained he confessed his real identity to be none other than Luong Lap Nam – a well-
known protégé of the Vietnamese revolutionary Phan Bội Châu and an
integral member of Phan's *Quang Phuc Hoi*, or Viet Nam Restoration
Association.[1] The detective took a statement from Luong, in which the
latter admitted "I am a revolutionary Annamite: all true Annamites are
anxious to liberate their country from French domination."[2] He justified his revolutionary orientation with a long list of grievances, including
French restrictions on indigenous education and travel, French policies
requiring the consumption of opium and alcohol, and the inability of
indigenous soldiers to rise to high rank. Luong insisted that each country
should be governed by its own subjects and compared his revolutionary
struggle with the successful Chinese struggle against the Manchu and
the ongoing South African and Indian struggles against the British. He
ended by insisting that he had broken no laws in Hong Kong and asked
that he be set free so that he could proceed to his intended destination in
Kwangtung (Guangdong).[3]

But British authorities did not release Luong. Instead, on January 14
they secretly transferred him to Gaston Liébert, the French consul in
Hong Kong, who had him whisked away on a ship under heavy guard.
Two secret agents accompanied Luong from Hong Kong to the French
enclave of Kuongtcheouwan (Guongzhouwan), where French authorities formally arrested him. From there, he was taken to Hanoi in French
Indochina, where he was tried for his role in a 1913 bombing in the

---

[1] Rapport de l'inspecteur de police Murphy au chef du service des detectives a Hong Kong,
December 17, 1914. Menées Austrio-Allemande en Indochine, Indo/nf/992, CAOM.
Luong Lap Nam also went by the name Luong Ngoc Quyen.
[2] Declaration de Luong-Lap-Ngam (Luong-Ah-Sam), December 17, 1914. Menées
Austrio-Allemande en Indochine, Indo/nf/992, CAOM.
[3] Declaration de Luong-Lap-Ngam (Luong-Ah-Sam), December 17, 1914.

northern province of Phu Tho.[4] Luong was convicted and sentenced to life with hard labor, and was finally transferred to the notorious Thai Nguyen prison in July 1916.[5] At the prison, he was considered so dangerous that he was kept shackled in solitary confinement. Anxieties about the threat he posed proved accurate, because a little more than a year later Luong played a critical role in the Thai Nguyen rebellion centered on the prison – the most significant rebellion in Indochina between 1880 and 1930 – and was killed by French forces on September 4, 1917.[6]

Like the Indian Nornendra Nath Battacharji (M.N. Roy) from Chapter 4, Luong Lap Nam was a revolutionary who sought any available means to rid his country of its colonial occupiers. Luong himself had helped Phan Bội Châu found the Viet Nam Restoration Association for this purpose in 1912, and when he was arrested he was acting in his capacity as head of the society's external relations.[7] Like many Ghadar party members, many of the most important Viet Nam Restoration Society members lived in exile in the years just prior to World War I, and in fact the Society itself was founded in Kwangtung, China. For these revolutionaries too, self-imposed exile allowed greater freedom to organize and to plan how they would overthrow their colonial rulers. And even more than the leadership of the Ghadar party, by the time of the outbreak of hostilities in 1914, leaders of the Viet Nam Restoration Association had nearly a decade of experience trying to marshal foreign resources and aid for their cause – first from Japan, then from Siam, and then from China.

Yet as we will see below, until the war began these appeals yielded only limited results. While groups in each state had offered – at least for a time – some combination of education, safe haven, or training, what the Viet Nam Restoration Association's leaders believed they needed to effect revolution was money, munitions, and soldiers. Then in 1914, the commencement of hostilities between France and Germany offered a new source of foreign aid willing to provide these items: Germany. Just as they had done for revolutionaries who hoped to ignite a revolution in India, German agents offered both money and arms to Phan's

---

[4] Arrestation à Hong Kong du rebel Annamite Luong-Lap-Nam – son envoi au Tonkin, January 13, 1915. Menées Austrio-Allemande en Indochine, Indo/nf/992, CAOM.

[5] Peter Zinoman, "Colonial Prisons and Anti-Colonial Resistance in French Indochina: The Thai Nguyen Rebellion, 1917," *Modern Asian Studies* 34, no. 01 (2000), 63.

[6] Patrice Morlat, *Les Affaires Politiques de l'Indochine, 1895–1923: Les Grands Commis, Du Savoir Au Pouvoir*, Collection Recherches Asiatiques (Paris: Harmattan, 1995), 200.

[7] Vinh Sinh and Nicholas Wickenden, trans., *Overturned Chariot: The Autobiography of Phan Bội Châu* (Honolulu: University of Hawaii Press, 1999), 138.

partisans for the explicit purpose of attacking French Indochina from both China and Siam. From the French point of view, then, Luong's arrest and imprisonment was a victory not only in terms of silencing a leader of an organized Vietnamese anticolonial movement operating on foreign soil but also in terms of eliminating a Viet Nam Restoration Association member with clear ties to enemy agents from Germany and Austria. Yet Luong was only one of the many Association members seeking to overturn French rule with the help of foreign resources during the war years, and his arrest did not halt collaboration between Vietnamese revolutionaries and German agents.

During the war, China served as an even more important point of contact between German agents and Vietnamese revolutionaries than Siam. China's neutrality (until August 1917) meant that, as in Siam, the extensive foreign diplomatic, consular, and commercial networks already in place before the war continued to function: German consulates existed side by side with those representing France and Britain, while German rail, shipping, and trading interests continued alongside those of their enemies. As a result, as in both the Dutch East Indies and Siam, it was a relatively "simple" matter to use German officials and sympathetic nationals already in place to carry out German policies geared toward undermining Allied colonial rule. This task was made infinitely easier because of the presence in China of well-developed networks of Vietnamese revolutionaries living in self-imposed or forced exile. There, revolutionaries were able to meet with German agents and to make arrangements for shipments of arms and money outside the direct, punishing gaze of colonial administrators. And unlike in Siam, where the government went out of its way to aid the Allies in apprehending those who sought to harm them, in China the government had no such commitment.

Moreover, while the story in this chapter is mainly about Vietnamese collaboration with Germans, representatives of the Central Powers in China also actively worked with other groups willing to cause trouble for either the French or the British – including especially Chinese "pirates" intent on plundering Indochina, and also Indian members of the Ghadar party who utilized China's neutrality to make contact with high-ranking German agents in cities like Shanghai. As such, the international and transcolonial networks that brought the war to British Malaya, the Dutch East Indies, and Siam form only part of the story about Southeast Asia during the war. Equally important were the networks that ran through China, which connected Vietnamese and Indian anticolonial revolutionaries to strategically placed Germans willing to provide them with money and weapons. The result, as we have seen in Chapters 1–5, was that global enmities extended the footprint of the war far beyond the European and Mediterranean theaters, not only to Allied and neutral territories in island Southeast Asia but also to Allied and neutral territories in mainland Southeast and East Asia.

This chapter argues that agents of the Central powers and anticolonial activists alike sought to use neutral China as a staging ground for revolutionary movements in Allied colonial territories. Its focus is on German connections with the Viet Nam Restoration Association, both because so little has been written about this part of the story (particularly in English), and also because it reminds us that it was not only the British who had to worry about such opportunistic partnerships. Moreover, East Asia was a critical focal point for anticolonial activists from Indochina even before the war. While at first such activists were drawn to Japan in the wake of the Japanese victory over Russia in 1905, decreased government tolerance for their presence – combined with the Chinese Revolution in 1911 – led many of them to China instead. Thus when the war broke out, there were already a number of Vietnamese revolutionaries in China who were in the process of using the new republic as a safe haven and training ground for exporting revolution back to Indochina. Under the circumstances, it was not difficult for German agents to make contact with Vietnamese revolutionaries, and vice versa, when the opportunity arose. In addition to Vietnamese–German collaboration, the chapter also explores reputed German schemes to promote disorder along the Sino-Vietnamese border using disaffected Chinese "pirates." Finally, it sketches the general outlines of German–Indian collaboration through China, the existence of which underlines the importance of China as a focal point for transnational, anticolonial networks in the region.

Although none of the revolutionary schemes between anticolonial activists and agents of the Central Powers in China was successful during the war years, as in earlier chapters success or failure is not the point. Instead, it is to demonstrate in yet another context the ways the war helped promote the globalization of regional anticolonial movements. It is also to show that these various efforts to collaborate were not simply isolated incidents but were instead deeply connected to one another – sometimes even by the same individuals, though most often by the diffusion of information – and were part of a global strategy to undermine Allied rule in whatever way possible. Indeed, the temporary partnerships that developed in China between Vietnamese or Indian revolutionaries on the one hand and German agents on the other was part of a pattern that extended throughout the region and beyond. As in other parts of Southeast Asia, then, even though very little fighting occurred as a result of the war, the war nevertheless came to the region in multiple and important ways.

China and Indochina in World War I

In spite of the many consequences of the war in both China and Indochina, the historiography focusing on either location is surprisingly lean. Only one English-language monograph, by Guoqi Xu, explores China's complicated and fraught experience of the war.[8] A few of the globally oriented histories of World War I, particularly Hew Strachan's *The First World War*, explore in some detail the Japanese campaign to conquer the German concession on the Shandong peninsula in 1914, as does the historiography on the Anglo-Japanese alliance that provided the opportunity for the campaign in the first place.[9] In addition, Guoqi Xu has contributed a helpful chapter on China's war experiences to Robert Gerwarth and Erez Manela's *Empires at War*.[10]

The historiography on Indochina in the context of the Great War is similarly slim, both in English and in French. Only one English-language monograph, by Kimloan Vu-Hill, explores the impact of the war on the region, and even then nearly half of the book is about the experience of the approximately 99,000 Vietnamese soldiers who served in Europe itself.[11] Richard Fogarty's *Race and War in France* includes the experience of Vietnamese soldiers in the larger context of French colonial subjects who were recruited to fight in Europe but does not offer an extended analysis of conditions in Indochina.[12] French-language sources are slightly more numerous, though many of these are unpublished dissertations.[13]

---

[8] Xu, *China and the Great War: China's Pursuit of a New National Identity and Internationalization*.

[9] Strachan, *The First World War*. For the Anglo-Japanese alliance, see Phillips Payson O'Brien, *The Anglo-Japanese Alliance, 1902–1922* (London; New York: RoutledgeCurzon, 2004).

[10] Guoqi Xu, Robert Gerwarth, and Erez Manela, eds. "China and Empire." In *Empires at War, 1911–1923* (Oxford: Oxford University Press, 2014).

[11] Vu-Hill, *Coolies into Rebels: Impact of World War I on French Indochina*. Hill also has an article on this topic, called "Strangers in a Foreign Land: Vietnamese Soldiers and Workers in France during World War I," in Nhung Tuyet Tran and Anthony Reid, eds., *Viet Nam: Borderless Histories* (Madison: University of Wisconsin Press, 2006), 256–89.

[12] Fogarty, *Race and War in France: Colonial Subjects in the French Army, 1914–1918*.

[13] Published sources include Emmanuel Bouhier, "Les Troupes Coloniales D'Indochine en 1914–1918," in Claude Carlier et al., eds., *Les Troupes Coloniales Dans La Grande Guerre* (Paris: IHCC-CNSV, Economica, 1997); Patrice Morlat, chapter 9, "La Mobilisation," in *Les Affaires Politiques de l'Indochine, 1895–1923*. Unpublished dissertations include Henri Eckert, Les Militaires Indochinois au Service de la France, 1859–1939 (Ph.d. Thesis, Université de Lille, 1998); Charles Fourniau, Les Contacts franco-vietnamiens de la 1ere a la 2e Guerre Mondiale (Multigraphie, Aix-en-Provence, 1987); Mireille Favre-Le Van Ho, Un Milieu Porteur de Modernisation: Travailleurs et Tirailleurs Vietnamiens en France pendant La Premiere Guerre Mondiale (These de l'Ecole Nationale de Chartes, 1986); and the much older Duong Van Giao, L'Indochine Pendant la Guerre de 1914–1918 (These, Paris, 1926).

And while there is a rich historiography on the late nineteenth to early twentieth centuries in Indochina in both English and French, the larger global context of World War I tends to play a relatively marginal role in these studies.[14]

Yet the dearth of works on the impact of World War I on East Asia should not be taken as an indication that the war was not important in either location. As Guoqi Xu has shown for China, the opening months of World War I resulted not only in the conquest of the German concession by the Japanese, but in a crisis of monumental importance when the Japanese government presented Yuan Shikai's new Chinese republic with the infamous Twenty-one Demands.[15] These demands – nearly all of which Yuan's government was forced to accept – were considered a national humiliation, and it was in part to redress this humiliation and win back the Shandong peninsula from the Japanese that China first sought to enter the war on the side of the Allies in November 1915.[16] Moreover, Xu demonstrates that when China finally did enter the war in August 1917 – a year after Yuan Shikai's death – the decision divided the government and led several factions to seek support from independent generals who commanded their own forces. In this way, the decision to enter the war also encouraged the warlordism and factionalism that characterized the early 1920s.[17] Finally, Xu argues – as does Erez Manela – that China's failure to win back the Shandong peninsula at the war's end after contributing 140,000 laborers to the European theater resulted in national outrage in the form of the May 4th Movement, and may well

---

[14] On the history of Vietnam in this era, see David Marr, *Vietnamese Anticolonialism: 1885–1925* (Berkeley: University of California Press, 1971); William Duiker, *The Rise of Nationalism in Vietnam, 1900–1941* (Ithaca: Cornell University Press, 1976); Christopher Goscha, *Vietnam or Indochina? Contesting Concepts of Space in Vietnamese Nationalism, 1887–1954* (Copenhagen: NIAS Books, 1995); Peter Zinoman, *The Colonial Bastille: A History of Imprisonment in Vietnam, 1862–1940* (Berkeley: University of California Press, 2001); Pierre Brocheux and Daniel Hémery, *Indochine: la Colonisation Ambigue, 1858–1954* (Paris: Découverte, 1995); Charles Fourniau, *Vietnam: Domination Coloniale et Résistance Nationale, 1858–1914* (Paris: Indes savantes, 2002); Pierre Montagnon, *France-Indochine: Un Siècle de Vie Commune, 1858–1954* (Paris: Pygmalion, 2004); Jean-Pierre Pecqueur, *Indochine-France: Conquête et Rupture, 1620–1954*, 1. éd, Évocations (Saint-Cyr-sur-Loire: A. Sutton, 2009); Thu Trang-Gaspard, *Hồ Chí Minh à Paris, 1917–1923*, Collection "Recherches Asiatiques" (Paris: L'Harmattan, 1992); and several of the essays in Pierre Brocheux, ed., *Histoire du l'Asie du Sud-Est: Révoltes, Réformes, Révolutions* (Lille: Presses Universitaires de Lille, 1981); Patrice Morlat, *La Répression Coloniale Au Vietnam, 1908–1940*, Recherches Asiatiques (Paris: Editions l'Harmattan, 1990); Morlat, *Les Affaires Politiques de l'Indochine, 1895–1923*. Of these, only Morlat's two monographs explore the global effects of the war on Vietnam in some detail.

[15] Xu, *China and the Great War*, 93.   [16] Xu, *China and the Great War*, 107.

[17] Guoqi et al., eds., "China and Empire," 222–228.

have encouraged some of China's leaders to turn toward communism during the 1920s.[18]

The war also had important short- and long-term consequences in Indochina. Most obvious in the short term was the recruitment of so many soldiers and workers to fight in Europe which, in some areas, generated resistance by local populations.[19] Additionally, like their counterparts in British Malaya, the French were compelled to withdraw many of their French soldiers and effective Vietnamese *tirailleurs* to France when the war began, leaving Indochina more militarily vulnerable than was normally the case.[20] As a result, colonial administrators noticed an increase in lawlessness and banditry in response to the weakening of the French presence.[21] In the longer term, Kimloan Vu-Hill and others argue that the return of thousands of Vietnamese soldiers and laborers to Indochina from service in Europe contributed to increased dissatisfaction with conditions in the colony after the War.[22] Perhaps even more important in both the short and long terms, the War provided an unprecedented opportunity for anticolonial activists to widen their field of international contacts in their search for support to defeat the French. While this search for international support did not begin with the War, it did for the first time suggest that France's European foes could be generous allies.[23] And although wartime efforts in this regard were not particularly successful, they would be revisited again in the context of international communism during the interwar period. On the French side, as Patrice Morlat notes, in the short term the crisis atmosphere produced by the war allowed the Government in Indochina, in March 1915, to declare martial law in the territory of Tonkin. What this meant was that the French now had free rein to deal with anticolonial actors through

---

18 Xu, *China and the Great War*, 130, 245, 276. Manela makes this argument with respect to China in *The Wilsonian Moment: Self-Determination and the International Origins of Anticolonial Nationalism* (New York: Oxford, 2007).

19 Zinoman, "Colonial Prisons and Anti-Colonial Resistance in French Indochina: The Thai Nguyen Rebellion, 1917," 84.

20 Michael Vann, White City on the Red River: Race, Power, and Culture in French Colonial Hanoi (Ph.D. Dissertation, University of Santa Cruz, 1999, 177–178). In Hanoi, Vann argues that the flight of white Frenchmen from Vietnam ironically created unprecedented economic opportunities for some Vietnamese entrepreneurs.

21 Gouvernor-Generale Ernest Roume à Monsieur Delcasse, Ministre des Colonies, 22 Fevrier 1916. Troubles en Cochinchine, Indo/nf/28/2, 1914, CAOM.

22 Vu-Hill, *Coolies into Rebels*, 9; Eckert, *Les Militaires Indochinoise au Service de la France*, 605.

23 Christopher Goscha's *Thailand and the Southeast Asian Networks of the Vietnamese Revolution, 1885–1954* (Richmond, Surrey: Curzon Press, 1999) insists on the long-standing "international context" of Vietnamese anticolonialism, beginning with the Can Vuong movement in the late nineteenth century. While his focus is on Thailand, he points to larger international networks in the 1914–1918 period.

military tribunals that were able to mete out swift and harsh punishment. As such, the war provided the opportunity for the French government to use violent repression on an even greater scale than before.[24] The consequences of this for Phan Bội Châu's Viet Nam Restoration Association were dire. In a twisted irony, given that Phan's group sought to profit from Franco–German enmity, the enhanced surveillance and summary justice afforded by the war allowed the French to kill or imprison nearly all of the Association's most important leaders – leaving the movement in a shambles.[25]

Given that Phan Bội Châu's Viet Nam Restoration Association was one of the most important early twentieth century anticolonial movements in Vietnam, most historians of Vietnamese anticolonialism are aware of the connections between the Association and German agents during World War I. Phan Bội Châu himself made no secret of it and made repeated references to the relationship in both his *Prison Notes* and his later autobiography.[26] At the same time, few historians have devoted much attention to these activities except to note that they produced little in the way of tangible results.[27] David Marr's classic study dismissed them by saying that funds provided by Germans were "used in ill-conceived attacks on French border posts, mere petty harassments that succeeded only in creating more dissension within the dwindling ranks of the *Quang Phuc Hoi*." Moreover, he argued, the "Germans remained unimpressed, membership drifted away, and the French linked up with certain Chinese warlords and bandit groups to arrange the killing or capture of the remaining leaders."[28] Patrice Morlat is one of the few who have taken these connections seriously, though his work has not been translated into English.[29]

[24] Morlat, *Les Affaires Politiques de l'Indochine, 1895–1923*, 195.

[25] Morlat, *Les Affaires Politiques de l'Indochine, 1895–1923*, 187.

[26] Phan Bội Châu's *Prison Notes* is available in English translation (along with Ho Chi Minh's *Prison Diary*) in Christopher Jenkins et al., eds., *Reflections from Captivity*, Southeast Asia Translation Series, v. 1 (Athens: Ohio University Press, 1978); Phan Bội Châu's autobiography was translated by Vinh Sinh and Nicholas Wickenden in *Overturned Chariot: The Autobiography of Phan-Bội-Châu* (Honolulu, HI: University of Hawai'i Press, 1999).

[27] Yves Le Jariel's otherwise excellent *Phan Bội Châu, 1867–1940: Le Nationalisme Vietnamien Avant Ho Chi Minh* (Paris: L'Harmattan, 2008) concludes that while these connections existed, they did not ultimately have much positive effect for the nationalist movement, as does David G. Marr's classic *Vietnamese Anti-Colonialism 1885–1925* (Berkeley: University of California Press, 1971). Christopher Goscha briefly discusses the connections from the Siamese side in Goscha, *Thailand and the Southeast Asian Networks of the Vietnamese Revolution, 1885–1954*.

[28] Marr, *Vietnamese Anti-Colonialism 1885–1925*, 229.

[29] Both Morlat's, *La Répression Coloniale Au Vietnam, 1908–1940* (1990) and *Les Affaires Politiques de l'Indochine, 1895–1923* (1995) discuss these connections in some detail, though they are not the main subject of either monograph.

While historians of Vietnamese anticolonialism have not paid much attention to German-Vietnamese conspiracies during the war, historians of World War I have given them no attention at all. They do not appear in any of the histories that track the global footprint of the war, or even in those that seek to shed light on German schemes to undermine colonial rule far from the main theaters of fighting. As a result, little is known about the various German-Vietnamese schemes that originated in China during the war, and until now no one has sought to place them in the larger regional context of German schemes in the rest of Southeast Asia. When we do this, we can see not only that World War I had a significant impact on both colonial Indochina and on China but also that German–Vietnamese collaboration was part of a larger regional pattern involving revolutionaries who sought outside help in their various quests for independence.

Vietnamese Anticolonialism and Foreign Support: The Background

Although it is clear that connections between Vietnamese revolutionaries and representatives of the Central Powers existed during World War I, the sources are fragmentary and at times contradictory regarding specific schemes and intelligence. For this reason, it is critical to understand the larger context within which these connections occurred – both in terms of the longer trajectory of Association attempts to involve foreign powers in its struggle against the French, and in terms of wider attempts by representatives of the Central Powers to encourage anticolonial revolutionaries to rebel against their colonial rulers.

The biggest problems with the sources are that they are one-sided and incomplete. As Christopher Goscha has noted with regard to revolutionary networks in Siam at this time, most of the evidence for these connections must be gleaned from French (and also, in this case, British) colonial documents, which of course were compiled by colonial administrators and diplomats. Such documents require a careful and critical reading, for these administrators and diplomats often had particular – and sometimes conflicting – motivations undergirding their interpretation of events. For example, a few of the key persons involved in the creation of these sources – including especially the French consul in Hong Kong, Gaston Liébert – were, like W.R.D. Beckett in Batavia, ambitious and patriotic, and were inclined to see conspiracies lurking around every corner. At the same time, others – like Governor General Joost von Vollenhoven (January 1914–April 1915) – routinely sought to downplay the internal problems caused by Vietnamese-German schemes in their reports back to the Minister of Colonies in Paris. Thus we have simultaneous impulses in the sources for both exaggeration and under-statement, even while nearly all of them convey a colonial point of view. The sources are also incomplete, because Gaston Liébert's transfer from the consulate in Hong Kong to New York in 1916 left a vacuum in what had been a steady stream of reports, telegrams, and correspondence on Vietnamese-German schemes between Liébert and the Governor General's office in Hanoi. As a result, while we have evidence for continuing schemes in 1916 and 1917 from the British sources, the flow of information in the French sources slowed considerably after Liébert's departure.

Another problem with the sources is that we know the intelligence they relied on was sometimes just plain wrong. A clear example of this problem were the multiple sightings and reports by Gaston Liebert's informers about Phan Bội Châu's actions in China between 1914 and 1916, discussed in more detail below, when we know that Phan was locked away in a Kwangtung prison for the duration of that period.

Notwithstanding these problems, the sources tell an important story when viewed in the larger context of the Viet Nam Restoration Association's attempts to win foreign support prior to the war, and of German actions in the region during the war. World War I was emphatically not the first occasion on which Vietnamese anticolonial activists looked to outside sources for help. Instead, it was the Japanese victory in the Russo-Japanese war a decade earlier that first caught the attention of anticolonial activists in Vietnam who had been seeking aid in their own struggle against the French. This was certainly true of Phan Bội Châu, who had been born to a poor scholarly family in Nghe An province in 1867.[30] Just prior to the Russo-Japanese war, Phan had helped organize a secret movement that sought to instigate a military revolution with the heir of the exiled princes of the Vietnamese ruling house – Cuong De – at its head.[31] Through reading the works of Chinese reformers like Liang Qichao, Phan became convinced that one of the keys to winning independence was to ensure the modernization of Vietnamese society along the lines of the Japanese modernization that had been occurring since

---

[30] Shiraishi Masaya and Vinh Sinh's co-edited *Phan Bội Châu and the Dong-Du Movement*, Lac-Viet Series (New Haven, CT: Yale Southeast Asia Studies, 1988) is very useful in this context.

[31] These princes were what was left of the Can Vuong (Save the King) movement, which was an insurgency that lasted from 1885 to 1896. Its purpose was to expel the French and place the young emperor Ham Nghi on the throne as the leader of an independent Vietnam. See Charles Fourniau, *Annam-Tonkin, 1885–1896: Lettrés et Paysans Viet-namiens Face à La Conquête Coloniale*, Travaux Du Centre D'histoire et Civilisations de La Péninsule Indochinoise (Paris: L'Harmattan, 1989), chapter 2; Claude Gendre, *Le Dê Thám (1858–1913): Un Résistant Vietnamien à La Colonisation Française* (Paris: Harmattan, 2007), 37–44.

the 1868 Meiji Restoration.[32] To that end, in 1904 he helped to found the *Viet Nam Duy Tan Hoi* (Viet Nam Modernization Association). And in 1905, just before the end of the Russo-Japanese war, the Association sent Phan to Japan with the goal of securing military aid for its cause.[33]

Yet Phan Bội Châu's hopes for immediate military aid from Japan were disappointed. Upon arriving in Japan and making contact with Liang Qichao – who was living in exile there – Phan was made to understand that it was too soon to ask for military intervention because the Vietnamese people were not yet ready. Instead, Liang and two sympathetic leaders of the Japanese Progressive Party suggested that young Vietnamese intellectuals come to Japan in order to educate themselves about modernity and to receive military and organizational training.[34]

Thus was born the *Dong-Du* (Travel East) movement with which Phan is famously associated.[35] The first young Vietnamese men went to Japan in 1905, and by 1906 nearly five hundred Vietnamese anticolonialists were studying at universities and military academies in Tokyo and Yokohama, with the blessing of a number of prominent Japanese politicians.[36] Yet only a year later, in 1907, the Japanese government signaled a major change in policy by indicating it would cooperate with the European powers in recognizing their colonial interests in Asia – including French interests in Indochina.[37] Suddenly the existence of hundreds of revolutionary anticolonialists at Japanese institutions became embarrassing for the Japanese government, and in 1909 the government cracked down to force colonized subjects from across Asia – including Phan Bội Châu and his partisans – to leave the country.[38]

Yet while the Dong-Du movement had been short-lived, it had far-reaching consequences. Those students who returned to Vietnam brought their training back with them, which in turn inspired many other

---

[32] Liang was one of the Chinese reformist writers whose works were collectively known as "New Books," and were themselves mainly filtered through Japanese writings about the West. Phan, *Overturned Chariot*, 9.

[33] Phan, *Overturned Chariot*, 11, 84; Yves le Jariel, *Phan Bội Châu*, 42.

[34] The two men were Count Okuma Shigenobu and Inukai Tsuyoshi, as recounted in Phan's autobiography. *Overturned Chariot*, 87.

[35] For more on the Travel East movement as it related to Phan, see Georges Boudarel, *Phan Bội Châu et La Societe Vietnamienne de Son Temps* (Paris: Extrait de France-Asie 199, 1969), chapter 2.

[36] Goscha, *Thailand and the Southeast Asian Networks of the Vietnamese Revolution, 1885–1954*, 29.

[37] Shiraishi Masaya, "Phan Boi Chau in Japan," in Shiraishi Masaya and Vinh Sinh, eds., *Phan Bội Châu and the Dong-Du Movement*, Lac-Viet Series (New Haven, CT: Yale Southeast Asia Studies, 1988), 73; Patrice Morlat, *La Repression Coloniale au Vietnam*, 19.

[38] Yves le Jariel, *Phan Bội Châu*, 60.

Vietnamese who had not had the opportunity to go to Japan.[39] More importantly for our purposes here, in the decade prior to World War I Japan was the temporary home to a wide variety of "Asian" revolutionaries and anticolonialists from many places besides Vietnam, including especially China and India.[40] Phan Bội Châu and others in the Dong Du movement came into contact with many of these individuals during their sojourn in Japan, and in 1907 Phan even helped to found the Society for East Asian Alliance to draw such individuals together. The strength of these ties was sometimes remarkable, as can be gleaned from a letter by a Ceylonese man found in Luong Lap Nam's possession at the time of his arrest in 1914. The author made it clear that the two had met while living in Japan, and that despite having left he had never forgotten Luong. He went on to add, after pledging his respect for the Japanese, that "we are the Asiatic laborers of the future: Chinese, Japanese, and Indians are brothers and I hope that the moment will soon come that the whole world will recognize this great truth . . . I hope that soon God will help us meet again as men nobly working for liberation from our respective empires."[41] Although it is only one letter, it indicates that anticolonial activists in Japan were familiar with the idea that colonialism was a global problem requiring global solutions.

Although the Society for East Asian Alliance included colonized and noncolonized people from many locations, Phan Bội Châu himself felt most drawn to the Chinese nationalists and revolutionaries with whom he made contact, both because he believed they came from a similar culture and because he thought they were suffering from the "same sickness" (colonial domination) as Vietnamese anticolonialists.[42] His relationships with Chinese nationalists from the province of Yunnan were particularly strong because of their common antipathy toward the French. Yunnan shared a long border with French Indochina, and Yunnanese activists were concerned about the possibility of French invasion as well as interference in their province.[43] Phan believed in a strong sense of solidarity between Vietnamese and Yunnanese activists, and famously wrote that the two groups, as "intimate brothers," would together rid themselves of the French. To accomplish this, he advocated that "While the Vietnamese grip the French throat, the Yunnanese hit their back; while the Yunnanese

---

[39] Phan, *Overturned Chariot*, 12–13.
[40] For India, see Fischer-Tiné, "Indian Nationalism and the 'world Forces'".
[41] V.K. Jaganayagam to Luong Lap Nam, June 15, 1911, Menées Austrio-Allemande en Indochine. Indo/nf/992, CAOM.
[42] Shiraishi Masaya, "Phan Boi Chau in Japan," 65, 76.
[43] Shiraishi Masaya, "Phan Boi Chau in Japan," 65, 76; Yves le Jariel, *Phan Bội Châu*, 104–105.

restrain the French arms, the Vietnamese hold their shoulders."[44] These contacts – forged as they were during a remarkable period of intercolonial collaboration in Japan – were later to become crucial to Phan as he increasingly turned his attention from Japan to China as the key to aiding Vietnam in its struggle against the French.

When Phan Bội Châu and his partisans were forced to leave Japan in 1909, Phan did not return to Indochina but rather traveled to Singapore and around Southeast Asia in order to find a way to smuggle arms into Indochina from abroad. Yet while he was able to purchase arms, he was not able to find a way to get them into Vietnam. Disgusted with his own failures, Phan went to Kwangtung (Guangdong) and donated the arms he had purchased to Sun Yat-Sen's revolutionary Chinese Guomindang party.[45] "My thought," Phan later recounted, "was that this would create warm sentiments that might be reciprocated after the other party had been successful."[46]

In autumn 1910, Phan and some of his compatriots decided to move to Siam in order to regroup, retrain, and contemplate next moves. In Siam, Phan enjoyed the hospitality of one of the king's brothers, who pledged to help support Phan's group with a food allowance and with the provisioning of farm land for them to live and work.[47] Phan then settled himself to the unfamiliar and difficult task of farming – a task completely unfamiliar to a classically trained Confucian scholar like himself – believing he would remain in Siam for years.

Late in 1911, however, Phan Bội Châu heard that Sun Yat-Sen's revolutionary army had captured the Chinese city of Wuhan, sparking a wave of events that led to the overthrow of the Qing dynasty and the establishment of a republican government – with Sun as its provisional president – in Nanking.[48] A friend advised Phan to return to China right away to take advantage of the situation, which he did post-haste. Back in China, Phan was quickly joined by the prince Cuong-De (who had been living in exile in Hong Kong) and a variety of his Vietnamese compatriots from both Siam and Vietnam.

It was at this point that Phan and his associates decided to scrap the Vietnam Modernization Association in favor of a new institution called the Viet Nam Restoration Association (Việt Nam Quang Phục Hội) which was directly modeled on Sun Yat-Sen's Guomindang Party's revolutionary principles. This new association – officially founded in

---

[44] Shiraishi Masaya, "Phan Boi Chau in Japan," 67.
[45] Phan, *Overturned Chariot*, 14. Phan recounts this episode in his life on pages 173–177.
[46] Phan, *Overturned Chariot*, 177.   [47] Phan, *Overturned Chariot*, 185.
[48] Jenkins et al., *Reflections from Captivity*, 50.

March 1912 – gave up the monarchism of the Viet Nam Modernization Association and stated its primary goal to be the restoration
of Vietnamese independence and the establishment of a democratic
republic.[49]

As in Japan, Phan's intention in coming to China was to approach Sun
Yat-Sen's new government for help in his own quest for Vietnamese independence. Unfortunately for Phan, however, his visit to Sun's temporary
capital at Nanjing in the spring of 1912 occurred at the very same time
Sun was handing his powers over to Yuan Shikai – a Qing dynasty general
who had negotiated the abdication of the last Qing emperor – in Beijing.
Sun in fact had no time to meet with Phan and left it to his associate to
share the disappointing news that the Guomindang was in no position
to help the Viet Nam Restoration Association at that moment. Instead,
he suggested that Phan take the next ten years to educate Vietnamese
students in China, after which the Chinese government might be able
to provide them some aid.[50] Having heard all this before in Japan and
determining not to wait so long to begin the revolution, Phan traveled to
Shanghai to try his luck with its Guomindang-appointed governor, Chen
Chi-Mei, with whom he had become friendly during his days in Japan.
Chen was more sympathetic, and gave Phan both money and weapons
for his cause.[51]

Phan returned to Kwangtung with Chen's contributions, and under the
benevolent protection of its governor, Chen Chiung-Ming, proceeded to
ready the Viet Nam Restoration Association for action.[52] By September 1912, the League had rented spacious headquarters, incorporated
a number of prominent Chinese into its leadership, and begun issuing
army scrip to raise money for itself. To generate publicity and enthusiasm, in September the League held its first congress of the Association
for the Revitalization of China and the Regeneration of Asia. With about
two hundred people in attendance, the congress made it clear that it
had a broad plan which began with assisting Vietnam people in their
struggle against the French but then would move to assisting Indians and
Burmans against the British, and finally to assisting Koreans against the
Japanese.[53]

By the end of 1912, however, it was clear that the Viet Nam Restoration
Association was running out of money. Phan believed that in order to gar-
ner continuing financial support, his organization needed to demonstrate

---

[49] Phan, *Overturned Chariot*, 191. Cuong De was still to be the president of the new
association, though without royal pretensions.
[50] Phan, *Overturned Chariot*, 193.   [51] Phan, *Overturned Chariot*, 194.
[52] Marr, *Vietnamese Anti-Colonialism 1885–1925*, 220.
[53] Phan, *Overturned Chariot*, 204.

its capacity for action rather than mere rhetoric.[54] As a consequence, Association leaders authorized a series of sensational acts of terror to be carried out in Indochina. The assailants were divided into three teams, one of which was to assassinate the French Governor-General, Albert Sarraut, and the other two of which were to assassinate the hated Vietnamese collaborators Nguyen Duy Han and Hoang Cao Khai. Yet while the teams succeeded in killing Nguyen Duy Han in Thai Binh and two French colonels in Hanoi in April 1913, they did not succeed in killing Sarraut. More importantly, the French response to the actions of the Association was swift and harsh, resulting in the arrest of 254 people, the execution of seven, and the imprisonment of fifty-seven.[55] Further attempts by the Association at disruption in 1913 resulted only in more repression, and in angry appeals by French diplomats to the Chinese government to stop sheltering known antagonists of the French colonial state.[56]

When we step back and view the period between 1905 and 1913 as a whole, what is clear is that Phan Bội Châu and his compatriots had already spent eight years trying to obtain aid from foreign governments in Japan, Siam, and – most recently – China to fuel the Association's revolutionary plans. Each of these attempts had begun hopefully. In Japan, Vietnamese students had received education and military training, and had taken part in a brief moment of cosmopolitan and collaborative anticolonialism. This experience increased their awareness about struggles against colonial rule in other places, and increased their connections with revolutionary leaders in places like India and China. In Siam, Phan and his associates had been given land on which to regroup, away from French persecution in Indochina. In China they had been received with sympathy by some of the leaders of the Guomindang party, and had been allowed to organize without being persecuted. From China also they were able to stage several violent attempts to wreak havoc within Indochina. As such, by the time the war broke out Phan and his compatriots had already made substantial progress building a revolutionary movement with its center outside of Vietnam.[57]

---

[54] Yves Le Jariel, *Phan Bội Châu, 1867–1940*, 114.
[55] Yves le Jariel, *Phan Bội Châu*, 126.
[56] Marr, *Vietnamese Anti-Colonialism 1885–1925*, 220. For more on colonial violence in this period, see also Michael Vann's "Fear and Loathing in French Hanoi: Colonial White Images and Imaginings of 'Native' Violence," in Martin Thomas (ed.), *The French Colonial Mind: Violence, Military Encounters, and Colonialism* (University of Nebraska Press, 2012).
[57] Goscha, *Thailand and the Southeast Asian Networks of the Vietnamese Revolution, 1885–1954*, 34.

At the same time, during this period Phan had grown discouraged by the lack of substantial military support or finances from any of these states, by the severity of French repression, and by the failings of his own people for not being ready to carry out a successful revolution. To make matters worse, circumstances in China for Phan's group of anti-colonialists were not stable, as Yuan Shikai's new government sought greater control over Chinese provinces and increasingly replaced sympathetic, Guomindang-affiliated military governors with men of his own choosing.[58] For example, in July 1913 Phan's benefactor in Kwangtung, Ch'en Chiung-ming, was forced to vacate his post as governor in favor of Lung Chi-kuang – a warlord and supporter of Yuan Shikai.[59] Unlike Ch'en, Lung was openly hostile to Phan and the Viet Nam Restoration Association, and quickly compelled its office to close. To make matters worse, in January 1914 Lung decided to throw both Phan Bội Châu and a close associate, Mai Lao Bang, into jail.[60] There they remained until spring 1917, sitting out most of the war in relative isolation from the flurry of activity associated with it. Meanwhile Cuong De, who had been in Hong Kong and was briefly imprisoned there himself, took the opportunity to make a long trip to Europe.[61]

From all appearances, the situation for the Viet Nam Restoration League looked pretty dismal at the beginning of 1914. Its leader, Phan Bội Châu, sat in a Kwangtung prison, while its figurehead, Cuong De, was in Europe. Many of its members had been apprehended by the French security police, and its schemes to assassinate key figures in Indochina had mostly failed. In fact, in early 1914 French authorities believed Cuong De was on the verge of turning himself in.[62] But then, just a few months later, the war broke out and offered the possibility of a change in fortune for the struggling Viet Nam Restoration Association through a new source of foreign collaboration: Germany.[63] And given the Association's history with actively exploring foreign sources of aid,

---

[58] Yves le Jariel, *Phan Bội Châu*, 141. Marr, *Vietnamese Anti-Colonialism 1885–1925*, 225.

[59] Phan, *Overturned Chariot*, 216.

[60] Lung's reason for imprisoning Phan Bội Châu and Mai Lao Bang are not entirely clear. Lung no doubt knew that the Viet Nam Restoration Association had been closely associated with Ch'en and other Guomindang supporters, who Yuan Shikai and his supporters considered rivals for power. In addition, Governor General Sarraut visited China in 1913 in part to request the extradition of Phan, Cuong De, and several other leaders of the Association, and Lung may have desired to keep Phan and Mai as bargaining chips in his dealings with the French. See Jenkins et al., *Reflections from Captivity*, 53; Phan, *Overturned Chariot*, 217–218; Morlat, *Les Affaires Politiques de l'Indochine*, 171–174.

[61] Marr, *Vietnamese Anti-Colonialism 1885–1925*, 224.

[62] Morlat, *Les Affaires Politiques de l'Indochine*, 182.

[63] Morlat, *Les Affaires Politiques de l'Indochine*, 187.

its leaders and members were already predisposed to welcome this new source even while their leader was in prison.

Vietnamese–German Collaboration During the War

Leaders of both the Viet Nam Restoration Association and representatives of the German government had each other in their sights as potential allies even before the war. As early as 1906, when Phan Bội Châu made a trip to Hong Kong from Japan, a friend had taken him to be formally introduced to the German consul there. According to Phan, "the relations in later years between members of our movement and the Germans arose largely from this occasion."[64] By 1912, when Phan was living in Kwangtung and building the Association, he recalled that he tried to draw close to the German community there after hearing rumors that a rupture with France was on the horizon.[65] And when the war broke out, German consular agents sought out known Vietnamese revolutionaries in China and Siam in much the same way they sought out Indian revolutionaries.[66]

As we know, most historians of Vietnamese anticolonialism who discuss the Vietnamese–German connection during World War I have concluded that the various schemes were not particularly important, since they only resulted in failure. Yet a more detailed exploration of the French and British colonial archives seen in their wider regional context suggests that the connection and the schemes deserve more attention. Certainly the archives reveal that Vietnamese–German connections went far beyond the oft-cited occasion when, in the autumn of 1915, the German consul in Siam gave Phan Bội Châu's representative 10,000 piastres to make trouble in Indochina.[67] Rather, they point to a wide variety of schemes over the course of the war that involved meetings between Viet Nam Restoration Association leaders and German consuls, financing for the making and distribution of bombs, and multiple instances of border raids.[68] And while it is true that none of these schemes was successful, for the members of the Viet Nam Restoration Association they represented the most effective way to strike the French at a time when the

---

[64] Phan, *Overturned Chariot*, 104.   [65] Phan, *Overturned Chariot*, 217.

[66] The evidence for this is clearest in Siam, as recounted by Phan Bội Châu in his memoirs, *Overturned Chariot*, 224–225; also Georges Boudarel, *Phan Bội Châu et La Societe Vietnamienne de Son Temps*, 48.

[67] This incident is discussed in Phan Bội Châu's autobiography, Marr's *Vietnamese Anticolonialism*, Yves le Jariel's *Phan Bội Châu*, and Christopher Goscha's *Thailand and the Southeast Asian Networks of the Vietnamese Revolution*, to name a few.

[68] Patrice Morlat's work supports this assessment, in both *La Repression Coloniale au Vietnam* (chapters 1–4) and *Les Affaires Politiques de l'Indochine* (chapters 4–9).

European powers were divided. For the Germans, they represented yet another method of harassing their enemies in the hope that one of the plans might distract significant attention away from the Western Front. It is also worth noting the investment the various parties placed in these schemes, since for Vietnamese revolutionaries participation quite often resulted in imprisonment or death – hardly a risk one would take without having some hope of contributing to an eventual success. And it is abundantly clear that the French took Vietnamese–German collaboration with the "utmost seriousness," for they expended large sums of money and countless hours of human labor to track, interpret, and thwart it.[69]

French concerns about the Viet Nam Restoration Association were hardly new in 1914. Since 1906, the French government in Indochina had been deeply concerned that first the Japanese and then the Chinese governments offered sanctuary for known antagonists to French colonial rule. In fact, the French expended considerable energies in exerting diplomatic pressure on both governments to change these policies, succeeding first with Japan in 1907, and then making some headway with Yuan Shikai's Chinese government in 1913. In 1913 Governor General Albert Sarraut (November 1911–January 1914) himself made a trip to China with the goal, at least in part, to seek extradition of Association leaders – including especially Phan Bội Châu and Cuong De.[70] For Sarraut, tracking the Viet Nam Restoration Association was a personal as well as a professional mission. In spite of the Association's small size, lack of adequate financing, and history of failed attacks, Sarraut believed it was among the most dangerous threats to French rule. As far as he was concerned, it was only in the international context that an organization like the Viet Nam Restoration Association could exist, and he argued that it was exiles like Phan Bội Châu who were behind most Vietnamese anti-colonial agitation.[71] As a result, in 1912 he created the Secret Exterior Police for the express purpose of following and pursuing the movements of Phan and his followers.[72] In addition, he created the Direction des

---

[69] Even though Marr did not believe that the connection with Germany turned out to be very important, he did acknowledge that the French took the threat with the "utmost seriousness." Marr, *Vietnamese Anticolonialism*, 238; Morlat, *Les Affaires Politiques de l'Indochine*, 187.

[70] Morlat, *Les Affaires Politiques de l'Indochine*, 165–171. Sarraut was Governor General from November 1911 to January 1914, and then again from January 1917 to May 1919.

[71] Christopher Goscha notes that French sources indicate that they believed there were about 1000 Vietnamese revolutionaries living in self-imposed exile in Japan, China, and Siam in 1912.

[72] Goscha, *Thailand and the Southeast Asian Networks of the Vietnamese Revolution, 1885–1954*, 41, 42. For an extended treatment of French colonial security forces in Vietnam, see Morlat, *La Repression Coloniale au Vietnam*.

Affaires Politiques et Indigènes which was, among other things, to serve as a coordinating center for both local and exterior information regarding Phan's revolutionary movement.[73] Beginning in 1912 also, Sarraut's government invested considerable energy and funds into establishing a network of paid informants in China, Hong Kong, and Bangkok who would work with the French consuls posted to each location to track the movement and activities of Vietnamese revolutionaries.[74] By the end of 1912, the government in Indochina had established cooperative relations with the French consulates in neighboring areas, and they had trusted informants who had penetrated Cuong De's inner circle. From the beginning of 1913, it was clear that the center of this new network linking informants, the consulates, and the government of Indochina was Hong Kong – thanks to the double efficiency of "BN," a Vietnamese secret agent who was located there, and to the enthusiasm and ambition of the just-returned French consul – Gaston Liébert – to that city.[75]

What this all means is that even before the outbreak of war the French government in Indochina had invested significant financial and human resources – including a raft of Vietnamese and Chinese undercover agents and informers – for the purposes of ensuring they knew what Phan's network was up to, and most especially of preventing its revolutionary plans from succeeding. They had also succeeded in gaining the cooperation of nearby French consuls in China and Hong Kong for lubricating the flow of information back to Indochina. As a result, by 1913 the French were already following the activities of Phan's partisans with a fair amount of precision, as it appeared that the intelligence transmitted by secret informants was generally sound.

Like the Ghadar party for the British, for the French the wartime collaboration between the Viet Nam Restoration Association and their German enemies was an extension of an existing threat rather than a wholly new one. Now, though, their fears that revolutionaries would wreak havoc

[73] Morlat, *Les Affaires Politiques de l'Indochine, 1895–1923*, 131. These efforts were followed in 1915 by the creation of the Sûreté Génerale (or the General Security Police), which together, according to Christopher Goscha, "created a counter-revolutionary intelligence network in Asia to destroy Phan Bội Châu's 'Village Abroad.'" Goscha, 42.

[74] Morlat, *Les Affaires Politiques de l'Indochine, 1895–1923*, 136–37. The centralization and regularization of this network was considered critical because heretofore each government office had their own group of spies, but the information gleaned from each was not centralized and thus did not contribute to an overall picture. Meanwhile, consuls posted in neighboring states and colonies had previously reported to the Ministry of Foreign Affairs in Paris and were not practiced in sharing information with the government in Indochina.

[75] Morlat, *Les Affaires Politiques de l'Indochine, 1895–1923*, 131, 145–147.

from outside the borders of Indochina were multiplied by the assistance of a powerful, wealthy, and motivated benefactor precisely at a time when the French military presence in Indochina was weakened by the demands of the war.[76] By March 1915, the French Minister of Colonies in Paris lamented that while the fortunes of the Viet Nam Restoration Association had seemed at an all-time low in early 1914, the war had changed everything. "Suddenly," he argued, "the revolutionary party found they had considerable resources and the means to take action."[77] And the cause of this change in fortune was unambiguous: according to the Minister, it was the subsidies paid by German consuls to Cuong De and the Viet Nam Restoration Association.

Key to the whole scheme, according to the Minister, was Dr. Ernst Voretzsch, the ex-German consul to Hong Kong. When Voretzsch was expelled from Hong Kong he went first to Bangkok and then to China, where he continued his work in trying to undermine French rule in Indochina. But it was not just the isolated case of Dr. Voretzsch that had the Minister concerned. Rather, "his colleagues at Canton and Yunnan-fu, who remain at their posts, are engaged in much activity against us, and take on any kind of work that presents itself to harm us."[78]

What was the evidence on which these allegations were based? The very same network of spies and informants who had been tracking the activities of the Viet Nam Restoration Association since 1912. This human intelligence work generated a copious amount of correspondence and telegrams between Indochina, Hong Kong, and France, and also between French officials in the Far East and their Allied counterparts. Taken at face value, this intelligence revealed extensive contacts between men like Cuong De and Phan Bội Châu and the various German consuls posted around southern China. It also revealed repeated attempts by revolutionaries to construct bombs for use in Indochina, as well as multiple plans to attack Indochina across the Chinese or Vietnamese border. And while there is no doubt that French intelligence about the Viet Nam Restoration Association spoke volumes about French preoccupations and interpretations, when used cautiously and in conjunction with corroborating sources they also expose the outlines of a pattern of collaboration between the Viet Nam Restoration Association and German agents during the war.

---

[76] Montagnon, *France-Indochine*, 171. At that time, such weakening was mostly because of the removal of French troops to Europe.

[77] Ministere des Colonies, Aide de l'agitation Annamite sur la frontiere de Chine, March 20, 1915. Troubles en Cochinchine, Centre des Archives d'Outre-Mer (CAOM), Indo/nf/28/2.

[78] Ministere des Colonies, Aide de l'agitation Annamite sur la frontière de Chine.

Contacts with Consuls

As the leaders of the Vietnam Restoration Association, Phan Bội Châu and Cuong De were obvious targets of French intelligence efforts. During the war years, paid informers tracked both men all over China and insisted on their repeated contacts with both German consuls and with Chinese "pirates" supposedly funded by German money. We know, of course, that Phan was in prison for most of the war, which means that he could not have been moving around China the way French intelligence described. This misconception seems to have been deliberately engineered by the Chinese General Lung Chi-kuang, governor of Kwang-tung, who had thrown Phan and Mai Son in jail in January 1914. When the arrests were made, Lung had originally communicated this to the French consular network and to the Governor General in Hanoi. French officials were overjoyed at the arrests and fully anticipated that Lung would extradite them to Indochina. Yet when it came the time to collect Phan and Mai Son, Lung's government informed the French that Phan had escaped. This intelligence came first to Liébert's network in Hong Kong and was repeated by him to the French authorities in Hanoi, who accepted it without question. So while the reasons for Lung's deception are not clear, one result was that the French believed Phan was a free man for most of the war.[79]

These detailed and frequent reports, then, clearly must give us pause. In the case of Phan Bội Châu, it is clear that whoever was being tracked around China could not have been the Association leader himself in the early years of the war. In the case of Cuong De, intelligence gathered by sources in China conflicted with intelligence gathered by the Hong Kong consulate, which revealed that the man being tracked by one set of informants or the other was not the right person.

In a period prior to extensive photographic documentation, it is at least possible that someone like Nguyen Thuong Hien (alias Mai-Son) – who assumed the leadership role in the Association in the absence of Phan Bội Châu – could have convinced informers for the French that he was in fact Phan Bội Châu.[80] There is certainly no indication – at

[79] This deception is clear from the correspondence between Liébert and the French consul at Canton between 19 and 22 January, 1914. Gaston Liébert Papers, Box 3, Folio 3. Cornell University Library, Division of Rare and Manuscript Collections. It was only in 1916, two years after Phan had been imprisoned, that the French discovered the mistake and the fact that Liébert's network was deeply flawed. Morlat, *Les Affaires Politiques de l'Indochine*, 207.

[80] For Nguyen's role in assuming leadership, see Marr, *Vietnamese Anticolonialism*, 228. If Phan Bội Châu himself was aware of these possible cases of mistaken identity, he does not offer an explanation in his autobiography.

least until the beginning of 1916 – that either Liébert or the French officials with whom he corresponded in Hanoi suspected that the man they were paying informers to watch was anyone other than Phan. Some informers, indeed, claimed not simply to have observed Phan or Cuong De, but to have spent time with them. A detailed example appeared in one of Liébert's reports in January 1915. This particular report summarized the intelligence of "our numerous emissaries" in China and included information on Phan Bội Châu, Cuong De, and other Association leaders – including Nguyen Thuong Hien.[81] Phan's whereabouts formed the centerpiece of the report, as one of the secret agents confirmed that he had dined with Phan on the night of December 18, 1914 in the city of Hangtcheou (Hangzhou), just south of Shanghai. The informer indicated that Phan was traveling under an assumed Chinese name (Tchan-hao-Seng) and was staying with a Chinese friend. At dinner on the 18th, the informer related a variety of news and information that Phan had supposedly told him while the two were sharing a meal. Among these items included Phan's sadness over the disunity he perceived in the Viet Nam Restoration Association, which he believed was holding the group back from executing its plans. He also expressed fear about making his relationships with Chinese revolutionaries public, since he didn't want Yuan Shikai's government to crack down on his Association any more than he had already done. More importantly, he discussed funds he had received from German consuls – particularly that he had already spent 40,000 [piastres?] for the recruitment and maintenance of three rebel bands in Yunnan, Kouangsi, and Kintcheou and was now short of cash. Finally, the informer claimed that Phan was anxious to return to southern China, but that he needed to wait in Hangtcheou for the arrival of some German friends who were presently at Swatow (Shantou) but who would shortly procure arms for him.[82]

French authorities continued to assume Phan remained a free man throughout 1915. Beginning in March 1915, someone informers believed to be Phan – the same man who had been at Hangtcheou – met and then traveled with Dr. Ernst Voretzsch to Peking. Voretzsch was well known to Liébert and also to British authorities, as both had served as foreign consuls in Hong Kong at the same time until the German consulate there was closed on August 12, 1914.[83] Once Voretzsch was forced to leave

[81] Secret letter from Gaston Liébert to the Political Affairs department, Indochina, January 14, 1915. Menées Austrio-Allemande en Indochine, Indo/nf/992, CAOM.

[82] Secret letter from Gaston Liébert to the Political Affairs department, Indochina, January 14, 1915. Menées Austrio-Allemande en Indochine, Indo/nf/992.

[83] Apparently Voretzsch was well liked by the British authorities in Hong Kong prior to the war, though he later became notorious for his anti-Allied schemes. "SMS Emden:

Hong Kong, he traveled to Siam and stayed for five months, where it was strongly suspected he played a role in the schemes (discussed in Chapter 5) to incite rebellion among British Indian troops.[84] From Siam, Voretzsch secretly returned to China in a neutral Norwegian ship, carrying the passport and assuming the identity of his former U.S. colleague in Hong Kong, George Anderson.[85] Once in China, Voretzsch apparently assumed the name and passport of his former Swiss colleague in Hong Kong, consul Nillson, and traveled to Shanghai where he was reported to have met with Phan Bội Châu. The two then reportedly traveled together from Shanghai to Peking in mid-January, where it was believed that Voretzsch presented Phan to the new German ambassador, Paul von Hintze – a man well known in his own right for creating an anti-Allied spy and intelligence network, first in Mexico and then in China.[86] The man believed to be Phan returned to Shanghai at the beginning of February, and then traveled back to Hangtcheou a couple of weeks later. Voretzsch also left Peking to return to Shanghai, where Liébert was sure he was plotting some "new move" against the Allies.[87]

Shortly thereafter, Liébert reported that Phan Bội Châu was traveling frequently between Hangtcheou and Shanghai, where he was supposedly meeting regularly with Voretzsch's Chinese secretary, Wou-sou-Lun. According to Liébert's informer, Phan and Wou-sou-Lun met often in a public garden, sometimes in the company of other Germans, after which Phan would travel back to Hangtcheou. The purpose of these meetings, according to Liébert, was arranging for the transfer of German money to Phan, which would then be used to purchase "arms, munitions, and explosives" from a group of Japanese who would smuggle the contraband into Tonkin.[88] In fact, Liébert advocated keeping a strict surveillance on a new weekly service run by a Japanese shipping company from Hong

Hong Kong's Favorite Foe," *South China Morning Post,* January 26, 2014. http://www.scmp.com/magazines/post-magazine/article/1411712/sms-emden-hong-kongs-favourite-foe.

[84] Secret letter from Liébert to the Political Affairs department of the Government of Indochina, March 2, 1915. Menées Austrio-Allemande en Indochine, Indo/nf/992.

[85] Voretzsch needed to travel secretly, and on a neutral ship, for fear of being stopped by British or Japanese warships. Liébert to Governor General Roume, May 12, 1915. Menées Austrio-Allemande en Indochine, Indo/nf/992, CAOM.

[86] Xu, *China and the Great War,* 111; Heribert von Feilitzsch, *In Plain Sight: Felix A. Sommerfeld, Spymaster in Mexico, 1908 to 1914* (Amissville, VA: Henselstone Verlag, 2012), 145.

[87] Voretzsch's part of the journey turned out to be no secret once he arrived in China, as the papers in Peking, Shanghai, and Hong Kong covered it well. Secret letter from Liébert to the Political Affairs department of the Government of Indochina, March 2, 1915. Menées Austrio-Allemande en Indochine, Indo/nf/992.

[88] Liébert to the Political Affairs Department of the Government of Indochina, March 15, 1915. Menées Austrio-Allemande en Indochine, Indo/nf/992.

Kong to Haiphong, which he believed might be involved in smuggling weapons.

By the end of March, another of Liébert's informants – who was keeping an eye on the movements of Cuong De in the city of Fatshan – reported that Cuong De had recently received a number of letters from Phan Bội Châu indicating that he had closed the arms deal with his Japanese friends.[89] According to the source, Phan intended to come south to join Coung De shortly but first needed to settle the issue of payment for the arms with the Germans. In response, Coung De supposedly wrote to Phan that he and his fellow revolutionaries would postpone any serious border uprisings in Tonkin until his arrival.[90]

Liébert's informer was insistent that Cuong De was in Fatshan at least through March 1915, whereupon he was supposed to have left for the frontier – presumably to join the bands of pirates and revolutionaries intent upon instigating border uprisings. Yet this intelligence was complicated at the end of March 1915 by conflicting reports that Cuong De had never been in the city of Fatshan at all, but was instead in Peking. Governor General Roume informed Liébert that "I have very serious reason to think that [your] agents have made an error in the identity of the person who has been living in Canton as Cuong De."[91] In reality, Roume argued, Cuong De was in Peking, a city he had hardly left since his return from Germany in 1914. Moreover, he believed the source of this information was indisputable, as it came from a European special agent in the Sûreté Génerale.[92] Liébert, however, adamantly stood by his source, responding "I can guarantee most categorically that your information on the subject of the presence of Prince Cuong De is absolutely false."[93] Liébert went on to explain that the Chinese informer locating Cuong De in Fatshan was one of their most trusted and intelligent, that he had known Cuong De for years, and that he saw Cuong De every week. He also claimed to have photographic evidence that the man in question in Fatshan was in fact Cuong De. In a follow-up letter the next day, Liébert added that he had excellent reason to believe not only that Cuong De was not in Peking, but that he had never traveled to Europe in 1913. Moreover, Liébert insisted that Cuong De had never been arrested

[89] Liébert to the Political Affairs Department of the Government of Indochina, March 22, 1915. Menées Austrio-Allemande en Indochine, Indo/nf/992

[90] Liébert to the Political Affairs Department of the Government of Indochina, March 22, 1915.

[91] Governor General Ernest Roume to Gaston Liébert, March 23, 1915. Menées Austrio-Allemande en Indochine, Indo/nf/992.

[92] Governor General Ernest Roume to Gaston Liébert, March 23, 1915.

[93] Liébert to Roume, March 29, 1915. Menées Austrio-Allemande en Indochine, Indo/nf/992.

in Hong Kong. Rather, he argued that a man named Cutrac – who had murdered a Vietnamese informer in 1912 – had been jailed there and mistaken for Cuong De.[94] Liébert also wrote the French ambassador in Peking to complain about the persistence of these "fanciful stories" about Cuong De which, he lamented, continued to endure in both Paris and Hanoi despite all the proof he had provided to the contrary.[95]

Liébert's blustering confidence aside, Cuong De's own memoirs record him leaving Hong Kong (after having spent eight days in jail there) for Europe in April 1913, only to return eight months later. The journey included two months in Berlin, during which Cuong De unsuccessfully sought useful contacts to aid the Vietnamese cause.[96] At the urging of his compatriots in China, Cuong De left Europe for Peking in April 1914 because Yuan Shikai's minister of war had indicated a willingness to consider an offensive strike against French Indochina.[97] Once back in China, however, the war broke out and the Chinese government grew preoccupied first with the Japanese conquest of the Shandong peninsula and then, in January 1915, with the diplomatic crisis spurred by Japan's Twenty-One Demands.[98] As a result, all promises to Cuong De and to Vietnam faded into the background. Disappointed and discouraged, according to Cuong De's memoirs and his biographer, a few months later – in May 1915 – Cuong De returned to Japan to live under the protection of his earlier benefactor, Inukai Tsuyoshi.[99]

If we are to believe Cuong De's memoirs, we know that Liébert's intelligence was wrong in nearly all of its assertions – including that Cuong De had not been arrested in Hong Kong, traveled to Europe, or gone to Peking. Thus, if the individual in Fatshan was not Cuong De, who then was it? And was Liébert's informer deliberately misleading, or was he convinced himself? Finally, does the inaccuracy of Liébert's intelligence with respect to the two most important leaders of the Vietnam Restoration Association throw all of his other intelligence into a dubious light?

[94] Secret letter from Liébert to Roume, March 30, 1915. Menées Austrio-Allemande en Indochine, Indo/nf/992. The Gaston Liébert papers at Cornell University demonstrate that Liébert was already arguing with a variety of French officials about the whereabouts of Cuong De as early as April 1914. Gaston Liébert Papers, Box 3, Folio 2. Cornell University Library, Division of Rare and Manuscript Collections.

[95] Secret letter from Liébert to the Peking Legation, March 30, 1915. Menées Austrio-Allemande en Indochine, Indo/nf/992.

[96] Tran My-Van, *A Vietnamese Royal Exile in Japan: Prince Cuong De, 1882–1951* (London and New York: Routledge, 2005).

[97] Marr, *Vietnamese Anti-Colonialism 1885–1925*, 236.

[98] Marr, *Vietnamese Anti-Colonialism 1885–1925*, 237. The editorial note in *Overturned Chariot* says the same thing, 227, n. 173.

[99] Tran My-Van, *A Vietnamese Royal Exile in Japan: Prince Cuong De, 1882–1951* (London and New York: Routledge, 2005).

In spite of the obvious (if unsolvable) problems in Liébert's informer network, we do know from a variety of other sources that the connection between the Viet Nam Restoration Association and German consuls was not fabricated. For one thing, we know that Phan Bội Châu had made contact with the German consulate years before the war, and we know by Phan's own admission that the German consul in Siam gave money to one of Phan's associates in 1915 for the express purpose of instigating a border uprising.[100] British intelligence, which we will explore below, also corroborated the extensive use of the German consular network in China to foment revolution in both British and French colonies. And finally, Phan Bội Châu's actions before and after his release from prison indicate that the idea of turning to the Germans for help was already quite familiar to him.

We know from Phan Bội Châu's memoirs that he was not completely isolated from the outside world while he was in prison, due to the help of a sympathetic Cantonese cook named Liu Ya-San. Liu periodically checked in at a friend's house to get news and letters from Phan's compatriots, and he also brought newspapers to the prison for Phan to read.[101] According to Phan, there was at least one occasion on which he personally gave instructions to Association members to accept an invitation by the German and Austrian ministers in Siam to meet.[102] The affair began with a letter to Phan in late autumn 1915 from a Vietnamese compatriot in Siam – Dang Tu Kinh – who informed Phan about the invitation and requested advice about how he should respond. The ministers had insisted on seeing the leaders of the movement, but neither Phan nor Cuong De was available for travel to Siam. Instead, Phan asked his trusted friend Nguyen Thuong Hien (alias Mai Son) – the same man who had assumed a leadership role in the Association once Phan was imprisoned – to travel to Siam in order to work out a deal on his behalf. When Mai Son arrived in Siam accompanied by Dang Tu Kinh, the German minister lost no time in offering ten thousand yuan for bringing about "some kind of sensational incident within your country that would cause our governments to take notice."[103] Mai Son accepted the money on Phan Bội Châu's behalf, which ended up funding various border attacks. Although Phan freely admitted that the attacks "ended

---

[100] This episode will be dealt with in more depth below.

[101] Phan, *Overturned Chariot*, 220–222.

[102] Phan recounts this incident by saying "there was one affair in particular that should be recorded, so that my compatriots may derive a lesson from it," leaving the possibility open that there may have been other incidents about which he did not comment. Phan, *Overturned Chariot*, 224.

[103] Phan, *Overturned Chariot*, 225.

in total failure," the point here is that he approved of and supervised the meeting with the German minister from his prison cell, and also that he authorized an individual to act on his behalf.

Once Phan was released from prison in March or April 1917, he continued to be involved in seeking out German help.[104] Shortly after regaining his freedom, Phan recalled receiving word from a fellow revolutionary in Japan that Germany and Japan were in the process of negotiating a secret alliance.[105] For this reason, Phan traveled to Japan to determine the truth of this rumor and to see if it could be used to the advantage of the Vietnam Restoration Association. While he was in Japan, however, the Chinese government finally declared war on Germany (August 14, 1917), which meant that diplomatic and commercial relations with all representatives of the Central Powers would soon be cut off. At that point, two of Phan's fellow revolutionaries who had been in Peking for the duration of the war were approached by a German in Tientsin (Tianjin) who offered assistance to the Association. According to Phan, this offer was initiated by the German ambassador in Peking, Paul Hintze, and was predicated on signing a written agreement between the Germans and the leaders of the movement. Phan deputized his two associates to negotiate the agreement and readied himself to travel to Tientsin to sign it. However, this affair also ended in failure, as his two associates were seized by British police as they passed through the British concession with a draft of the agreement, having been betrayed by an informer to the Surété.[106]

What all this means is that in spite of what was surely faulty intelligence gathered by the French consul in Hong Kong, there was nevertheless justification for claiming interaction between Viet Nam Restoration Association members and German consuls. Not only that, it is clear that the goal of this interaction was to undermine French rule in Indochina. Thus, while we may never know whether or not Liébert's intelligence bespoke activities carried out on behalf of Phan and Cuong De, its fundamental premise, underscoring connections between the Vietnamese revolutionaries and the Germans, was sound.

---

[104] Phan was released from prison when Lung Chi-Kuang – the military governor of Kwangtung – was himself driven from the city by his enemies. Phan, *Overturned Chariot*, 227.

[105] This in fact was partially true, as early in 1917 Japan made overtures to Germany for a separate peace, mostly for the purpose of winning concessions from the Allies. This was not the first occasion on which Germany and Japan had flirted with the idea of a separate peace. See Frank W. Ikle, "Japanese-German Peace Negotiations during World War I," *The American Historical Review* 71, no. 1 (October 1, 1965), 75–76.

[106] Phan Bội Châu, *Overturned Chariot*, 231–232. One of the men, Truong Quoc Uy, managed to escape, but the other – Le Ap Ton – was handed to the French and later died in prison.

Bombs and Weapons

Both French intelligence as well as corroborating sources indicate that the members of the Viet Nam Restoration Association meant to translate their collaboration with France's enemies into violent and immediate action. Like Indian Ghadar nationalists, one of the great hopes of the members of the Viet Nam Restoration Association was to smuggle arms directly in to Indochina for use in uprisings against French rule, both on the border and in the interior. As we have already seen, even before the war Phan Bội Châu had done his best to get arms and munitions to his fellow countrymen who were in revolt and had traveled not only to Singapore but also to Thailand for this purpose before giving up and donating the weapons to Sun Yat-Sen's Guomindang Party. Unfortunately for the Association and other Vietnamese anticolonialists, arms smuggling did not prove any easier during the war, and as a result such schemes met with little success. But they did reveal a number of efforts by Vietnamese revolutionaries to make bombs themselves for import into Indochina, which French authorities believed were funded with German money.

The Governor General in Indochina began to receive reports about groups of "Annamite revolutionaries" making and smuggling bombs in late 1914, just a few months after the war broke out. In this instance Liébert's intelligence – obtained via several of his own secret agents in China – appeared sound and played a crucial role in bringing these schemes to light. In December 1914, for example, he reported that "a group of about twenty Annamite rebels and several of their Chinese friends" were in Yunnan under the direction of Phan Bội Châu's close associate Phan Ba Ngọc.[107] According to Liébert's sources, these men had recently imported dynamite from Canton to Nanning and were using it to make bombs intended for smuggling into Tonkin. More alarming still, from the French point of view, was not only that some of these bombs had already been sent, but that the German consul in Yunnan was "secretly directing these plots."[108] Although this group had reportedly originally sought to smuggle most of the bombs to Tonkin by land across the Chinese frontier, by the end of December it seemed they found the

---

[107] Telegram from Liébert to Governor General Sarraut, December 5, 1914. Menées Austrio-Allemande en Indochine, Indo/nf/992, CAOM. Phan Ba Ngọc had studied at the Peking Military Academy and was one of the original members of the Executive Committee in the Viet Nam Restoration Association. Phan Bội Châu, *Overturned Chariot*, 197, 193.

[108] Telegram from Liébert to Governor General Sarraut, December 5, 1914. Menées Austrio-Allemande en Indochine, Indo/nf/992.

land border too well guarded and were attempting instead to take the bombs via Chinese junks from coastal Pakhoi (near Beihei) to Tunghing, a port town just across the Indochinese border near Mong Cai.[109] This was not the only group involved in such activities, added Liébert. Another group of about ten men, also working near Nanning, were also allegedly fabricating bombs for the same purpose. This group included Dang Tu Man, a member of the Viet Nam Restoration Association who, by Phan Bội Châu's own account, had gained experience making bombs and grenades for the party prior to the war in Hong Kong.[110] Finally, a third group under the leadership of Tran Huu Luc – who was later executed for his role in conspiring with Germans – was reported to be making bombs in Siam for the purpose of transporting them across the border to Laos.[111]

That at least some of these schemes were credible – and that some of the bombs made their way into the heart of Indochina – can be gleaned from arrest reports. In early 1915, for example, a delegate from the French consul's office in Yunnan noted that intelligence from his office had led the Résident Supérieur in Hanoi to uncover a violent anti-French plot in that city during the previous November. When the bust was made, a group of Vietnamese men was found right in the midst of a work-shop stocked with materials needed for making bombs. These men were brought before the Council of War at Yen-Bay at the end of November, after which eighteen were condemned to death. The law came down swiftly on these men, for after their condemnation the executions took place only four days later, on December 2.[112]

Another arrest that provided evidence for bomb-making schemes – among other things – was that of Luong Lap Nam in late December 1914. Luong was a well-known young protégé of Phan Bội Châu, and a founding member of the Vietnam Restoration Association. He had long been wanted by the French, and thus his chance arrest at the hands of the British in Hong Kong was greeted with both enthusiasm and urgency by French authorities. As we saw at the beginning of the chapter, Luong was secretly released by the British into the hands of Liébert, who spirited him away to the infamous Thai Nguyen prison. Prior to this secret extradition, however, police had seized and searched Luong's

---

[109] Telegram from Liébert to Governor General Sarraut, December 20, 1914. Menées Austrio-Allemande en Indochine, Indo/nf/992.

[110] Phan Bội Châu, *Overturned Chariot*, 212.

[111] Telegram from Liébert to Governor General Sarraut, December 5, 1914.

[112] Letter from the delegate to the Minister of Foreign Affairs in Yunnan to the Deputy Superintendent to the Chief of Military Services, March 20, 1915. Troubles et Com-plots en Indochine, Indo/nf/28/3, CAOM.

belongings. The upshot, as Liébert wrote to the Governor General in Hanoi, was not that the materials found in Luong's possessions told them "anything we didn't already know about the organization and projects of the Annamite rebels, but that they confirm the information we already had."[113]

Among these materials were a number of letters – some written by Luong and others written to him – that explicitly discussed invasion plans and bomb-making schemes. One of these, written by Luong and addressed to several Chinese friends, asked for money to form an army that would be used to invade French Indochina. He added that the army would begin at the border post of Langson and then move south, ending with the optimistic assurance that the country could be retaken within a dozen days.[114] Another letter, from a man named Gia Than to three recipients, indicated that the author was in the process of learning how to make bombs. Once he had learned the necessary steps, he vowed, he would immediately organize a group for the purpose of assassinating seven "notable traitors" of the Association, "so that no one would dare do anything against us."[115] In addition to these letters, Luong's possessions included a map of Yunnan province, a packet containing nineteen revolutionary brochures, a false identity card, and photographs of various revolutionary Chinese and Vietnamese.[116]

Another arrest – of Hoang Trong Mau, one of Phan Bội Châu's most important deputies – gave teeth to the belief that Vietnamese revolutionaries were operating with funds from German consuls in China. As had been the case with Luong Lap Nam, it was Liébert's network once again that provided the intelligence leading to his arrest. In this case, two of his Chinese agents befriended Hoang and his friend Le Duc Nhuan while they were in the region of Guangxi and working in close connection with German consuls. The agents confirmed that Hoang not only had been one of the principal organizers of the 1913 acts of terror in Hanoi and Thai Binh, but that he had organized a border raid in 1914 and a bomb attack in 1915. When Hoang and Le decided to travel to Shanghai via Hong Kong in May 1915, the Chinese informers alerted Liébert, who was waiting for them.[117]

[113] Secret letter from Liébert to the Political Affairs Department of the Government of Indochina, January 13, 1915. Menées Austrio-Allemande en Indochine, Indo/nf/992.

[114] Copy of a confiscated letter from Luong Lap Nham to Chinese friends, January 13 (no year given). Menées Austrio-Allemande en Indochine, Indo/nf/992.

[115] Summary of a letter Gia Than to Y-Long, Nghia-Hing, and Hien-Hing, no date. Menées Austrio-Allemande en Indochine, Indo/nf/992.

[116] Appendix 4 to the material sent January 13 from the French Consulate in Hong Kong to Hanoi. Menées Austrio-Allemande en Indochine, Indo/nf/992.

[117] Yves le Jariel, *Phan Bội Châu*, 151–152.

Although evidence for German funding of the Vietnamese bomb makers in question here is only circumstantial, French authorities certainly believed there was a connection between the two. Having already obtained what they believed to be clear evidence that Vietnamese revolutionaries were meeting regularly with German consuls, it followed that subsequent anti-French activity on the part of the Viet Nam Restoration Association was made possible via German financial support for supplies and transport. Furthermore, this belief was strengthened by the numerous attacks initiated from China and Siam into Indochina – many of which French authorities were convinced were organized and funded by German consuls intent on disrupting French rule.

Border Attacks

There is very little dispute in any of the sources – whether from French intelligence, Phan Bội Châu's memoirs, arrest reports, or secondary sources – that German consular representatives provided funds for members of the Viet Nam Restoration Association, in conjunction with armed Chinese "pirates," to organize border attacks from both China and Siam.[118] As we have seen, these attacks are often dismissed in the secondary sources as "ill-conceived" and ineffective stunts that were unimportant both singly and in the aggregate. In contrast, I argue that even with incomplete archival sources, it seems clear that in the first three years of the war the attacks were frequent, quite costly, alarming to the French government, and the source of serious diplomatic tension between the French and Chinese governments. And while attacks across the Chinese frontier had been a problem for the French since the conquest of Tonkin, the incidents that occurred during the war seemed to be doubly menacing because of the possibility they were funded and armed by Germans.[119]

An example of one of the more serious attacks occurred early in the war at the French military post of Muong Hou, at Laos's northern border with Yunnan. Whether it was ill-conceived or not, it was not a minor

---

[118] The use of the somewhat problematic term "pirates" – also sometimes referred to as bandits – was not new to this period. It is used similarly to the ways "dacoit" was employed by the British in India, which denoted a type of nonpolitical banditry. The reason the term is problematic as it was used by the French is that sometimes "pirates" were clearly not only causing trouble but were also politicized. A good example is De Tham, who was known as the "chief pirate" working against the French in the late nineteenth and early twentieth centuries. However, De Tham was not simply a bandit, as he was affiliated first with the Can Vuong movement and then with Phan Bội Châu's revolutionary movement before his assassination in 1912. See Gendre, *Le Dê Thám (1858–1913)*.

[119] For problems with cross-border attacks dating from the conquest, see Fourniau, *Annam-Tonkin, 1885–1896*, 19–25.

affair: the assault took over a year to repulse, required the deployment of a significant and expensive military force from French Indochina, and involved Chinese military aid as well as diplomatic intervention from Yuan Shikai's Chinese government. Throughout, the French were convinced that the attack was funded and maintained by representatives of the Central Powers in Yunnan, who were also believed to be working with the Viet Nam Restoration Association.[120] And although the French eventually dislodged the rebels from Muong-hou, many of them simply slipped back over the Chinese border to regroup and fight another day.

According to the stories of both the French Ambassador at Peking and the Governor General of Indochina, in December 1914 an armed group of "malefactors" – composed mostly of Chinese opium traders – crossed the border from China and seized the remote French outpost of Muong Hou. Upon hearing of the attack, the French government sent a force of *tirailleurs* to dislodge the invaders. But the force did not reach Muong Hou until March, and once there not only was the French captain wounded, but the force discovered that it was outmatched in numbers and arms and had to retreat.[121]

At that point, the Governor General decided that a clear demonstration of force was necessary and determined to send a much larger force to the area as an example to other would-be attackers.[122] But such a force could not be arranged until the end of the rainy season the next autumn, as the roads were impassable. This, of course, left the attackers at Muong Hou intact and in territory claimed by the French for nearly an entire year. Meanwhile, in August 1915 the French ambassador at Peking, Monsieur Conty, received permission to send the French consul at Yunnan-fu – Monsieur Lépissier – close to the border with Laos to investigate the situation. Once there, Lépissier discovered clues that the rebels at Muong Hou had not only been recruited but resupplied from Yunnan with the concurrence of the Chinese provincial government and with the financial and logistical backing of representatives from Germany and Austria. Particularly suspicious, according to Lépissier, was the fact that numerous caravans carrying people and arms from Yunnan were found to be moving in the direction of the Laotian frontier. The French believed an

[120] Patrice Morlat believes this attack was likely funded with German money. Morlat, *La Répression Coloniale Au Vietnam, 1908–1940*, 29.

[121] M. Conty, Ambassador of the Republic of France in Peking, to M. Delcasse, Minister of Foreign Affairs, October 6, 1915. Menées Revolutionnaires Sur La Frontiere du Tonkin, Indo/nf/992.

[122] There was a changing of the guard in terms of Governor Generals during this affair. When the attack began in December 1914, Joost van Vollenhoven served in this role. By the time it was over in late 1915, Ernest Roume had taken his place as of April 1915.

old Austrian officer named Pawelka, who had worked for the Chinese customs service in Yunnan-fu, was the main organizer behind these caravans. When the war broke out, Pawelka suddenly resigned his service in order to begin leading voyages into the Chinese interior. In addition, Conty also received information from the British ambassador, Sir John Jordan, that certain Austrians and Germans – including Pawelka – were involved in schemes that not only threatened French Indochina but British Burma as well.[123] Such schemes, added the Governor General, were not simply the brainchild of individual patriotic Austrians determined to damage the Allies. Rather, on the basis of his own intelligence and British reports, he concluded that there was no doubt that the "pirates" who had occupied Muong Hou "had been not only encouraged, but largely funded and provisioned with arms and munitions by the German consulate at Yunnan-fu."[124]

It was not clear to the French whether or not members of the Viet Nam Restoration Society were involved with this particular attack. In an effort to tie them together circumstantially, however, he noted that the same Germans involved in the Muong Hou scheme were also in "constant contact with notorious Annamite rebels."[125] In particular, he had reports that the German ex-consul to Hong Kong, Dr. Voretzsch, whom we have seen in a variety of contexts already, was in the southern Yunnanese city of Nan-Ning-Fou with Phan Bội Châu at the same time as the Muong Hou affair was developing. While of course we know Voretzsch could not have been with Phan, if the intelligence about Voretzsch's whereabouts were correct it is possible that he could have been with a different representative of the Viet Nam Restoration Association. In any case, the Governor General argued that even though it was difficult to know the precise intentions of "dangerous characters" like Phan and Voretzsch, their "mere presence near the frontiers of [Indochina] signify evil intentions."[126]

Armed with what they believed to be credible evidence of Austro-German support of anticolonial activities – including those taking place

[123] Conty to Delcasse, October 6, 1915. Menées Revolutionnaires Sur La Frontière du Tonkin, Indo/nf/992.
[124] Governor General Roume to Minister of Colonies, February 22, 1916, Troubles et Complots en Indochine, Indo/nf/3, CAOM. The British ambassador at Peking was also convinced of the involvement of the German consul at Yunnan-fu, a Mr. Weiss, in the plans that involved Pawelka. Sir John Jordan to Earl Grey, Foreign Office, Report 54393, November 25, 1915. Straits Settlements Original Correspondence: Foreign, CO 273/432, TNA.
[125] Governor General Roume to Minister of Colonies, February 22, 1916. Troubles et Complots en Indochine, Indo/nf/3, CAOM.
[126] Governor General Roume to Minister of Colonies, February 22, 1916.

at Muong Hou – Monsieur Conty and Sir John Jordan made a joint appeal to the Chinese Ministry of Foreign Affairs, asking the government to give formal instructions to the provincial government in Yunnan to "energetically oppose all actions contrary to good neighborly relations" between China on the one hand, and France and Britain on the other.[127] The timing for such a demand was excellent, because the Chinese government had recently been humiliated by having to accept most of the Twenty-one Demands made by Japan after its conquest of the Shandong peninsula.[128] In response to this humiliation, Yuan Shikai's regime was preoccupied with the possibility of joining the war on the side of the Allies in order to have a say at the bargaining table when the war was over. In fact, it was only shortly after Conty and Jordan's protestations, on November 6, 1915, that the Chinese government informed the Allies for the first time that it was ready to join the war.[129]

Given the timing of Conty and Jordan's visit, they found the Chinese central government to be quite accommodating to their wishes. With regard to Muong Hou, Conty demanded that the Chinese government take measures that would support the French counter-offensive at the outpost, which was projected to take place in November 1915. First, he asked that the Yunnan police keep on the lookout for certain individuals believed to be involved in anticolonial schemes. Second, he asked the Chinese government to take measures that would prevent the rebels at Muong Hou – when pushed back by French forces – from escaping to safety across the Chinese border. In order to ensure that these measures were taken, he asked for a special military delegate to be sent personally by Yuan Shikai to Yunnan in order to supervise the situation.[130] Yuan Shikai responded by appointing Colonel Tang Pao Tchao to these duties, who was well-liked in French circles. He also offered, if the French found themselves outnumbered again as a result of a shortage of troops caused by the war in Europe, to send an imposing force to reinforce them. This, however, Conty refused, as he thought it would be bad for French prestige if the Chinese were to assemble more powerful forces in the campaign than the French themselves.[131]

The campaign to retake Muong Hou was not a minor affair, nor was its outcome completely successful. Provisioning the force took the better

---

[127] Conty to Delcassé, October 6, 1915. Menées Revolutionnaires Sur La Frontière du Tonkin. Indo/nf/992.

[128] Japan issued the Twenty-one Demands on January 18, 1915.

[129] Xu, China and the Great War, 107. China did not join the Allies at this time, however, due to the opposition of the Japanese.

[130] Conty to Delcassé, October 6,1915. Menées Revolutionnaires Sur La Frontière du Tonkin, Indo/nf/992.

[131] Conty to Delcasse, October 6, 1915.

part of eight weeks, beginning at the end of September 1915, and required no fewer than eight hundred horses and mules in order to keep the supply lines running. Rice stores had to be brought from the Tonkin delta, and four columns of French-led *tirailleurs* had to be outfitted and readied, all at great cost.[132] The force itself was composed of four columns, one of which marched north and then west along the Chinese border in order to attack the rebels from the north, and the other three of which marched from the south to surround the rebels from the south, east, and west. The northern column reached the vicinity of Muong Hou on December 17 and encountered strong defenses that took eleven days to dislodge and then only with the help of a heavy mountain gun. The southern columns, meanwhile, began their assault in the vicinity on December 1 and only successfully retook the post on January 4 after heavy fighting and the loss of two French officers and several dozen *tirailleurs*.[133] Once repulsed, a large number of the rebels were able to escape back across the border to Yunnan. Back in China, they were quickly folded into a Yunnanese rebel movement that had risen up against the Chinese central government with the result, as Roume ruefully noted, that French efforts to cooperate with the Chinese government in bringing the Muong Hou rebels to heel were "partly lost."[134] Even more unfortunately, according to Roume, was that now the "pirates" had the facilities and the safety to regroup on the other side of the frontier, "especially if, as we envisage, the Germans continue to aid them."[135]

Although the attack on Muong Hou was among the largest in scale and the longest-lived, it was not the only border area in the fall and winter of 1914–1915 to suffer from anti-French activity. Another was an attack by a band of Chinese "pirates" in the northeastern Laotian province of Sam Nua and in the Black River Valley in November and December 1914. On November 11, the band attacked the post at Sam Nua, killed the French commander, and stole cash valued at 102,000 piastres. Although they were pursued by troops of the *Garde Indigene*, they retreated and then attacked another post at Son La. There, however, a troop of *tirailleurs* who had just arrived were able to repulse the attackers and inflict heavy losses, eventually chasing them first to Dien Bien Phu and then across the Chinese border. In a report to the Paris authorities the acting Governor

---

[132] Roume said that the total cost of the campaign "will not be less than fifteen hundred thousand [quinze cent mille] francs," though that number seems quite high. Governor General Roume to Minister of Colonies, February 22, 1916, Troubles et Complots en Indochine, Indo/nf/3, CAOM.

[133] Governor General Roume to Minister of Colonies, February 22, 1916, 18–19. Troubles et Complots en Indochine, Indo/nf/3, CAOM.

[134] Governor General Roume to Minister of Colonies, February 22, 1916, 20.

[135] Governor General Roume to Minister of Colonies, February 22, 1916, 20.

General of Indochina at the time, Joost von Vollenhoven, insisted that the attack had absolutely no political character whatsoever.[136] However, a French official working in Yunnan disagreed completely.[137] After reading telegraphic exchanges between van Vollenhoven and Gaston Liébert in Hong Kong, he noted that Liébert had warned the Governor General a month in advance that attacks would soon be made in the area by a combination of Chinese pirates and members of the revolutionary Annamite party (the Viet Nam Restoration Association). Liébert even had warned the Governor General that one of the leaders of the attacks was a known revolutionary named Phan Ba Ngoc (a man we have seen before in the context of making bombs), who possessed intelligence about which border posts were poorly defended. According to the French official, the large number of raids that suddenly arose in the region indicated that these were not simply attacks made for the sake of plunder, but rather for "a more extensive purpose" tied in with the goals of the Viet Nam Restoration Association.[138]

The attacks on Sam Nua and Son La were far from the end of these border threats. In December 1914 Liébert reported from Hong Kong that bands of Chinese "pirates" had congregated on the border of Yunnan and what the French called Deux-Kouangs (Kouang-tong and Kouang-si), and were ready to cross into Tonkin. In response, Governor General van Vollenhoven indicated that the colonial government was taking the possibility of such an incursion from that location very seriously, and that preparations to oppose it were under way.[139] At the end of January 1915, Liébert reported with alarm that Vietnamese rebels under the direction of Cuong De were headed toward the border area of Moncai. Further, he reported that these rebels had assembled about 4,000 armed Chinese men to slip across the border to Indochina in small groups through the forests of the region. Once across, Liébert warned, the idea was for rebels already on the interior of Tonkin to coordinate their attacks with those coming from the outside.[140] Just a few days later, in February 1915,

---

[136] Joost von Vollenhoven was acting Governor General of Indochina between January 1914 and April 1915.

[137] Report from the Delegate for the Minister of Foreign Affairs in Yunnan to the Deputy Superintendent to the Chief of Military Services, March 20, 1915. Troubles et Complots en Indochine, Indo/nf/3, CAOM.

[138] Report from the Delegate for the Minister of Foreign Affairs in Yunnan to the Deputy Superintendent to the Chief of Military Services, March 20, 1915.

[139] Letter from Monsieur Liébert, Consul-General Hong Kong, to Monsieur Delcassé, Minister of Foreign Affairs, December 27, 1914; Letter from van Vollenhoven to Liébert, January 21, 1915. Menées Austrio-Allemande en Indochine, Indo/nf/992, CAOM.

[140] Liébert to van Vollenhoven, January 26, 1915. Menées Austrio-Allemande en Indochine, Indo/nf/992, CAOM.

two attacks on posts occurred on the same day in the provinces of Phu Tho and Ninh Binh, to the west and south of Hanoi, respectively. In mid-March, Liébert warned of a situation in the region of Thanhoa (Annam province) in which Vietnamese revolutionaries had succeeded in winning over a large portion of Indochinese *tirailleurs* stationed there. According to his sources, the *tirailleurs* and the revolutionaries – along with a bunch of Chinese pirates – were hiding out in the forests of the region with 500 guns and four cannons.[141] And by the end of March, Liébert reported that not only was Cuong De still in constant contact with the German consul in Canton for the purpose of obtaining money, but also that Vietnamese rebels who had been in Siam were preparing to enter Cochinchina – by way of Cambodia – with the purpose of stirring up local populations against the French. While Liébert did not think this last situation was particularly dangerous, he added that it "nevertheless demands a constant vigilance on our part."[142]

Given what we know about the reliability of Liébert's sources with regard to Vietnamese-German schemes, it is not possible to know for sure whether or not Cuong De was personally involved in the border attacks prior to his departure for Japan in May 1915, though such involvement does seem unlikely. What we do know is that repeated border attacks did occur, that they were often carried out by paid Chinese "pirates" or "bandits," and that members of the Viet Nam Restoration Association – funded with German money – appeared to be involved in at least some of them.

As with bomb-making schemes, arrests of well-known individuals involved with the Viet Nam Restoration Association help to shed further light on the clandestine networks behind these attacks. One such occasion was the arrest of Tran Huu Luc (originally Nguyen Thuc Duong), who had trained in Japan and China and, in 1912, had gone to Siam to create a company of armed expatriate Vietnamese in the name of the Viet Nam Restoration Association.[143] French intelligence indicated that just after the war broke out in September 1914, Tran had gone to the German and Austrian consuls in Bangkok and obtained a subsidy of 10,000 piastres for the purpose of creating border uprisings in Indochina. This money was then transported to China, where on March 13, 1915 it was used to organize and fund a border attack at the French post of Tulang in northern Tonkin. The attack itself comprised about one hundred men, most of

---

[141] Liébert to van Vollenhoven, March 12, 1915. Menées Austrio-Allemande en Indochine, Indo/nf/992, CAOM.

[142] Liébert to von Vollenhoven, March 22, 1915. Menées Austrio-Allemande en Indochine, Indo/nf/992, CAOM.

[143] Phan, *Overturned Chariot*, 154.

whom were Vietnamese. When the men attacked, they were dispersed by an opposing French-led force, and then retreated back across the Chinese border.[144] Although the attack came to nothing, according to Governor General Roume its real importance lay in the capture of its leaders and what they revealed about anti-French activities during the war. As we know, by 1915 the Siamese government was cooperating with French and British demands for the extradition of anticolonial agents operating on Siamese soil. Tran and five of his compatriots were among the unlucky men who were arrested by Siamese police as a result of this cooperation. They were charged with obtaining money for the border incursion from German agents and conspiring against French rule, and were brought back to Hanoi for judgment. Tran Huu Luc appeared before the Council of War for several days giving testimony that confirmed his involvement with German agents in Siam, and then he was executed. In the meantime, Roume admitted, his testimony shed the most complete light thus far on "the rebel alliance with our European enemies."[145]

Tran Huu Luc's arrest did not stop members of the Viet Nam Restoration Association from continuing to attempt to conspire with representatives of the Central Powers. We already know that later in 1915 Phan Bội Châu authorized yet another plot involving German money from the minister in Siam, which was obtained by his personal emissary Mai Son (Nguyen Thuong Hien). In addition to offering Mai Son another 10,000 yuan, the German minister promised that this initial money would just be a first installment if the Viet Nam Restoration Association were able to succeed in making a big impact with the initial funds.[146] Once back in China, Association members split the money three ways for the purpose of carrying out border attacks on Mong-cai, Lang-Son, and Hokow.[147] Although each of the efforts failed, they are further evidence that Vietnamese-German conspiracies were not simply the fanciful inventions of French authorities.

Reports of frontier disturbances continued right through 1915 and into 1916. A letter written by the French consul in Yunnan-fu in March 1915 reported that Cuong De had already received 100,000 piastres for the purposes of stirring up agitation in Indochina from the now well-known ex-German consul of Hong Kong, Dr. Voretzsch.[148] By the end of

---

[144] Governor General Roume to Minister of Colonies, February 22, 1916, 26. Troubles et Complots en Indochine, Indo/nf/3, CAOM.

[145] Governor General Roume to Minister of Colonies, February 22, 1916, 26.

[146] Phan says yuan, but it may have been piastres.

[147] Phan, *Overturned Chariot*, 227. Phan does not discuss these schemes any further until he himself was released from prison in 1917.

[148] Letter from French consul in Yunnan-fu to the Minister of Colonies, March 20, 1915. Troubles en Cochinchine, Indo/nf/28/2.

January 1916, Governor General Roume telegrammed the French Minister of Colonies that incidents of "intrigues" on the Sino-Indochinese
frontier were numerous, and that they were being encouraged by the
German consuls at Canton and Pakhoi, who were providing various rebel
groups camped on the border with arms.[149] A letter from Paris written
in the same month went even farther, arguing that armed rebel bands of
petty criminals and pirates "who infest the frontier, have been organized
and even commanded by Germans and Austrians," making them therefore very dangerous.[150] Moreover, the author envisioned more frequent
and tenacious attacks in the future, which would seek to do as much
harm as possible. The situation, he believed, was only exacerbated by the
fact that China itself was undergoing considerable turmoil, which made
the frontiers even more unstable and difficult to control.

Reports about border attacks from both China and Siam died down
after 1916. Nevertheless, they reveal that such attacks were frequent for
at least the first three years of the war, and that they required regular –
and sometimes quite costly – responses from French-led military forces
in Indochina. It is also clear that German funds were behind at least
some of these attacks, and that Germans worked with both Vietnamese
revolutionaries and Chinese "pirates" to bring them about. Finally, in
spite of the fact that the French eventually repulsed all of these attacks
and that no general revolution resulted from them, they caused genuine
and repeated alarm to the French government in Indochina – to the
point where French officials were willing to mobilize their allies in China
to bring about a satisfactory solution.

Diplomatic Outrage

In fact, by early 1916 the French considered the Chinese government's
apparent toleration of German scheming with Vietnamese rebels so
untenable that Governor General Roume wrote that the only way to
deal effectively with the problem was for the Allied powers to take measures "outside the state."[151] The Minister of Colonies in Paris responded
to Roume's letter with some alarm, writing to the Minister of Foreign
Affairs that the situation in Indochina had now become quite serious with
regard to intrigues by the Central Powers. Given the situation, he urged
that representatives of all the Allies in China come together to demand

---

[149] Telegram from Governor General Roume to Minister of Colonies, January 21, 1916.
Menées Austrio-Allemande en Indochine, Indo/nf/992.
[150] Letter from Paris, January 20, 1916, on La frontière sino-annamite et le projet de
recrutement d'une armée Indochinoise. Troubles en Cochinchine, Indo/nf/28/2.
[151] Roume to Ministère de Colonies, January 29, 1916. Menées Austrio-Allemande en
Indochine, CAOM, Indo/nf/992.

action by the Chinese government against any and all Germans or Austrians found to be intriguing against Indochina or otherwise funding armed rings of bandits.[152]

But representatives of all the Allies in the Far East had already taken the matter into their own hands and had begun to meet together to discuss possible collective ways of dealing with the problem. Their motives did not necessarily stem from concern for the French, but rather from the fact that all of the Allies save Japan were experiencing similar problems. The British, for their part, were busy trying to thwart German schemes to incite revolution in India and Burma, while the Russians were dealing with the same problem on their railways in Manchuria. In the meantime, the Japanese were interested in assisting with the problem in the hopes that a solution might extend their influence in China. Thus in early January 1916, the Japanese foreign minister held a meeting in Tokyo for all Allied representatives, in which he outlined a plan for the Allies to create an international police force to deal specifically with German intrigue, to isolate and restrict German concessions in Tientsin and Hankow, and to require all German and Austrian officials working for Chinese customs and other government industries to be dismissed.[153] Back in Peking, however, the French, British, and Russian ambassadors met alone to discuss the proposal. The mood was gloomy. Each feared that the Japanese would overstep their authority and seek to expand their influence in China if they created an international police force. Further, they acknowledged that isolating German concessions or dismissing officials would require the permission of the Chinese government, which they believed would not be forthcoming.[154] In short, given the internal situation in China and the fact that it was still a neutral state, the collective representatives of the Allied powers did not believe they would be able to obtain more than lip service by the Chinese government to shut these schemes down.

In the end, the French determination to take matters "outside the state" resulted in little more than continued official complaints to the Chinese central government. Like the British in the Dutch East Indies in the same period, they found there was little they could do to compel the Chinese government to put an end to German "intrigues." Moreover, French officials no doubt understood that the instability in the Chinese

---

[152] Ministère de Colonies a Ministre des Affaires Etrangères, January 31, 1916. Menées Austrio-Allemande en Indochine, CAOM, Indo/nf/992.

[153] Telegrams from Ambassador Sir J. Jordan (Peking), January 4, 1916, and from Ambassador Sir C. Greene (Tokyo), January 5, 1916, Report #1292. Straits Settlements Original Correspondence: Foreign, 1916, CO 273/449.

[154] Telegram from Ambassador Sir J. Jordan (Peking), January 4, 1916, Report #1292. Straits Settlements Original Correspondence: Foreign, 1916, CO 273/449.

government during much of the war made it impossible to impose its will on the various provinces where the intrigues were taking place. In early 1916, the provinces of Yunnan, Guangxi, and Guizhou were in open rebellion against Yuan Shikai's government, and Yuan himself died in June.[155] Much to the chagrin and frustration of the French, then, representatives of the Central Powers continued to work with anticolonial activists and to subvert Allied colonial rule in neighboring territories with relative impunity until the Chinese government finally declared war on Germany on August 14, 1917.

"Fighting for the Hegemony of the World"

Whether or not it was any consolation, the French were not alone in their frustrations with German schemes in China. The British in particular readily agreed that Germans in China had created a complex network of conspiracies and alliances with any and all anticolonial activists who sought to undermine colonial rule in an Allied colony. A memo written by the British Foreign Office to the Japanese ambassador to Britain late in 1915 asserted that "The information at the disposal of His Majesty's Government tends to show that the whole German consular organization, in addition to a number of German firms and private individuals in China, have been engaged since the outbreak of war in a propaganda aimed at enlisting Chinese sympathy on the side of the Central Powers and at damaging the commercial position and military prestige of the Allies."[156] While this chapter is mostly about German-Vietnamese schemes in China, a brief exploration of the British experience provides further evidence that Germans were involved in similar activities against other Allied powers at precisely the same time.

German-fueled "intrigues" against British rule in China centered on conspiracies with participants in the Indian Ghadar movement, as they did also in the Dutch East Indies and in Siam. Between 1914 and 1916, British officials became convinced that "all the evidence goes to show that the German consulate-general in Shanghai is the centre of a widespread organisation for fomenting sedition and raising an armed rebellion in India."[157] The evidence in question was wide-ranging and included confessions of arrested German agents as well as the intelligence of

---

[155] Guoqi et al., eds., "China and Empire," 222.

[156] Confidential memorandum communicated to Japanese Ambassador, December 28, 1915, Report #4469. Straits Settlements Original Correspondence: Foreign, 1916, The National Archives, CO 273/449.

[157] Confidential Memorandum Communicated to the Japanese Ambassador, December 28, 1915, report 4469. Straits Settlements Original Correspondence: Foreign, 1916, CO/273/448, TNA. Also Popplewell, *Intelligence and Imperial Defence*, 177.

undercover Indian agents in Tokyo and Manila.[158] It also included intercepted telegrams between known German agents in Batavia and the interpreter for the German consul in Shanghai regarding arms shipments, as well as a map seized during an arrest of a German agent that located "the actual points on the Indian coast where an Indo-German rebel force was to disembark."[159] From these various sources, British authorities deduced that the German consul in Shanghai, Knipping, bore the final responsibility for approving the expenditure of funds relating to Indian intrigues.[160] Not only that, they were convinced that "the constant passage of German agents through Shanghai is connected with a scheme to obtain and equip five ships laden with arms and ammunition," and that Germans and "disaffected Indians" were to make up the core of a fighting force after disembarking in India.[161]

British sources also backed up French intelligence that the German consulate in Yunnan province was also up to no good. In late 1915, the Foreign Office cited the case of the notorious Austrian Pawelka, who had been found earlier that year conveying "arms and ammunition to the Tongking frontier" under the direction of Dr. Weiss, the German consul at Yunnan-fu. That individuals like the notorious Pawelka and Dr. Ernst Voretzsch might also be involved in anti-British intrigues also became clear in spring 1915, when French authorities arrested two Chinese men in Saigon for trying to induce the exiled Burmese prince, Myngoon-Min, to lead an uprising to take back his country from the British. Myngoon-Min had been living quietly in Saigon for years, however, and quickly denounced the Chinese messengers. Upon interrogation, the Chinese men revealed that they had been sent by Voretzsch, who as we know was believed to have extensive connections with Phan Bội Châu (or someone acting in his place).[162] Moreover, in October 1915 Shanghai Municipal

---

[158]   Key confessions came from a man named Moses Silberstein, who had been recruited to work for the Central Powers as a spy. Silberstein was arrested in Peshawar and on interrogation gave up details about an intricate espionage network headed by consul-general Knipping in Shanghai. Another critical arrest was Max Kindling, who gave away further details about Knipping's activities after being arrested by the Shanghai Municipal Police. See Nigel West, *Historical Dictionary of World War I Intelligence* (Plymouth, UK: Rowman & Littlefield, 2014), 286–287.

[159]   Confidential Memorandum Communicated to the Japanese Ambassador, December 28, 1915, report 4469.

[160]   Ramnath, *Haj to Utopia*, 77. A.C. Bose makes the same assertion in "Activities of Indian Revolutionaries Abroad, 1914–1918," in Amitabha Mukherjee, ed., *Militant Nationalism in India, 1876–1947* (Calcutta: Institute of Historical Studies, 1995), 306.

[161]   Confidential Memorandum Communicated to the Japanese Ambassador, December 28, 1915, report 4469.

[162]   Liébert to the Governor General in Indochina, May 12, 1915. Menées Austrio-Allemande en Indochine, Indo/nf/992. One of the Chinese men had been born in Singapore.

Police arrested two Chinese men who were in the midst of trying to ship 129 pistols and 12,000 rounds of ammunition to Calcutta at the request of a German firm. Finally, British authorities believed they had evidence that Germans living in China were deliberately spreading disaffection among the Indian Sikhs who lived and worked in Shanghai.[163]

British authorities grew so convinced that Shanghai was the linchpin in German intrigues in the Far East that they allowed David Petrie – who, as we know from Chapter 5, had been called upon to establish a comprehensive Far Eastern intelligence agency in 1915 – to establish his headquarters in Shanghai. Originally, Petrie's organization was going to be centered in Singapore, with consuls around the region employing secret agents whose reports would filter back to him. However, between May and August 1916 Petrie toured Singapore, the Philippines, China, and Japan, and decided that the area needing most supervision was China, given that there was virtually no check on Indians passing through its cities, nor on German consuls stationed there.[164] As he was establishing his headquarters, Petrie – along with the British ambassador in Peking, Sir John Jordan – also advocated that the ambassador in China be given new powers to deal with the problems caused by German intrigues. Specifically, they successfully requested an Order-in-Council that would allow the ambassador to summarily deport any British subject "who at any time or place since the beginning of the war" had been engaged in "intrigues with enemy subjects directed against the peace and security of the King's dominions," or "aiding, abetting, or counseling the waging of war against the King."[165] According to Petrie, these powers were especially important in a place like China, where the activities of Indian revolutionaries "have been directed not to the commission of criminal acts in China itself, but in India, and it is there ... that evidence exists of the conspiracy of which they are a part." Petrie went on to say that "it is only in light of this evidence that the real significance of their conduct elsewhere can be made to appear."[166] Rather than rely on Chinese law to hold and convict these men – a problem experienced by both the French and the British during the war years in China – these

---

[163] Confidential Memorandum Communicated to the Japanese Ambassador, December 28, 1915, report 4469. For an excellent treatment of Shanghai's place in revolutionary Indian networks, see chapter 3 in Cao Yin, Red Turbans on the Bund: Sikh Migrants, Policemen, and Revolutionaries in Shanghai, 1885–1945 (Ph.D. thesis, National University of Singapore, 2015).

[164] Popplewell, *Intelligence and Imperial Defense*, 269, 268.

[165] Letter from Sir John Jordan to Earl Grey, September 12, 1916, Report 50898. Straits Settlements Original Correspondence: Foreign, CO 273/449, TNA.

[166] David Petrie to Sir John Jordan, August 16, 1916, Report 50898. Straits Settlements Original Correspondence: Foreign, CO 273/449, TNA.

new powers allowed the British to remove suspected revolutionaries at will.

British intelligence also corroborated French intelligence about German attempts to undermine French rule in Indochina. In early 1917, the British consul's office in Yunnan-fu intercepted several letters written by the German consul in that city to T'ang Tu Chun, the military governor of the province. These letters were unambiguous. The first, from February 1917, lamented Chinese "impotence" with regard to foreign intervention by Britain, France, and Japan, and advocated that T'ang "should take this opportunity to reorganize the army and recover China's lost territory, either by attacking the French in Annam or the Japanese in Formosa; subsequently Hong Kong could be recovered by attacking Great Britain."[167] If this course of action were to be taken, the consul added, "my Government will undertake to assist China with arms and ammunition for a period of five years, and in future we shall fight together as allies and cordial relations will be established for ever between our respective countries."[168] In the end, this attempt to induce the Chinese government to attack its neighboring territories – which one British reader called "curiously bare-faced" – was entirely unsuccessful. The Chinese government under Duan Qirui, at great internal political cost, declared war on Germany on August 14, 1917.[169] As a result, representatives of the Central Powers were considered enemy aliens and were no longer permitted to remain in China. Until that time, however, the British were convinced – along with the French – that the Germans were using every means possible in their goal of "fighting for the hegemony of the world."[170]

Conclusion

Although China was thousands of miles away from the main theaters of fighting, as in Singapore, the Dutch East Indies, and Siam the war nevertheless came in multiple ways to the country and the region. China's neutrality made it possible for representatives of the Central Powers to repeatedly attempt to undermine Allied power in neighboring colonies

---

[167] Herbert Goffe, Consul-General in Yunnan-fu to B.F. Alston, Peking Legation, February 20, 1917. China: Situation at Yunnan-Fu: Intrigues of German Consul (Herr Weiss), 1917, IOR IOR/L/PS/11/122, 1811.

[168] Herbert Goffe, Consul-General in Yunnan-fu to B.F. Alston, Peking Legation, February 20, 1917.

[169] Guoqi et al., eds., "China and Empire," 222–223.

[170] B.F. Alston, Peking Legation, to Minister of Colonies, May 2, 1917. China: Situation at Yunnan-Fu: Intrigues of German Consul (Herr Weiss), 1917, IOR IOR/L/PS/11/122, 1811.

by funding revolutionary groups seeking an end to French or British rule, and by providing weapons and arms for border attacks. While little has been written about German collaboration with Vietnamese revolutionaries, such efforts at collaboration occurred regularly for most of the war. Both parties were motivated: the Germans as part of their larger war aim to distract Allied attention from the Western Front, and the Vietnamese as part of their pattern of seeking outside help in their struggle to rid Indochina of the French.

When viewed in its wider regional context, German–Vietnamese collaboration echoed German efforts to undermine British rule from China as well. And as we know, this was not a strategy limited to China. Rather, it was deeply connected – sometimes by the same people – to similar strategies employed in both the Dutch East Indies and Siam. While in the end none of the schemes succeeded, they nevertheless caused alarm among both French and British colonial authorities and resulted in the diversion of significant resources and time toward efforts to thwart them. In the long run, the creation of new or improved security networks to deal with these threats would have a lasting impact on the region well after the war was over. Not only that, the crisis atmosphere produced by the war allowed both British and French colonial authorities the license to pursue their anticolonial opponents with a violence and vigor that would have been unacceptable to metropolitan sensibilities in a time of peace. We have seen in Chapters 1–5 what this meant for Ghadar revolutionaries: the evisceration of their organization, the arrest of many of their leaders, and the failure of their plans. A similar fate befell Phan Bội Châu's revolutionaries as well. Indeed, although Phan had worked with the Germans in the hopes of finally obtaining the means for a successful revolution, in the end the partnership sped up the virtual destruction of Phan's movement.

Conclusion

This book began with the short-lived and relatively obscure mutiny of the 5th Light Infantry on the island of Singapore in February, 1915. In spite of its obscurity, as a story the mutiny is dramatic and intense, encapsulating as it does hope, fear, violence, tragedy, revenge, treachery, and death. Adding to the drama are the strange and sometimes counter-intuitive partnerships that characterized it, whether between Indian soldiers and German captives, or between British, French, Russian, and Japanese troops. In short, it is the kind of story that – through the prism of a moment of crisis – simultaneously brings the past to life and captures our attention.

But the mutiny is more than a good story. Rather, it represents in microcosm the ways global currents set in motion by World War I played out over a wide swath of Southeast Asia. We know that the mutiny was caused in part by revolutionary and pan-Islamic propaganda spread by Ghadar networks, which themselves originated in California and were funded by the German Foreign Office. We also know that the leaders of the mutiny had access both to the *Ghadar* newspaper as well as Ghadar supporters in the city of Singapore, both of which reached the island in the first months of the war. Moreover, the leaders of the mutiny had direct contact with Germans like August Diehn and the crew of the sunken *Emden*, who were keen to aid the German war effort in whatever way they could. And it was not only the causes of the mutiny that were linked to larger global currents related to the war. As we saw in Chapter 2, the response to the mutiny by nearby colonial powers, independent states, and non-British communities in Singapore were deeply shaped either by wartime alliances or by the desire to stay out of the war. These responses – particularly the military aid provided by Britain's French, Russian, and Japanese allies – had real consequences for the rebellious soldiers, for they all but ensured that the mutiny would fail.

Taken as an isolated event, the story of the mutiny is a perfect vehicle for tracing the many ways Singapore was connected to the wider world at war via print media, the movement of individuals, or national, imperial, or ideological alliances. But the significance of the mutiny goes beyond recognizing these wide-ranging connections between an island in Southeast Asia and a world war whose most ferocious battles were being waged thousands of miles away in Europe. For the Singapore mutiny was not an isolated event. Rather, when we view it in the context of the larger region, we can see that the same currents that helped cause a mutiny there were also active in the surrounding region, whether in the Dutch East Indies, French Indochina, Siam, or China.

In fact, a wider focus on Southeast Asia clearly shows that Ghadar revolutionaries were active throughout the region, particularly in neutral states like the Dutch East Indies, Siam, and China where British power was weak or at least moderated by a sovereign power. As we saw in Chapters 3–6, these neutral states played key strategic roles in facilitating and enabling Ghadar networks between the United States and India during the war, whether wittingly or not. Thus while the Singapore mutiny may have been the most dramatic event in the region caused by Ghadar propaganda, the lion's share of the action by Ghadar revolutionaries actually took place in places like Batavia, Bangkok, and Shanghai, to name only a few locations.

One of the reasons so much Ghadar activity took place on neutral territory in Southeast Asia was because German agents – including consuls, business owners, and contractors – were able to act with relative freedom in such locations. This meant they were able to meet and conspire with Ghadar revolutionaries in person, and to exchange both money and weapons. And German agents conspired not only with Indian revolutionaries but also with Vietnamese anti-French revolutionaries similarly intent on taking advantage of French weakness during a time of war. As we saw in Chapters 5 and 6, in both Siam and China Vietnamese revolutionaries and German agents used neutral neighboring states as launching points for anticolonial activity in the region.

In addition to the importance of the neutral states for facilitating connections between anticolonial activists and German agents in the region, the war affected the neutral states in other ways as well. In the Dutch East Indies, we have seen that British restrictions on global shipping and communications had a profoundly negative effect on the economy and on personal freedoms. Perhaps even more importantly, the delicate balancing act of remaining neutral during the war forced the Dutch government in the Indies to spend vast amounts of time and money on the numerous (and not altogether inaccurate) complaints by both sides about the improper use of Indies territory in the prosecution of the war. In Siam, the government was faced with similar complaints but, unlike the Dutch East Indies, allowed itself to be pushed toward an active alliance with the Allied powers. In China, representatives of Allied and Central powers complained bitterly about breaches in Chinese neutrality while also seeking the aid of the government in furthering their own war aims. Eventually, the Chinese government too chose the side of the Allies, though the reasons had less to do with ideological sympathy than with winning back its territories in the Shandong peninsula from the Japanese. In all these ways, then, this First World War lived up to its name in Southeast Asia, for its impact was felt in every location where representatives of the belligerent countries were found, no matter how far from the fighting.

In addition to demonstrating the importance of World War I in Southeast Asia, one of the deeper purposes of this book has been to highlight the messy and interlinked nature of modern colonialism. I argue that it is not adequate to view the structure of colonialism principally in terms of metropole–colony relations. Rather, by exploring the region of Southeast Asia at a time of crisis in the early twentieth century, we can clearly see the importance not only of metropole–colony relations but also of intercolonial contact and movement, as well as connections between colonies and independent states.

This book has traced such intercolonial and extracolonial connections most clearly with regard to two groups of anticolonial revolutionaries and to the global consular network. In the case of anticolonial revolutionaries, we have seen how Ghadar revolutionaries and the members of the Viet Nam Restoration Association strategically moved across colonial borders both to other colonies and to independent states in order to organize more freely and effectively. Ghadar revolutionaries, for example, moved from India to North America and then dispersed around the world, not only to British colonies but to strategically located independent states such as China, the Dutch East Indies, and Siam – each of which was meant to serve as a way-station for revolutionaries who would eventually bring about revolution in India. Members of the Viet Nam Restoration Association, for their part, moved first from Indochina to Japan, established themselves in Siam and China, and maintained strong connections in the British colony of Hong Kong. In each instance, their movement across colonial borders and to neighboring independent states was part of a strategy to avoid French persecution and to obtain aid for fomenting revolution in Indochina.

In the case of the global consular network, we have seen on numerous occasions how consuls knit both the colonial and noncolonial worlds together with their steady and multidirectional communications. Consuls of every nationality not only kept in regular contact with their ambassadors (if there were one, as in China or Siam) and metropolitan

Foreign Offices but also with consuls in other states and colonies as well as with nearby colonial administrators. By virtue of their office they were also necessarily in contact with representatives of their host state or colony, and thus they functioned, literally, as conduits of communication between and among colonies and independent states. When an event like the Singapore mutiny occurred, then, it was the consular network that ensured most of the world knew about it within hours after it happened, and it was the consular network that received critical communications about how the various Allied and neutral states would respond. Consuls were also critical for keeping the British informed about Ghadar revolutionaries who moved from the United States to China and from Siam to the Dutch East Indies. Similarly, consuls kept the French informed about the activities of the Viet Nam Restoration Association in China, Siam, and Hong Kong. What all this demonstrates, then, is just how linked colonies were to each other and to the wider world, and how frequently both people and ideas moved across colonial borders.

Such cross-border connection and movement is, I would argue, part of what makes this book not only a history of World War I or of empire but also a world history. World histories, indeed, are not simply comprehensive accounts of the whole world. Rather, world histories tell stories about connections – whether between people, places, ideas, or events – over large geographical areas or long periods of time. Perhaps most importantly, world histories tell stories that cannot be understood only in the context of local or regional perspectives. Rather, in order to appreciate their full significance, such stories must be placed in their larger, global context. As I have argued here, it is not possible to fully understand the Singapore mutiny, anticolonial collaboration with German agents, or the complexities of alliances and loyalties in Southeast Asia without attention to the world at war between 1914 and 1918. When viewed this way, the movements and events that form the basis of each chapter should not be seen simply as local stories, but rather as parts of a single story. The mutiny, therefore, is part of the same story as the *S.S. Maverick* and the *Henry S.*; the Ghadar invasion force set to invade from Siam is part of the same story as the cross-border attacks of the Viet Nam Restoration Association; and the desperate search for Narendra Nath Battacharya is part of the same story as the arrest of Luong Lap Nam. Although historians have not often written these stories as though they were connected, this book has argued not only that we can trace these connections in hindsight but also that a variety of anticolonial revolutionaries and colonial administrators understood these connections at the time.

This book has argued that the legacies of the war on Southeast Asia were long-lived. In the short term, the crisis of the war allowed colonial authorities to demand – and to win – permission to summarily punish anticolonial revolutionaries, often with extraordinary violence. The French government in Indochina, for example, used the war as an opportunity to set up military tribunals to deal with captured members of the Viet Nam Restoration Association. As a result, the government was able to execute key members of the Association days after capture, all while avoiding long trials. The British government in Singapore, for its part, responded to the mutiny in 1915 by the quick execution of forty-two men only a few weeks after the formal inquest had begun, and in Siam and China used the opportunity of war to deal quickly with captured revolutionaries.

In the longer term, the existence of anticolonial groups who sought collaboration with German agents contributed to the rise of new colonial security networks in the region. As we saw in Chapter 6, the French government in Indochina redoubled its efforts to use its fledgling security networks to coordinate information about the Viet Nam Restoration Association not only between government departments, but between consuls in neighboring states and colonies. And as we saw in Chapter 5, the British determination to thwart revolutionary Ghadar networks resulted in the creation of the Far Eastern Intelligence Agency, which also sought to bring consuls into the habit of collecting and sharing information with government agents. Even the Dutch, who remained neutral during the war, set up a new *Politieke Inlichtingendienst* (Political Intelligence Department) in 1916 in order to guard against threats to Dutch neutrality in the East Indies.

During the war, the French and British security agencies helped to destroy – or at least neutralize – both Ghadar and the Viet Nam Restoration Association. Indeed, the development of revolutionary networks stimulated the growth of colonial networks designed to shut them down, while the crisis of the war allowed colonial governments to use violence and imprisonment on a very wide scale to rid themselves of their enemies. In a twist of irony, then, the very revolutionary movements that had sought to use the war as their moment of opportunity instead found that the war had hastened their demise. Just as important, the colonial security agencies that grew out of the needs of the war would only grow more efficient after its end. By the 1920s, they would fulfill a new function in fighting communism around the region.

Nearly a century after the end of the war, we are still accounting for its enormous human cost. In recent years, historians have focused increasing attention on the impact of the war outside Europe, in places as far afield as China, sub-Saharan Africa, and India. It seems, in fact, that nearly every location in the world felt its impact in both large and small ways. As I hope this book has demonstrated, this was certainly the case in Southeast Asia, for although wartime events in the region did not have a significant impact on the outcome of the war, the war had a momentous impact on the region.

Select Bibliography

ARCHIVES

The National Archives, Kew, England.
The India Office Library, London, England.
Centre des Archives d'Outre-Mer, Aix-en-Provence, France.
Archief Nationaal, Den Haag, the Netherlands.
Singapore National Archives, Singapore.
Cornell University Library, Division of Rare and Manuscript Collections.

PUBLISHED PRIMARY SOURCES

Jenkins, Christopher, translator. *Reflections from Captivity: Phan Bội Châu's "Prison Notes" and Ho Chi Minh's "Prison Diary."* Southeast Asia Translation Series, vol. 1. Athens: Ohio University Press, 1978.

Phan, Bội Châu. Translated by Vinh Sinh and Nicholas Wickenden. *Overturned Chariot: The Autobiography of Phan-Bison No.* SHAPS Library of Translations. Honolulu, HI: University of Hawai'i Press, 1999.

Sareen, T.R. *Secret Documents on Singapore Mutiny 1915, vols. 1 and 2.* New Delhi: Mounto Publishing House, 1995.

Select Documents on the Ghadr Party. New Delhi: Mounto Publishing House, 1994.

Tran, My-Van, translator and editor. *A Vietnamese Royal Exile in Japan: Prince Cuong De, 1882–1951.* London and New York: Routledge, 2005.

SECONDARY WORKS

Abbenhuis, Maartje. *Art of Staying Neutral: The Netherlands in the First World War, 1914–1918.* Amsterdam: Amsterdam University Press, 2006.

Adas, Michael. "Contested Hegemony: The Great War and the Afro-Asian Assault on the Civilizing Mission Ideology." *Journal of World History* 15, no. 1 (2004): 31–63.

Aksakal, Mustafa. *The Ottoman Road to War in 1914: The Ottoman Empire and the First World War.* Cambridge Military Histories. Cambridge, UK; New York: Cambridge University Press, 2008.

Anderson, Clare. *Subaltern Lives: Biographies of Colonialism in the Indian Ocean World, 1790–1920.* Cambridge: Cambridge University Press, 2012.

Andrade, Tonio. "A Chinese Farmer, Two African Boys, and a Warlord: Toward a Global Microhistory." *Journal of World History* 21, no. 4 (December 2010): 573–591.

Andrew, Christopher and Jeremy Noakes, editors. *Intelligence and International Relations, 1900–1945*, Exeter Studies in History. Liverpool: Liverpool University Press, 1987.

Ansari, K.H. "Pan-Islam and the Making of the Early Indian Muslim Socialists." *Modern Asian Studies* 20, no. 3 (January 1, 1986): 509–537.

Aydin, Cemil. *The Politics of Anti-Westernism in Asia: Visions of World Order in Pan-Islamic and Pan-Asian Thought*. Columbia Studies in International and Global History. New York: Columbia University Press, 2007.

Baker, Christopher John and Pasuk Phongpaichit. *A History of Thailand*, 2nd ed. Cambridge; New York: Cambridge University Press, 2009.

Ban, Kah Choon. *Absent History: The Untold Story of Special Branch Operations in Singapore, 1915–1942*. Singapore: Raffles, 2001.

Andaya, Barbara Watson. "From Rūm to Tokyo: The Search for Anticolonial Allies by the Rulers of Riau, 1899–1914." *Indonesia* 24 (October 1, 1977): 123–156.

Barrett, Tracy. *The Chinese Diaspora in South-East Asia: The Overseas Chinese in IndoChina*. London: I.B. Tauris, 2012.

Bauduin, F. *Het Nederlandsch Eskader in Oost-Indië*. 'S-Gravenhage: Martinus Nijhoff, 1920.

Best, Antony. "India, Pan-Asianism and the Anglo-Japanese Alliance." In Phillips Payson O'Brien, editor. *The Anglo-Japanese Alliance, 1902–1922*, 236–248. London: RoutledgeCurzon, 2004.

Bose, Sugata. *A Hundred Horizons: The Indian Ocean in the Age of Global Empire*. Cambridge, MA: Harvard University Press, 2006.

Brocheux, Pierre, Daniel Hémery, Ly Lan Dill-Klein, Eric Jennings, Nora A. Taylor, and Noémi Tousignant. *Indochina: An Ambiguous Colonization, 1858–1954*. Berkeley: University of California Press, 2011.

Brückenhaus, Daniel. "'Every Stranger Must Be Suspected': Trust Relationships and the Surveillance of Anti-Colonialists in Early Twentieth-Century Western Europe." *Geschichte Und Gesellschaft* 36, no. 4 (2010): 523–566.

The Transnational Surveillance of Anti-Colonialist Movements in Western Europe, 1905–1945. Ph.D. Dissertation, Yale University, 2011.

Burton, Antoinette. *At the Heart of the Empire: Indians and the Colonial Encounter in Late-Victorian Britain*. Berkeley: University of California Press, 1998.

editor. *Archive Stories: Facts, Fictions, and the Writing of History*. Durham, NC: Duke University Press, 1995.

Carlier, Claude et al., editors. *Les Troupes Coloniales Dans La Grande Guerre: Actes Du Colloque Organisé Pour Le 80e Anniversaire de La Bataille de Verdun Par Le Comité National Du Souvenir de Verdun, Le Mémorial de Verdun, l'Institut D'histoire Des Conflicts Contemporains, Le 27 Novembre 1996 à Verdun Au Centre Mondial de La Paix*, Hautes études Militaires 5. Paris: IHCC-CNSV, Economica, 1997.

Chakrabarti, Hiren. *Political Protest in Bengal: Boycott and Terrorism, 1905–1918*. Calcutta: Papyrus, 1992.

Chandran, J. "British Foreign Policy and the Extraterritorial Question in Siam 1891–1900." *Journal of the Malaysian Branch of the Royal Asiatic Society* 38, no. 2 (208) (December 1, 1965): 290–313.

"Lord Lansdowne and the 'Anti-German Clique' at the Foreign Office: Their Role in the Making of the Anglo-Siamese Agreement of 1902." *Journal of Southeast Asian Studies* 3, no. 2 (September 1, 1972), 229–246.

Ching-hwang, Yen. *The Chinese in Southeast Asia and Beyond: Socioeconomic and Political Dimensions*. Singapore: World Scientific Publishing Company, 2008.

Das, Santanu. *Race, Empire and First World War Writing*. Cambridge; New York: Cambridge University Press, 2011.

Dickinson, Frederick R. "The Japanese Empire." In Robert Gerwarth and Erez Manela, editors. *Empires at War, 1911–1923, 197–213*. Oxford: Oxford University Press, 2014.

Di Paola, Maria Teresa, Ulbert Jörg, and Prijak Lukian. "Between Trade and Intelligence: The Messina British Consulate in a Fast Changing World." In *Consuls et Services Consulaires Au XIXe Siecle = Die Welt Der Konsulate Im 19. Jahrhundert = Consulship in the 19th Century*, 157–173. Hamburg: DOBU, Dokumentation & Buch, 2010.

Doran, Christine. "Gender Matters in the Singapore Mutiny." *Sojourn: Journal of Social Issues in Southeast Asia* 17:1 (April 2002), 76–94.

Dua, Enakshi. "Racialising Imperial Canada: Indian Women and the Making of Ethnic Communities." In Antoinette Burton, editor. *Gender, Sexuality, and Colonial Modernities*. London and New York: Routledge, 1999.

Duara, Prasenjit. "Nationalists Among Transnationals: Overseas Chinese and the Idea of China, 1900–1911." In *Ungrounded Empires: The Cultural Politics of Modern Chinese Transnationalism*, edited by Aihwa Ong and Donald Nonini. New York: Routledge, 1997.

"The Discourse of Civilization and Pan-Asianism." *Journal of World History* 12, no. 1 (2001): 99.

"Transnationalism and the Predicament of Sovereignty: China, 1900–1945." *American Historical Review* 102, no. 4 (October 1997): 1030.

Duncanson, Dennis J. "Ho-Chi-Minh in Hong Kong, 1931–32." *The China Quarterly* 57 (January 1, 1974): 84–100.

Eckert, Henri. *Les Militaires Indochinoise au Service de la France*. Ph.D. Dissertation, University of Paris Sorbonne, 1998.

Ellinwood, DeWitt C. and S.D. Pradhan, editors. *India and World War 1*. Columbia, MO: South Asia Books, 1978.

Esenbel, Selcuk. "Japan's Global Claim to Asia and the World of Islam: Transnational Nationalism and World Power, 1900–1945." *The American Historical Review* 109, no. 4 (October 1, 2004): 1140–1170.

Esherick, Joseph and C.X. George Wei, editors. *China: How the Empire Fell*. Asia's Transformations 41. London; New York: Routledge, 2013.

Fawaz, Leila Tarazi. *A Land of Aching Hearts: The Middle East in the Great War*. Cambridge, MA: Harvard University Press, 2014.

Fischer, Fritz. *Germany's Aims in the First World War*. New York: W.W. Norton, 1967.

Fischer-Tiné, Harald. "Indian Nationalism and the 'world Forces': Transnational and Diasporic Dimensions of the Indian Freedom Movement on the Eve of the First World War." *Journal of Global History* 2, no. 03 (2007): 325–344.

Fogarty, Richard Standish. *Race and War in France: Colonial Subjects in the French Army, 1914–1918*. Baltimore: Johns Hopkins University Press, 2013.

Formichi, Chiara. "Pan-Islam and Religious Nationalism: The Case of Kartosuwiryo and Negara Islam Indonesia." *Indonesia* 90 (October 2010), 125–146.

Islam and the Making of the Nation: Kartosuwiryo and Political Islam in Twentieth-Century Indonesia. Leiden: KITLV Press, 2012.

Foster, Anne. *Projections of Power: The United States and Europe in Colonial Southeast Asia*. Durham: Duke University Press, 2010.

Fourniau, Charles. *Annam-Tonkin, 1885–1896: Lettrés et Paysans Vietnamiens Face à La Conquête Coloniale*, Travaux Du Centre D'histoire et Civilisations de La Péninsule Indochinoise. Paris: L'Harmattan, 1989.

Fraser, Thomas G. "Germany and Indian Revolution, 1914–18." *Journal of Contemporary History* 12, no. 2 (April 1, 1977): 255–272.

Frémeaux, Jacques. *Les Colonies dans la Grande Guerre: Combats et Éprouves des Peuples d'Outre-Mer*. Paris: 14–18 Editions, 2006.

Frost, Mark Ravinder. "Emporium in Imperio: Nanyang Networks and the Straits Chinese in Singapore, 1819–1914." *Journal of Southeast Asian Studies* 36, no. 01 (2005): 29–66.

Gendre, Claude. *Le Dê Thám (1858–1913): Un Résistant Vietnamien à La Colonisation Française*. Paris: Harmattan, 2007.

Gerwarth, Robert and Erez Manela. *Empires at War, 1911–1923*. Oxford: Oxford University Press, 2014.

Ghosh, Durba. "Terrorism in Bengal: Political Violence in the Interwar Years." In *Decentring Empire: Britain, India, and the Transcolonial World*, Ed Durba Ghosh and Dane Kennedy. Himayatnagar, Hyderabad: Orient Longman, 2006.

"Another Set of Imperial Turns?" *The American Historical Review* 117, no. 3 (June 1, 2012): 772–793.

Goscha, Christopher. *Thailand and the Southeast Asian Networks of the Vietnamese Revolution, 1885–1954*. Richmond, Surrey: Curzon Press, 1999.

Gould, Harold A. *Sikhs, Swamis, Students, and Spies: The India Lobby in the United States, 1900–1946*. New Delhi: Sage Publications, 2006.

Greene, Stephen Lyon Wakeman. *Absolute Dreams: Thai Government under Rama VI, 1910–1925*. Bangkok: White Lotus Press, 1999.

Gyory, Andrew. *Closing the Gate: Race, Politics, and the Chinese Exclusion Act*. Chapel Hill: The University of North Carolina Press, 1998.

Hanioğlu, M. Şükrü. *A Brief History of the Late Ottoman Empire*. Princeton: Princeton University Press, 2008.

Harper, Tim. "Singapore, 1915, and the Birth of the Asian Underground." *Modern Asian Studies* 47, no. 06 (2013): 1782–1811.

Harper, W.R.E. and Harry Miller, *Singapore Mutiny*. Singapore: Oxford University Press, 1984.

Heehs, Peter. "Terrorism in India during the Freedom Struggle." *Historian* 55, no. 3 (1993): 469.

Hevia, James Louis. *The Imperial Security State: British Colonial Knowledge and Empire-Building in Asia*. Cambridge: Cambridge University Press, 2012.

Hill, Kimloan, Nhung Tuyet Tran, and Anthony Reid, editors. "Strangers in a Foreign Land: Vietnamese Soldiers and Workers in France during World War I." In *Viet Nam: Borderless Histories*, 256–289. Madison: University of Wisconsin Press, 2006.

Ho, Enseng. *The Graves of Tarim: Genealogy and Mobility Across the Indian Ocean*. Berkeley: University of California Press, 2006.

Hopkirk, Peter. *Like Hidden Fire: The Plot to Bring Down the British Empire*. New York: Kodansha, 1997.

Hoyt, Edwin P. *The Last Cruise of the Emden: The Amazing True World War I Story of a German Light Cruiser and Her Courageous Crew*. Guilford, CT: Lyons Press, 2001.

Ikle, Frank W. "Japanese-German Peace Negotiations during World War I." *The American Historical Review* 71, no. 1 (October 1, 1965): 62–76.

Jarboe, Andrew. "Soldiers of Empire: Indian Sepoys in and Beyond the Imperial Metropole During the First World War, 1914–1919." Ph.D. Dissertation, Northeastern University, 2013.

Jarboe, Andrew Tait and Richard Standish Fogarty. *Empires in World War I: Shifting Frontiers and Imperial Dynamics in a Global Conflict*. London; New York: I.B. Tauris. Distributed in the U.S. and Canada exclusively by Palgrave Macmillan, 2014.

Jenkins, Christopher, Khánh Tuynh Tryn, Sanh Thông Huông, David G. Marr, Bôi Châu Phan, and Chí Minh Hi, editors. *Reflections from Captivity*. Southeast Asia Translation Series, vol. 1. Athens: Ohio University Press, 1978.

Johnston, Hugh J.M. *The Voyage of the Komagata Maru: The Sikh Challenge to Canada's Colour Bar*. Vancouver: University of British Columbia Press, 2014.

Jones, Alun. "Internal Security in British Malaya, 1895–1942." Ph.D. Dissertation, Yale University, 1970.

Jones, Raymond A. *The British Diplomatic Service, 1815–1914*. Waterloo, Ontario: Wilfred Laurier University Press, 1983.

Kersten, Albert E., Bert van der Zwan, Ulbert, Jörg, and Prijak, Lukian. "The Dutch Consular Service in the 19th Century." In *Consuls et Services Consulaires Au XIXe Siecle = Die Welt Der Konsulate Im 19. Jahrhundert = Consulship in the 19th Century*. Hamburg: DOBU, Dokumentation & Buch, 2010.

Kuhn, Phillip A. *Chinese among Others: Emigration in Modern Times*. Lanham: Rowman & Littlefield Publishers, 2009.

Kuwajima, Sho. *Mutiny in Singapore: War, Anti-War, and the War for India's Independence*. New Delhi: Rainbow Publishers, 2006.

"Indian Mutiny in Singapore, 1915: People Who Observed the Scene and People Who Heard the News." *New Zealand Journal of Asian Studies* 11, no. 1 (June 2009), 375–385.

Laffan, Michael. "An Indonesian Community in Cairo: Continuity and Change in a Cosmopolitan Islamic Milieu." *Indonesia* 77 (April 1, 2004): 1–26.

"'Another Andalusia': Images of Colonial Southeast Asia in Arabic Newspapers." *The Journal of Asian Studies* 66, no. 03 (2007): 689–722.

Laffan, Michael Francis. *Islamic Nationhood and Colonial Indonesia: The Umma below the Winds*. London; New York: RoutledgeCurzon, 2003.

Lauterbach, Julius. *£1000 Belooning Dood of Levend: Avontuurlijke Vlucht door de Hollandsche Kolonien van den Voormaligen Prijsofficier van de 'Emden'*. Amsterdam and Rotterdam: Van Langenhusen, 1918.

Le Jariel, Yves. *Phan Bội Châu, 1867–1940: Le Nationalisme Vietnamien Avant Ho Chi Minh*. Paris: L'Harmattan, 2008.

Liebau, Heike. *The World in World Wars: Experiences, Perceptions and Perspectives from Africa and Asia*. Leiden, the Netherlands; Boston: Brill, 2010.

Locher-Scholten, Elspeth. *Beelden van Japan in Het Vooroorlogse Nederlands Indië*. Leiden: Werkgroep Europese Expansie, 1987.

Lorin, Amaury. *Paul Doumer, Gouverneur Général de l'Indochine: 1897–1902: Le Tremplin Colonial*, Recherches Asiatiques, Paris: Harmattan, 2004.

Louro, Michele. "Where National Revolutionary Ends and Communism Begins: The League Against Imperialism and the Meerut Conspiracy Case." *Comparative Studies of South Asia, Africa, and the Middle East* 33:3 (December 2013), 331–344.

Lüdke, Tilman. *Jihad Made in Germany: Ottoman and German Propaganda and Intelligence Operations in the First World War*. Münster; London: LIT; Global [distributor], 2005.

Mackenzie, John. *Propaganda and Empire: The Manipulation of British Public Opinion, 1880–1960*. Manchester: Manchester University Press, 1984.

Manela, Erez. "Dawn of a New Era: The 'Wilsonian Moment' in Colonial Contexts and the Transformation of World Order, 1917–1920." In Sebastian Conrad and Dominic Sachsenmaier, editors. *Competing Visions of World Order: Global Moments and Movements, 1880–1910*, 121–149. New York: Palgrave MacMillan, 2007.

The Wilsonian Moment: Self-Determination and the International Origins of Anticolonial Nationalism. Oxford: Oxford University Press, 2009.

Manjapra, Kris. "The Illusions of Encounter: Muslim 'Minds' and Hindu Revolutionaries in First World War Germany and After." *Journal of Global History* 1 (2006): 363–382.

M.N. Roy: Marxism and Colonial Cosmopolitanism. New Delhi: Routledge, 2010.

Age of Entanglement: German and Indian Intellectuals Across Empire. Cambridge: Harvard University Press, 2013.

Marchand, Suzanne L. *German Orientalism in the Age of Empire: Religion, Race, and Scholarship*. 1st pbk. ed. Publications of the German Historical Institute. Cambridge: Cambridge University Press, 2010.

Marr, David. *Vietnamese Anticolonialism: 1885–1925*. Berkeley: University of California Press, 1971.

Masaya, Shiraishi and Vinh Sinh, editors. *Phan Bội Châu and the Dong-Du Movement*, 52–100. Lac-Viet Series. New Haven, CT: Yale Southeast Asia Studies, 1988.

McKale, Donald M. *War by Revolution: Germany and Great Britain in the Middle East in the Era of World War I*. Kent, OH: Kent State University Press, 1998.

McKenna, R.B. and C.F. Yong. "The Kuomintang Movement in Malaya and Singapore, 1912–1925." *Journal of Southeast Asian Studies* XII (1981): 118–132.

McKeown, Adam. *Melancholy Order: Asian Migration and the Globalization of Borders*. New York: Columbia University Press, 2008.

McMeekin, Sean. *The Berlin-Baghdad Express: The Ottoman Empire and Germany's Bid for World Power*. Cambridge, MA: Belknap Press of Harvard University Press, 2010.

McVey, Ruth. *The Rise of Indonesian Communism*, 1st Equinox ed. Jakarta: Equinox Publishing, 2006.

Menezes, S.L., Alan Guy, and Peter Boyden, editors. *Soldiers of the Raj: The Indian Army 1600–1947*, 100–117. Coventry: Clifford Press Ltd., 1997.

Metcalf, Thomas R. *Imperial Connections: India in the Indian Ocean Arena, 1860–1920*. Berkeley: University of California Press, 2007.

Meyer, Charles. *Les Français En Indochine, 1860–1910*, La Vie Quotidienne, Paris: Hachette, 1996.

Harper, R.W.E. and Harry Miller. *Singapore Mutiny*. Singapore: Oxford University Press, 1984.

Milner, A.C. "The Impact of the Turkish Revolution on Malaya." *Archipel* 31, no. 1 (1986): 117–130.

Mockaitis, Thomas Ross. "The British Experience in Counterinsurgency, 1919–1960." Ph.D. Dissertation, The University of Wisconsin – Madison, 1988.

Montagnon, Pierre. *France-Indochine: Un Siècle de Vie Commune, 1858–1954*. Paris: Pygmalion, 2004.

Morlat, Patrice. *La Repression Coloniale au Vietnam*. Paris: l'Harmattan, 1990.
    Les Affaires Politiques de l'Indochine, 1895–1923: Les Grands Commis, Du Savoir Au Pouvoir, Collection Recherches Asiatiques. Paris: Harmattan, 1995.

Motadel, David. "Islam and the European Empires." *The Historical Journal* 55, no. 03 (2012): 831–856.

Mukherjee, Amitabha, editor. *Militant Nationalism in India, 1876–1947*. Calcutta: Institute of Historical Studies, 1995.

Murfett, Malcolm. *Between Two Oceans: A Military History of Singapore from First Settlement to Final British Withdrawal*. Singapore: Marshall Cavendish Academic, 2004.

Neiberg, Michael S. *Fighting the Great War a Global History*. Cambridge, MA: Harvard University Press, 2005.

Ngo, Van. *Viêt-Nam, 1920–1945: Révolution et Contre-Révolution Sous La Domination Coloniale*. Paris: L'Insomniaque, 1995.

Noer, Deliar. *The Modernist Muslim Movement in Indonesia, 1900–1942*. Kuala Lumpur; New York: Oxford University Press, 1973.

Noor, Farish. "Racial Profiling Revisited: The 1915 Indian Mutiny in Singapore and the Impact of Profiling on Religious and Ethnic Minorities." *Politics, Religion, and Ideology* 12, no. 1 (2011).

O'Brien, Phillips Payson. *The Anglo-Japanese Alliance, 1902–1922*. London; New York: RoutledgeCurzon, 2004.

O'Malley, Kate. *Ireland, India and Empire: Indo-Irish Radical Connections, 1919–64*. Manchester; New York: Manchester University Press; distributed exclusively in the USA by Palgrave, 2008.

Omissi, David E., editor. *Indian Voices of the Great War: Solders' Letters, 1914–18*. Houndmills, Basingstoke, Hampshire; New York: Macmillan Press; St. Martin's Press, 1999.

Özcan, Azmi. *Pan-Islamism: Indian Muslims, the Ottomans and Britain, 1877–1924*. The Ottoman Empire and Its Heritage, vol. 12. Leiden; New York: Brill, 1997.

Pecqueur, Jean-Pierre. *Indochine-France: Conquête et Rupture, 1620–1954*, 1st ed. Évocations. Saint-Cyr-sur-Loire: A. Sutton, 2009.

Phan, Văn Trư ut. *Une Histoire de Conspirateurs Annamites à Paris, Ou, La Vérité Sur l'Indochine*. Montreuil, France: Insomniaque, 2003.

Popplewell, Richard J. *Intelligence and Imperial Defence: British Intelligence and the Defence of the Indian Empire, 1904–1924*. Cass Series – Studies in Intelligence. London; Portland, OR: Frank Cass, 1995.

Porch, Douglas. *The French Secret Services: A History of French Intelligence from the Dreyfus Affair to the Gulf War*. New York: Farrar, Straus, and Giroux, 2003.

Puri, Harish K. *Ghadar Movement: Ideology Organisation and Strategy*. Amritsar: Guru Nanak Dev University, 1993.

Qureshi, M. Naeem. *Pan-Islam in British Indian Politics: A Study of the Khilafat Movement, 1918–1924*. Social, Economic, and Political Studies of the Middle East and Asia, vol. 66. Leiden; Boston: Brill, 1999.

Rai, Rajesh. "The 1857 Panic and the Fabrication of an Indian 'Menace' in Singapore." *Modern Asian Studies* 47 (2013): 365–405.

Ramnath, Maia. *Haj to Utopia: How the Ghadar Movement Charted Global Radicalism and Attempted to Overthrow the British Empire*. Berkeley: University of California Press, 2011.

"Two Revolutions: The Ghadar Movement and India's Radical Diaspora, 1913–1918." *Radical History Review* 92 (2005): 7–30.

Raucher, Alan. "American Anti-Imperialists and the Pro-India Movement, 1900–1932." *Pacific Historical Review* 43, no. 1 (February 1, 1974): 83–110.

Ray, Dalia. *The Bengal Revolutionaries and Freedom Movement*. New Delhi: Cosmo Publications, 1990.

Raza, Ali, Franzisca Roy, and Benjamin Zachariah. *The Internationalist Moment: South Asia, Worlds, and World Views*. London: Sage, 2014.

Reid, Anthony. "Nineteenth Century Pan-Islam in Indonesia and Malaysia." *The Journal of Asian Studies* 26, no. 2 (1967): 278.

Rosenberg, Emily, editor. *A World Connecting, 1870–1945. A History of the World*. Cambridge, MA: Belknap Press of Harvard University Press, 2012.

Salmon, Claudine. "The Contribution of the Chinese to the Development of Southeast Asia: A New Appraisal." *Journal of Southeast Asian Studies* XII (1981): 260–275.

Samson, Anne. *World War I in Africa: The Forgotten Conflict Among European Powers*. London: I.B. Tauris, 2012.

Shiraishi, Takashi. *An Age in Motion: Popular Radicalism in Java, 1912–1926*. Ithaca: Cornell University Press, 1990.

"A New Regime of Order: The Origin of Modern Surveillance Politics in Indonesia." In James Siegel and Audrey Kahin, editors. *Southeast Asia Over Three Generations: Essays Presented to Benedict R. O'Gorman Anderson.* Ithaca: Cornell Southeast Asia Program Publications, 2003.

Singh, Bhai Nahar and Kirpal Singh. *Struggle for Free Hindustan (Ghadr Movement) Vol. 1–1905–1916.* New Delhi: Atlantic Publishers and Distributors, 1986.

Sinha, Mrinalini. *Colonial Masculinity: The 'Manly Englishman' and the 'Effeminate Bengali' in the Late Nineteenth Century.* Manchester: Manchester University Press, 1995.

Snow, Karen. "Russia and the 1915 Mutiny in Singapore." *South East Asia Research* 5 (1997).

Sondhaus, Lawrence. *World War I: The Global Revolution.* Cambridge; New York: Cambridge University Press, 2011.

Sowry, Nathan. "Cross-Colonial Cooperation in Nineteenth-Century Java: Examining the Sepoy Conspiracy of 1815 in a World History Context." *The Middle Ground Journal* 6 (2013).

Stolte, Carolien and Harald Fischer-Tiné. "Imagining Asia in India: Nationalism and Internationalism (ca. 1905–1940)." *Comparative Studies in Society and history* 54, no. 1 (January 2012): 65–92.

Storey, William Kelleher. *The First World War: A Concise Global History,* 2nd ed. Exploring World History. Lanham: Rowman & Littlefield, 2014.

Strachan, Hew. *The First World War in Africa.* Oxford; New York: Oxford University Press, 2004.

The First World War. New York: Penguin Books, 2005.

"The First World War as a Global War." *First World War Studies* 1, no. 1 (2010): 3–14.

Streets, Heather. *Martial Races: The Military, Race, and Masculinity in British Imperial Culture* (Manchester: Manchester University Press, 2004).

Streets-Salter, Heather. "The Singapore Mutiny of 1915: The Local Was Global." *Journal of World History* 24, no. 3 (2013), 539–576.

Tagliacozzo, Eric. *Secret Trades, Porous Borders: Smuggling and States Along a Southeast Asian Frontier, 1865–1915.* New Haven: Yale University Press, 2005.

"The Indies and the World: State Building, Promise, and Decay at a Transnational Moment, 1910." *Bijdragen Tot de Taal-, Land-, En Volkenkunde* 166 (2010), 270–292.

Tagliacozzo, Eric and Wen-Chin Chang, *Chinese Circulations: Capital, Commodities, and Networks in Southeast Asia.* Durham, NC: Duke University Press, 2011.

Tarling, Nicholas. "The Merest Pustule: The Singapore Mutiny of 1915." *The Malaysian Branch of the Royal Asiatic Society* 55 (1982): 26–59.

Taylor, Philip M. "The Foreign Office and British Propaganda during the First World War." *The Historical Journal* 23, no. 4 (December 1, 1980): 875–898.

Thomas, Martin. *The French Empire between the Wars: Imperialism, Politics and Society.* First published in 2005. Studies in Imperialism. Manchester: Manchester University Press, 2005.

Tjepkema, A.C. "Strategic Dilemmas of a Small Power with a Colonial Empire: The Netherlands East Indies, 1936–1941." In Herman Amersfoort and Wim Klinkert, editors. *History of Warfare, Volume 65: Small Powers in an Age of Total War, 1900–1940.* Leiden: Brill Press, 2011.

Trang-Gaspard, Thu. *H ung-Gaspardrfare, Volume 65:,* Collection "Recherches Asiatiques." Paris: L'Harmattan, 1992.

Trocki, Carl A. *Singapore: Wealth, Power and the Culture of Control.* Asia's Transformations. London; New York: Routledge, 2006.

van Dijk, K. *The Netherlands Indies and the Great War 1914–1918.* Verhandelingen van Het Koninklijk Instituut Voor Taal-, Land- En Volkenkunde 254. Leiden: KITLV Press, 2007.

van Der Vat, Dan. *Gentlemen of War: The Amazing Story of Commander Karl von Muller and the SMS Emden.* New York: Book Sales, 1984.

van der Veur, Paul W. *The Lion and the Gadfly: Dutch Colonialism and the Spirit of E.F.E. Douwes Dekker.* Verhandelingen van Het Koninklijk Instituut Voor Taal, Land- En Volkenkunde 228. Leiden: KITLV Press, 2006.

van Miert, Hans. *Een Keol Hoofd en Een Warm Hart: Nationalisme, Javanisme, en Jeugdbeweging in Nederlands-Indië.* Amsterdam: De Bataafsche Leeuw, 1995.

Vann, Michael. White City on the Red River: Race, Power, and Culture in French Colonial Hanoi. Ph.D. Dissertation, University of Santa Cruz, 1999.

Vu-Hill, Kimloan. *Coolies into Rebels: Impact of World War I on French Indochina.* Paris: Les Indes savantes, 2011.

Westad, Odd Arne. *Restless Empire: China and the World since 1750.* New York: Basic Books, 2012.

Winichakul, Thongchai. *Siam Mapped: A History of the Geo-Body of a Nation.* Honolulu: University of Hawaii Press, 1994.

Woodward, David R. *Hell in the Holy Land: World War I in the Middle East.* Lexington, KY: The University Press of Kentucky, 2006.

Wyatt, David. *A Short History of Thailand, 2nd ed.* New Haven: Yale University Press, 2003.

Xu, Guoqi. *China and the Great War: China's Pursuit of a New National Identity and Internationalization.* Studies in the Social and Cultural History of Modern Warfare. New York: Cambridge University Press, 2005.

Guoqi, Xu, Robert Gerwarth, and Erez Manela, editors. "China and Empire." In *Empires at War, 1911–1923,* 214–234. Oxford: Oxford University Press, 2014.

Yamamoto, Nobuto. "Print Power and Censorship in Colonial Indonesia, 1914–1942." Ph.D. Dissertation, Cornell University, 2011.

Zinoman, Peter. "Colonial Prisons and Anti-Colonial Resistance in French Indochina: The Thai Nguyen Rebellion, 1917." *Modern Asian Studies* 34, no. 01 (2000): 57–98.

Index